STAKEHOLDING AND THE NEW INTERNATIONAL ORDER

Stakeholding and the New International Order

STELLA MAILE
DEREK BRADDON
University of the West of England

ASHGATE

Published by
Ashgate Publishing Limited
Gower House
Croft Road
Aldershot
Hants GU11 3HR
England

Ashgate Publishing Company
Suite 420
101 Cherry Street
Burlington, VT 05401-4405
USA

Ashgate website: http://www.ashgate.com

British Library Cataloguing in Publication Data
Maile, Stella
    Stakeholding and the new international order
    1.Economic policy 2.Mixed economy 3.Civil society
    4.Globalization 5.Mixed economy – Great Britain 6.Civil
    society – Great Britain 7.Great Britain – Economic policy –
    1979-1997 8.Great Britain – Economic policy – 1997-
    I.Title II.Braddon, Derek, 1949-
    338.9'2

Library of Congress Control Number: 2003105083

ISBN 1 84014 153 0

Printed and bound in Great Britain by MPG Books Ltd, Bodmin, Cornwall

Contents

1   Introduction   1

2   Stakeholding in context: some global dilemmas   7

3   Economic theory and the stakeholding alternative   31

4   Challenging orthodoxy: new insights into capitalism
      and market behaviour   52

5   The business process revolution: workers, producers,
      consumers   80

6   New world disorder   104

7   Communitarian orthodoxy and the Third Way   124

Bibliography   *150*
Index   *158*

Chapter 1

Introduction

In the mid-1990s, stakeholding appeared to be both a politically and ideologically contentious concept. This was largely due to the diverse national contexts from which it emerged and its identification with an array of different welfare states and economic and organisational models. What was regarded as the closer, co-operative relations and trust-inducing characteristics of German, Scandinavian and Japanese approaches to workplace relations and welfare, inspired debate focused upon re-evaluating economic policies to take into consideration the needs of communities, employees and others affected by the daily operations of business and markets.

In Britain, the stakeholding debate brought into the foreground the merits of a re-cast Keynesianism committed to near full employment, appropriate capital and corporate restraints, long term investment and universal protection for the unemployed or physically or mentally infirm. Such a strategy would require the fostering of a particular type of relationship between government, the financial sector, the business community and trade unions, versions of which were seen formerly in Germany and the Scandinavian countries. Although Japanese variants were also identified within the short-lived stakeholding debates of the late 1990s, it was principally the Rhenish and Scandinavian models which seemed to hold promise as role models for the ideas popularised by, for example, Will Hutton (1995).

It would appear now that such models have been abandoned by those once impressed by the stakeholding concept. Despite constant references to the lessons provided by German economic co-determination, that country has come under pressure to reform its industrial relations system by de-coupling the close relationship between government and the trade unions to make it more 'investor friendly' for a globalised world. The Scandinavian economies, too, are conforming to the political and economic orthodoxy of recent years: the single-minded drive for enhanced 'enterprise' and competition.

In the UK, rather than learning from our European neighbours in an attempt to counter the worst excesses of neo-liberal economic policies, we continue to work within the doctrine of Anglo-Saxon approaches to workplace relations and integration, these promoting individualism and personal effort to the detriment of collective bargaining. Within the various policy-making branches of the European Union, the focus is increasingly upon the importance of individual adaptation to 'flexible labour markets' and competition. Stakeholding economics now appears to have been sacrificed on the altar of a re-born neo-liberalism. Given this inflection, it is perhaps revealing that Hutton's work tends to focus on society over and above economy while recognising the enmeshment of one with the other.

In his earlier writings, Hutton argued that a stakeholding approach would require keeping a close eye on the operations of markets and business activities and a regulatory framework out of keeping with the dominant economic policies of neo-liberalism. The latter became viewed as a *fact* of globalisation, beyond the capacity of individual nation states to challenge. This resulted in a shift of attention away from the importance of re-casting the principles of classical economics as a means of combating dire social inequalities to a preoccupation with the social and cultural problems of globalisation. Instead of re-thinking the relationship between the operations of financial markets and local or national communities (Hutton, 1995; Plender, 1997) these same communities are being encouraged to adapt to the inevitabilities of 'economic globalisation'.

As part of this development, the stakeholding debate became displaced by a surge of interest in Third Way politics, with stakeholding appearing only as a supplementary term in political rhetoric. The Third Way does not question the fundamental logic of neo-liberal or orthodox economic policy but rather seeks to modify its more extreme excesses as these occur at societal and cultural levels. The inevitability of economic globalisation is broadly accepted (Hall, 1998; Held, 1995; Jessop, 2001; Giddens, 2000).

Perhaps not surprisingly, the Third Way (not socialism, not free-market capitalism) draws largely from Anglo-Saxon economic models, and was already heavily inscribed with managerial and entrepreneurial discourses we now identify with what has become known as 'Thatcherism'. To temper the aggressive individualism of that period, it has now become important to recognise the skills and contributions of employees as 'social capital'. The impact of neo-liberalism on all areas of social and political life as this occurs at the level of both the nation state and civil society requires a corresponding reshaping of democracy and cultural practices.

According to some globalisation theorists, stakeholding was rejected because, as an example of neo-Keynesianism, it relies upon the autonomy of the nation state to pursue its economic policies unilaterally. They contend that such autonomy has been seriously undermined by growing global economic integration (Held, 1995). Elaborating on this and other arguments in this book, we attempt to locate our discussion of stakeholding and its apparent demise in a range of political, strategic and economic developments that define a new post-Cold War 'global' environment. We argue that stakeholding has been subordinated to the *management* of societal and political fragmentation in the face of continued support for neo-liberalism.

In this respect it cannot be divorced from the impact of shifting geo-political relations and tensions which are the basis of emerging forms of international governance, or from the economic, political and social struggles to deliver some kind of meaningful and lasting 'peace dividend' from the cessation of the super-power arms race. Notwithstanding, it would be impossible to discuss the rise and fall of the stakeholding debate without placing it within broader discussions of the various attempts on the part of major international players to re-shape and play upon different notions of 'democracy'.

Civil society

Civil society is taking a prominent focus in terms of social and political changes occurring at the sub-state level and also in relation to states' attempts to accommodate, intervene and manage these changes (Held, 1995; Giddens, 2000). Governments keen to pursue a Third Way programme are focusing upon the re-ordering of a variety of organisations and institutions which operate within civil society, including non-governmental organisations (NGOs) and the voluntary sector. From the perspective of liberal democracy, civil society should be considered as an arena for open and fair debate, beyond the narrow confines of sectional interests. It is also an arena whose activities may be harmonised with those of national and global interests.

Civil society is a very broad arena and includes a range of institutions operating outside the formal remit of the nation state. This necessarily includes business as well as broader social and grass-roots organisations. This broad interpretation of civil society may implicate it as a vehicle for enhancing popular democratisation. Alternatively, the already heightened profile of business in the context of neo-liberal economics may be given additional political and ideological power in attempts to deal with what are often regarded as the specifically *managerial* problems of globalisation. These include the pressures of societal breakdown, social and economic exclusion; fragmentation of communities and problems associated with the growing numbers of itinerant workers and refugees crossing national borders.

The re-constitution of social and political problems as a *managerial* issue, via the appropriate deployment of managerial *techniques,* has been a central feature of welfare state restructuring. The rationale of the private sector has been held up as a model for public and welfare institutions to emulate as they deal with reduced budgets and greater demands on resources (see Clark and Newman, 1997). The Third Way has been shown to play a pivotal role in the new managerialism that has a softer, 'socially inclusive' rhetoric while underscoring the continued importance of business and free-markets creating conditions for individual self-empowerment, equal opportunities and raised living standards (Newman, 1999).

Although there are those who suggest that there is too much complexity in terms of welfare and economic models to suggest an international managerialism (Flynn, 2000), attempts on the part of international non-governmental organisations, representing powerful vested interests, to internationalise economic and cultural systems cannot be ignored. It is becoming increasingly apparent that powerful international bodies are actively intervening in civil society by setting the rules of political and economic engagement.

In relation to this, we need to ask ourselves how far attempts to engage citizens in various forms of 'participation' in a variety of organisations at the national and international or at the local and global level, (whether they involve citizens expressing their opinions on council tax levels at the local council offices or attempts to pay lip-service to the expressed needs of people in rural planning projects in sub-Saharan Africa), can truly represent the average stakeholder constantly referred to in governmental and inter-governmental publications. Anthony McGrew, for example, suggests that it is easier for some NGOs and transnational social movements, acting within the sub-state level, to influence political agendas than others:

> Not only are there inequalities between different regions of the world - Africa, for instance, is home to few transnational movements or NGOs with a global influence - but these are often compounded by economic, gender, information and ethnic inequalities which transcend national borders. Diverse as it is, transnational civil society remains decidedly unrepresentative of the world's peoples (McGrew, 1997).

A preoccupation with the complexities of the modern 'global' world can serve to detract from stark inequalities and structural power dynamics which remain for all the rhetoric of difference, whether it is difference in cultural traditions, identities or (and this is particularly pertinent for stakeholding debates) capitalisms. Paradoxically, although complexity is taken as read, it is the Anglo-Saxon forms of capitalism which are often represented as the pinnacle of economic progress and the model for future human development.

The fundamental tension between liberal democratic discourses of equality and freedom and the inherent economic inequalities of global capital (see, for example, Gray, 1998) necessitate a search for new approaches to unfolding economic, social and international conflicts, the discourse of 'difference' being part of attempts to resolve the economic, political and social dilemmas of the modern age with the ostensible aim of building new types of democracy. In reality, as John Pilger has argued, this search for a 'New Democracy' is about getting leaders in a country, targeted for investment or for other purposes, to want what America wants (Pilger, 1999: p.67).

It has been suggested (Keane, 1998, Held, 1995) that a fundamental precondition of a genuinely democratic political culture would be the implementation of new international laws formulated to both regulate and uphold civil and/or citizens' rights and freedoms. Stakeholding would require similar attention to international and national law, if it were to have any political potency. Others have argued that we would need to review our political structures and processes that appear to have lost touch with the views of citizens.

As we argue, in spite of rhetoric to the contrary, the relentless pursuit of 'free-trade' in the name of democracy may limit the scope for new ways of organising social relations that fully acknowledge difference and provide opportunities for the expression of a variety of voices and experiences which are affected by a range of high profile issues ranging from welfare state restructuring to defence and foreign policy.

The road ahead

Our aim in this book is not to provide a comprehensive treatment of all the features outlined above but rather to locate issues of stakeholding in a range of debates surrounding globalisation; the dilemmas and challenges of a post-Cold War world and the meaning of this for issues of 'containment' and economic and political change. We begin to do this in Chapter 2, where we also explore the various economic, cultural and political dimensions of globalisation, and the challenge they present to national government. In particular, we examine the ways in which international agencies and governments, led by the US, attempt to deal with the insecurities of a post-Cold War world through processes of military containment and intervention; cultural and economic integration. We then contrast this vision of the world with more contentious arguments surrounding globalisation as a system of inherent economic, social and political inequalities, driven largely by neo-liberalism.

Chapter 3 focuses upon the meaning of stakeholding and its evolution from the economic and welfare models of particular countries to the more individualistic and arbitrary usage of the term in America and Britain – rejecting Keynesianism and adopting the ideals of a 'born-again market economics'. Chapter 4 attempts to relate the foregoing discussion to contemporary insights into capitalism and market behaviour. The limited adoption of new economic theory is placed within the context of the pressures of neo-liberalism and its reverberations in a variety of institutions across Europe, particularly welfare states restructured to meet the needs of 'the new economy'.

Chapter 5 follows this theme by focusing upon the rationality of the business sector and the ways in which it attempts to deal with pressures of globalisation while chapter 6 looks to the ways in which key players in the post-cold war environment address issues of hegemony and containment, through the rhetoric and practices now associated with the new governance. This chapter also examines the real potential of stakeholding in what appears to be a "new world disorder" of shifting international relationships and attempts to maintain some degree of control over the potentially anarchic developments of a post-Cold War world.

Finally, in Chapter 7 we assess the dilution of the economic dimensions of stakeholding in prevailing neo-liberal policy and its declining political and ideological relevance for key constituencies which came to prefer a 'pragmatic', 'grounded' and politically anodyne Third Way approach. We also briefly discuss what would have to entail before the representation of more diverse interests could take place. We conclude that the skewed nature of economic and political interests played out at national and international levels, vitiates against the more progressive stakeholding models which were applauded in the mid 1990s but which are themselves being seriously undermined by powerful financial and business lobbying groups who would appear to be driving economic policy. Such interests are obscured by the overly culturalist bias of the Third Way which tends to treat society as an amorphous, complex and equally mixed bag of interests. Ultimately this feeds the sense of uncertainty and chaos often identified with globalisation. The representation of stakeholder interests in policy necessitates a commitment to the prioritisation of 'choices' which in turn requires serious open and engaged public debate. We also need political leaders who are not bound to the programmes of sectional interests and who are prepared to listen and respond to critical debate. If the concept of stakeholding has anything to offer in the current climate it is the potential identification of powerful vested interests as well as those lacking significant levels of power.

Chapter 2

Stakeholding in context: some global dilemmas

Some commentators would argue that the modern world does not seem to know where it is going or what it is aiming for. Book titles like 'Runaway World' (Giddens, 2000), or 'On the Edge' (Hutton and Giddens, 2000), contrast starkly with the more proactive and *enterprising* 'Thriving on Chaos' of 1980s management gurus Peters and Waterman. The genie of neo-liberalism has been let out of the bottle and it appears no longer possible to control it. There is a feeling that something has gone terribly wrong. Any decent taxi driver will tell you that 'the world seems to have gone mad'. Many of our students, who are working their way through university, talk of seeing their co-workers as barely human, money-making machines, while programmes on stress and social alienation are proliferating.

We are living with the consequences of over twenty years of declining quality public expenditure and investment and rampant consumerism. Issues which dominate the news: international crime and terrorism; environmental catastrophe; famine and the 'new' epidemic diseases of CJD, HIV and Aids are truly global events which are often felt to resonate with experiences of insecurity close to home.

Tensions, conflicts and contradictions are everywhere; tensions between 'globalisation' and local interests, between public service providers and their consumers suffering deteriorating quality, between the need to find security and the constant appeal to risk and gambling with credit. Even personal relationships, the area which some authors believe to offer us a model of ideal, democratic communication, the ideal of the 'pure relationship' is confused by the insecurity arising from subjection to a tenacious, fast disappearing discourse of marriage, stability and family life. These confusions reverberate in government rhetoric.

On the one hand, the universal political discourse common to the Enlightenment project is now presented as inappropriate, politically naïve and impractical. Paradoxically, although globalisation purportedly knows no frontiers or boundaries, and all countries may benefit from this powerful force, the perceived need for continued US 'control' was clearly reinforced in President Clinton's Millennial New Year's Day speech.

James P. Rubin, former US State Department spokesman, is optimistic about the power of America to continue influencing foreign policy; this foreign policy being associated with framing 'democracy'; helping Europe to develop their own military capabilities, (in a way which does not undermine the over-riding security role of the Nato alliance); ensuring China meets its conditions of membership of the World Trade Organisation by engaging with them in developing new programmes, exchanges and monitoring mechanisms; influencing the development and deployment of satellites and defence systems in South Korea and Russia; in addition to the containment of and possible intervention in Iraq 'to minimise the damage' their policies may cause 'other interests in the region'. Interestingly, given the prevalence of managerial discourses in political rhetoric, the role of the US President here is cast in terms of the careful manager of a large complex organisation:

> the reality of globalisation, the resentments it creates and the opportunities for progress or catastrophe that it promises, entails a whole new level of complexity for the new President (James. P. Rubin, Weekend Financial Times, November 25/26, 2000).

This advice was given in the face of the far more difficult problems associated with managing domestic policy in the aftermath of the legal wranglings over the outcome of the Presidential election. It is advice focused upon the highly political strategies that need to be pursued to regain legitimacy at home. As Rubin suggests:

> the new President...may gravitate towards the international arena for early action, both because he is able to do so and because success might help put the bitter election disputes behind him (Weekend FT, November 25/26, 2000).

The renewed bombing of Iraqi command and control facilities by some 80 US and UK aircraft in February, 2001 has already seen this potential 'gravitation' realised. Even more so, the unprecedented impact and scale of the terrorist attack on the United States on September 11, 2001 led to the US seeking a global coalition against terrorism. Within days, the political leaders of the UK, France and Japan had met with the US President to pledge the support of their respective nations while those of China and Russia were swift to associate themselves with the new anti-terrorist coalition that looked set to radically transform international relations in the immediate future. We will return to the issue of terrorism and its global geo-political implications later in the book.

In countries throughout Europe, (Italy being one of the most extreme examples) as well as in the United States, Australia and New Zealand, centralisation of government authority is growing (see Travers, 2001). As has often been noted, in the UK, the executive is becoming more powerful than the House of Commons (Corfe, 2000; Gray, 1998). Clearly issues of government legitimacy in the face of declining support for parliamentary politics (especially in the US) are becoming quite pronounced in a range of discussions on such matters as nationality, social cohesion and devolution. Any concepts from stakeholding to the 'Third Way' must demonstrate a capacity to capture these conflicting pressures.

These issues are a far cry from the idea that globalisation is a largely apolitical, technologically-driven phenomenon. Policies are clearly highly political both in terms of the vested interests that garner the greatest support from government, and in terms of rather old-fashioned ideological issues; issues of regaining legitimacy, issues surrounding ways to generate mass appeal among increasingly socially diverse citizens.

Directionless markets

Once we accept or even embrace the prevailing orthodoxy on markets as the only viable political or economic alternative and reject analysis of their causal features in favour of an ungrounded cultural analysis, political, individual and social problems are experienced as social and individual confusion. A reluctance to question the material or economic contributory factors to such confusion is related to the ways in which the market generates its own legitimacy. Once in place, policies and technologies designed to enhance market efficiency, over and above all else, serve to change the relationship between business and society, generating organisational practices which shift the boundaries between home and work, between producers and consumers, men and women and even between nations so that it becomes more and more difficult to conceive of a life outside corporate structures and rationalities. These then become perceived as a natural part of everyday life and fundamental to human nature.

Furthermore, as sociologists have recognised for some time, a sense of anxiety is associated with the various environmental, political and social risks which are an endemic feature of modern global capitalism. The effects of such risks become impossible to calculate in terms of their source or levels of destruction. Growing inter-dependencies between different spheres and levels of life are such that problems can no longer be contained within their source of origin but their shockwaves are felt throughout entire social, political and economic systems. A clear example is the destruction of the World Trade Centre in New York on September 11th, 2001. The catastrophic effects of global and international political, religious and economic dynamics, no longer contained within national borders, were felt – more than just emotionally - throughout the world. They also affected the tourism industry (an approximate 11,000 jobs were lost subsequently in tourism alone in the UK), the airline industry, stock market confidence and, in turn, exacerbated a prevailing feeling of insecurity.

The inter-dependencies of economies and polities also provide some insight into some of the causes of activities which appear on the surface to be highly arbitrary and irrational but might also be seen as a rational, (albeit cruel and barbaric), attack on a world dominated by symbols of Western culture and global finance whose interests appear to stand beyond the lives of minority causes or struggles. The Palestinians, under-represented in Western foreign policy and subject to continual aggressive incursions into their territories, suffering from extreme poverty and sub-standard housing, health and educational opportunities, are one part of humanity which, along with their allies, are constantly on the point of explosion, both metaphorically and physically. As individuals and groups we are often unconsciously complicit in such experiences which seem both near in their potential consequences for us and yet far away in terms of what are also barbaric living experiences and the conditions, daily humiliations and want which give rise to them.

From the perspective of business, the twin developments of globalisation and localisation (which some sociologists have referred to rather inelegantly in terms of 'glocalisation') are part of the internal logic of modern day global colonialism that must not only shape cultures (as of course it always has done) but also accommodate and respond to a growing consciousness of the relative power of public pressure groups, consumer groups and more culturally diverse societies. Businesses are compelled to please and appease in the context of saturated markets, consumer pressures and public relations. Operating in global markets, they must seek ways of accommodating narrow business concerns with broader political and social ones. Not sufficient that their products are of good quality or competitively priced - goods and services have to be 'ethical', (or at least appear to be) environmentally friendly and socially just as well. This is a lesson which OPEC, for example, appears to have learned. Reporting in the Times (March 12th, 2002), Michael Knipe noted:

> In the December agreement between the OPEC and non-OPEC countries, the organisation has reduced its supplies to consumer nations by 1.5 million barrels a day for the first six months of this year....Chakib Khelil, Algeria's Minister of Energy, who was OPEC's President last year, said the organisation's decisions following the destruction of the World Trade Centre.... demonstrated the organisation's commitment as a responsive and responsible member of the world community.

In some senses this apparent PR exercise is also associated with the spreading of risks and the careful management of markets after the demand for energy plummeted post-September 11th. Again, as reported by Michael Knipe: "OPEC's aim is to keep the price at between $22 and $28 a barrel."

In the same article Ali-Naimi, Saudi Arabia's Minister of Petroleum stated:

> but there is a market which ultimately determines the price...... All the producers, whether they are OPEC or non-OPEC, are in the same boat. All of us lose when the price crashes and gain when the price is at the desired reference. What we want to avoid is being in a confrontational mode, either with non-OPEC producers or with the consumers.

OPEC is now presented rather glowingly in terms of its role in creating world political and economic stability after decades of having a bad reputation following the OPEC crisis in 1974. These kinds of developments which may be read in terms of cartel behaviour and price fixing are perceived to offer real benefits to local communities. Giddens argues for the positive social potential of multinational corporations who are learning, if they are to prosper, that they must be protective of and sensitive to local communities. In terms of their political and social significance, the part played by businesses in shaping individual lifestyles and biographies is of particular note here since it is they, more than abstract entities of technology and/or IT, which are acquiring additional political significance in the context of declining support for parliamentary institutions and politicians (see Giddens, 1998).

This is a significant development in the face of trends towards reduced turn-out in formal elections (particularly local) where mainstream political issues apparently fail to capture the social imagination (see, for example, The Independent 20th October, 1999 and The Economist July 17[th,] 1999, 'Is Democracy in Trouble?'). There are clear long-term implications for the viability of liberal democracy (Kondrake, 2001).

In the neo-liberal world, business is synonymous with the pursuit of free markets, the just and natural allocation of resources and the allocation of reward for individual effort and talent. Yet, here again, there is little that is laissez-faire about the role of business (particularly as regards transnational corporations) in the reshaping of the relationship between state and civil society. Business is regarded as a benign 'partner' in the life of thriving local communities under centre-left governments throughout Europe and in those from Nigeria to Nepal.

While representative democracy is waning, business as a major influence on policy and culture is in the ascendancy. A 1999 Times poll of the most powerful people in British society placed Bill Gates in second place after Tony Blair, closely followed by Alan Greenspan. Both Gates and Greenspan are highly influential in international business, economics and politics. Microsoft, for example, supplies the software for 90% of the world's personal computers. Greenspan is chairman of America's Federal Reserve Board and exerts a major influence on the world's financial markets. Not deterred by Greenspan's close association with Republicanism (Greenspan was first appointed to advise the Reagan administration in 1987), both Blair and Clinton drew on his insights for 'modern' economic policy. There are close political and business networks operating at the international level, largely through high profile business lobbying groups who have unfair advantage over influence on politicians, simply because, unlike other lobby groups, they can afford to pay public relations experts and advisors to do their work for them (Balanya, Doherty, Hoedeman, Ma'anit and Wesselius, 2001).

In the richer parts of the world, governments have deliberately courted business (Pilger, 1998; Ramsay, 2000) to gain its electoral support. Having accepted that there are no political alternatives to capitalism, across a spectrum of European governments there is a growing enclave of erstwhile social democrats who argue for the need to look to civic institutions, the voluntary sector and the private sector to address social and economic problems. Given the influence of business on governments, it should be no surprise that, borrowing from the Human Resource

Management language of the modern business world, the role of the state is being recast as:

> that of providing opportunities for individuals and communities while placing responsibilities on them to take those chances (Phillip Webster, Political Editor The Times, May 24th 2000).

The implications of this for political vision or social experience are vast. In the context of flexible employment patterns and the resulting collapse of boundaries between business, public and private spheres, all areas of life are in danger of becoming saturated by the language and ideas of big business. This is ever more likely as the 'individual' biography becomes the site of marketing strategies for producers and consumers alike, thus narrowing citizens involvement in public life to the filling in of consumer surveys about products and 'services'. New types of governance involve state and quasi-governmental institutions intervening in and drawing on public, private sector, voluntary and grass-roots organisations as a strategy to ensure the deployment of government policies which can no longer rely upon strongly funded welfare states to deal with the perceived social and political fall-out of 'globalisation'. All of this is a further development on Beck's depiction of the private sphere as something quite other to traditional conceptualisations of it:

> the private sphere is not what it appears to be: a sphere separated from the environment. It is the outside turned inside and made private, of *conditions* and *decisions* made elsewhere, in the television networks, the educational system, in firms, or the labour market, or in the transportation system, with general disregard of their private, biographical consequences (Beck, 1992, p.133).

Beck relates these processes to the conditions of the 'risk society': a society which is increasingly dependent upon individualisation is also associated with the proliferation of ecological, social and political risks. For example:

> Unemployment disappears, but then reappears in new types of risky underemployment. This all means that an ambiguous, contradictory development is set in motion in which advantages and drawbacks are intermeshed, a development whose far-reaching consequences and risks are not calculable for political consciousness and action either (Beck, 1992, p.144).

A vicious cycle is perpetuated – as governments attempt to deal with the socially fragmenting consequences of neoliberal economic policy, they reinforce individualism (in the current rhetoric, in the form of individual responsibility which was once seen in social or collective terms) to the detriment of group or collective effort. Intervention in individual lives becomes much more important to government strategy which must literally tell people how they should conduct themselves to meet the responsibilities formerly associated with stronger welfare states or international relations. In the richer parts of the world, on at least two levels, the growing impact of corporate and political strategies designed to cater for a neoliberal order, individualisation occurs under conditions of *reduced* individual autonomy (Beck, 1992, p.131). This momentum is intricately tied in with the blurring of boundaries between home, leisure, work and public space, increasingly subject to the institutional pressures of global capital. Compulsive consumerism, linking 'free markets' with 'choice', coincide with the intensification of work processes. Whole communities and lifestyles have been transformed by aggressive corporate mergers and workplace restructurings.

The proliferation of large shopping malls both encroaches upon and changes the social and cultural potential of public space as an arena of meaningful communication (Sennet,1998). Shopping malls are designed in such a way that people will not sit about and waste time talking when they could be consuming. Most shopping malls have a notable lack of benches to sit on for example, sitting can only take place in coffee bars (more consumption) and bistros. Further confusion is created by the fact that modernity relies paradoxically on individualisation via the constitution of personal biographies while homogenising the experiences of 'individuals', who become the bearers of societal risks, not least of which are under-employment and 'the generalisation of employment insecurity'. Furthermore, risks are quite arbitrarily distributed, resulting in an

> ambiguous, contradictory development.... in which advantages and disadvantages are individually meshed (Beck, 1992, p.144).

Due to the ways in which modern political economy both celebrates and denigrates the individual in flexible employment and manufacturing systems, it is perhaps not too surprising that rampant individualism should, according to some commentators, infect the body politic. This is especially true in a culture that is saturated with self-help manuals and psychological discourses emphasising 'self-empowerment' to the detriment of duty or sacrifice to broader social goals (Lasch, 1980).

On the other hand, for want of a healthy and thriving political and social arena (which can only be such for retaining autonomy from vested governmental or elite interests), it is not surprising that even the poorest sections of society will internalise the injuries done to them by economic activities based on greed and callousness. Irresponsible investment practices on the part of multinationals can cause havoc in specific communities and in their residents' private lives and, without recourse to a thriving social sphere, people have to retreat into personal self-help or become depressed and suicidal (depression is the fastest growing illness, globally). Not that we are against self-help if it actually helps people. The important point is that it is becoming more and more difficult for people to locate the roots of their dissatisfactions in an economy which appears to be rootless and they may find themselves feeling similarly ungrounded or fragmented. The classical sociologist Emile Durkheim had a name for it, 'anomie' (a concept which Will Hutton seems particularly taken with).

Sociologists Lasch and Urry understand this increasingly intangible world in terms of an 'economy of signs and space' where the invisible movements of finance, cultural artefacts and symbols dominate our culture. All of this occurs in an economy which, though still dominated by manufacturing (still accounting for some 62% of global trade according to the Financial Times) is also characterised by the rapid growth of 'services - banking, insurance, consultancy, accountancy, films, music and other cultural services, airlines and shipping' (FT World Desk Reference, 2002). We consume for the style, the glamour and the symbolic value of goods as much, if not more than, for their actual utility, an empty exercise which can never ultimately satisfy the voids created by the very dynamics and processes of consumption. Baudrillard talked of this constant quest to consume things for what they signify, rather than their function, in terms of a world of *general hysteria*:

> The world of objects and of needs would thus be a world of *general hysteria*. Just as the organs and functions of the body in hysterical conversion become a gigantic paradigm which the symptom replaces and refers to, in consumption, objects become a vast paradigm designating another language through which something else speaks. We could add that this evanescence and continual mobility reaches a point where it becomes impossible to determine the specific objectivity of needs, just as it is impossible in hysteria to define the specific objectivity of an illness, for the simple reason that it does not exist. The flight from one signifier to another is no more than the surface reality of a desire, which is insatiable because it is founded on a lack. And this desire, which can never be satisfied, signifies itself locally in a succession of objects and needs (Baudrillard on the consumer society, cited in Poster (ed), 2001, p.48).

One of the problems with popular conceptualisations of stakeholding is its associated assumptions about the *needs* and *interests* of different groups. This fails to register *the ways* in which such needs and desires a) may not be consciously accessible due to the material conditions and cultures which limit speech and a sense of right and b) fails to account for the ways in which the setting of questions by quasi-governmental institutions will already pre-empt or shape what can be talked about. As we shall argue later, the last point is particularly salient in the context of emerging forms of governance that are being extended into civil societies throughout the world. The expression of anxieties, needs and desires is delimited by the overarching presence of governments at national and supranational levels in civil society which must bow to the logic of a heavily consumerist society. Within this consumerist society, as already indicated by Baudrillard, it becomes more and more difficult to access the needs or interests which the stakeholding project aims, (in rhetoric at least), to address. Indeed it becomes increasingly difficult to keep a grip on any sense of reality. As Catherine Casey usefully summarises, from this Baudrillardian perspective:

> there is not much prospect for meaningful collective practice, because such referents are imploded, and the condition is now one of hyper, simulated reality, that cannot be "known" outside itself (Casey, 1995:11).

The intermeshing of economy and culture makes for a complex political and social landscape as signs and symbols fly at us through our PCs and TVs and other channels of advertising to play on the collective psyche and to feed the sometimes strange and manic anxieties and desires which compel us to consume. There may not be much that is new about the role of advertising here but within the political landscape in which we find ourselves dominated by the political ideas and culture of consumerism, it acquires a new significance.

Added to the confusions generated by a consumerist culture is a political culture in which the centres of power are increasingly obscured by the *complexities* of the modern economy. Robert Reich (The Observer, 24th October, 1999, 'Challenge to US Democracy') argues that the ubiquity of power is a defining feature of new corporate and business interests:

> new power centres are far less visible than the old. Big corporations, big labour, big government, and the military couldn't be missed. But institutional investors, venture capitalists, the Fed, and big entertainment-telecommunications all deal in intangibles, and they do it without anyone being aware. Americans' lives are affected no less, but Americans *know far less* (our italics); hence one of the greatest challenges this democracy faces.

This leads to a feeling of chaos at both social and individual levels due to:

> the indeterminate, unruly and self-propelled character of world affairs; the absence of a centre, of a controlling desk, of a board of directors, of a managerial office....This disorder sets it radically apart from another idea which it ostensibly replaced, that of 'universalisation' - once constitutive of the modern discourse of global affairs....the new term refers primarily to the global *effects,* notoriously *unintended and unanticipated,* [our italics] rather than global initiatives and undertaking (Bauman, 1998, p. 69).

Due to their greater competition and fluidity, Hutton suggests that financial markets, 'tend to be followers rather than leaders' of public opinion and it would *appear* that almost anyone can now influence public opinion. As an Observer article states:

> pop-stars to grass-roots political activists may have a profound influence on the values and lifestyles which we admire, helping to sustain whole industries in a world of 'post-ideological politics', where traditional positions of power are in decline (The Observer, 24th October, 1999).

Simply through our daily acts of consumption, we will have effects on the economy and, by implication, on jobs and cultures. But the very notion of power needs some deconstruction before we embrace the exciting possibilities opened up by the activities of financial markets. Such forms of potential *empowerment* must be understood in relation to two fundamental interpretations of *power* and here, according to Dowding (1996) it is also important to distinguish intentional conscious behaviour from unintentional or unconscious behaviour.

Relatedly, 'power' may be defined loosely as *power to influence* or to have *power over* (somebody). The former opens up the possibility of anybody, at any time, influencing the society in which we live. But it is important to acknowledge the ways in which a whole history of choices made not only at the individual level, but also the broader political and structural levels, are constrained and influenced by *perceptions* of desire, need and external conditions. These conditions can be changed in such a way as to influence the kinds of choices people make. According to Dowding:

> changing the set of choices open to an individual is an important way of altering individual and collective power (Dowding, 1996, p.24).

'Need' is a modal term which can only be explained by reference to something else. Significantly, one cannot talk about need without reference to one's present situation. This seems in some ways an obvious but often overlooked point when it comes to exploring the critical value of ideas relevant to stakeholding. Dowding's insights relate to the fact that he manages to give due acknowledgement to the role of values and the subjective identifications surrounding them (for example, ideas surrounding 'needing' a family). Yet he is also careful to distinguish the objective nature of need from the subjective elements of desire which surround it. Desire, anchored by specific contexts (these latter, in turn being shaped by those with *power over*) then acquires the quality of need. Needs entail the tools or resources required to map desires to present situations but the ways in which this might be done are not always known.

> Any set of desires entails a set of needs which holds whether or not the person who has the desires actually knows or understands her needs…as our desires change, so do our needs…The process of forming preferences itself creates needs which we may not understand, or may deny when they are pointed out (Dowding, 1996, p.22).

Desires and needs are influenced by a broader culture which, in turn, will be in some way shaped by governmental choices. A concern with shaping cultural values is closely bound up with influencing perceptions of need. Even if alternative needs are expressed, they may not be heeded. The actions of political leaders often give cause for doubt in this respect. According to Elliot and Atkinson:

> The destabilisation of companies, communities, even whole countries, such as Mexico in 1995 and Thailand in 1997 did not shake the faith in the scientific rationale behind the free movement of globalised capital, any more than the millions starving to death in the famines of the 1930s made Stalin question mass collectivisation (Elliot and Atkinson, 1998, pp.222-3).

The consumer society and the complex levels of desire and longing which it evokes is, perhaps, more confusing for those in the richer parts of the world than it is for those who have to deal daily with the stark realities of underdevelopment, poverty and extreme forms of political corruption and injustice. *Need* as opposed to *desire* is a sharper distinction if there is a lack of clean water, basic housing materials, food or shelter. Needs are not so heavily coloured by the driving desires of consumerism which characterise the West for example (although even here disparities in terms of disposable income are ever widening within the shadows of those dazzling symbols of modern consumerism like Coca-Cola or IBM which may be seen on the horizons of many a poor country). Having said that, we would not wish to paint a picture of people living in such countries as simple victims of globalisation.

The reality principle: economic 'globalisation'

It is important to recognise the political and cultural dynamism of particular countries and regions and the extent to which new countries are becoming active players in the global economy. Gray notes the degree to which the system of global trade relations 'tends to project features of disorganized capitalism into every country' (Gray, 1998, p.73) with ambiguous outcomes. It may be possible, for example, to positively experiment with ideas which might emerge from the development of new types of capitalism as more countries enter into global economic relations (Gray, 1998, p.60). Adrian Wooldridge argues in a special issue of The Economist that de-regulation and the reduced costs of capital and technology favour smaller locally based companies. Local companies are proving themselves resistant to foreign competition, their competitive advantage being enhanced by knowledge of local needs:

> Bajaj Auto, India's leading scooter maker, succeeded in defending its local market from Japanese firms because it understood that, given the country's appalling roads, what Indians needed was cheap bikes that you could take to a convenient repair shop as soon as anything went wrong with them. Honda may have offered superior technology but it was Bajaj's nationwide distribution system and easily repairable bikes which assured its success.... ('Global warriors strike back', The Economist Special Issue, 'The World in 2001', Nov.2000).

To overstate the levels of interdependence and integration which popularly defines economic globalisation (see European Commission 1997, p.45) would be a mistake. As noted in the FT:

> The wealthy countries of the developed world, with their aggressive, market-led economies and their access to productive new technologies and international markets dominate the world economic system. At the other extreme, many of the countries of the developing world are locked in a cycle of unpayable debt, rising populations, and unemployment... (FT World Desk Reference, 2002, p.58).

Reasons for lack of integration or inequalities in economic and technological advancement are quite complex and cannot be separated from the shifting geo-political environment wrought, for example, by the fall of the Berlin Wall, or the ways in which privatisation and investment processes introduced into different parts of the world have been received, and are complicated by the growth of new types of self-interested elites. They may place a block on innovation and economic progress. The old guard communists of, say, Albania; the corrupt officials of Indonesia; the asset-stripping managers of Russia and the self-interested enclaves of power which characterise countries like Panama or Peru (see FT World Desk Reference, 2002) tend to hoard the wealth of their respective countries. The withdrawal of communist support throughout different parts of the world has generated untold levels of social fragmentation and poverty throughout, for example, Africa. The problem of 'third world' debt also hinders the integration and economic success of many poorer countries from India to Honduras, from Iraq to Afghanistan while extensive arms-trading takes away money which could be spent on health, education and infrastructural development.

Western imposed trade embargos and sanctions also play their part in perpetuating economic and political inequalities. Sanctions against Iraq on the back of the Gulf War have, arguably, resulted in thousands of deaths; the embargo placed on Cuba by the US has had knock-on implications for investment into that country. Again, many Liberians live in extreme rural poverty in a country hampered by years of war and the sanctions placed on its diamond trade by the UN (Financial Times World Desk Reference, 2002). Often such practices are dependent upon the latest developments in international relations and security. The Taliban of Afghanistan were supported and armed to the hilt by the Western alliances at one stage in its fight against communism and then attacked for its undemocratic dealings the next. Iraq, too, was once a useful strategic player in the Middle East and the beneficiary of Western arms sales yet, in turn, became the new enemy in the 1990s and part of what has been termed by President Bush: 'the axis of evil'.

The intricate machinations of the global arms trade occur alongside development work in a surreal geo-political landscape of bombs and food parcels. It is now widely accepted that sometimes economic aid intended for development in poorer countries is used by their governments to purchase military capabilities, often designed to suppress all or part of their own population. Some analysts allege that, in the confused, caring-sharing, war- hungry policies of what was supposed to be a Third Way, even institutions like the World Bank attempt to involve themselves in development projects in order to secure low-waged workforces and infrastructures suitable for investment, under the guise of local empowerment and the spreading of knowledge and skills (Cammack, 2002).

A recent newsworthy item (and there are many cases which are not regarded as newsworthy) relates to the government of Tanzania which leads one of the world's poorest countries. The government was criticised for purchasing a £28 million military air traffic control system from UK company, BAE Systems, with it would appear, British aid money. However the Department of Trade and Industry, supported by Tony Blair, argued that it had British commercial interests at heart, the sale being seen in terms of saving 250 British jobs (The Guardian, March 20th, 2002).

In the economies in transition, marketisation and privatisation programmes have not always delivered the anticipated economic success envisaged but have frequently resulted in the creation of large swathes of people struggling to survive on the derelict manufacturing sites and crushed welfare states which characterised the collapse of communism. Russia, for example, although having made some significant progress in the 1990s, suffers from under-investment and Russian companies, according to a recent report in the Financial Times, keep 'billions of US dollars in Western bank accounts, an outflow of capital which damages the economy'. China is becoming a viable global economic player, extending its markets throughout the world. If it is to continue to succeed, however, it must bow to the arguably inhumane policies advocated by the World Trade Organisation which stipulate the importance of labour market flexibility at all costs; this having enormous social consequences for people living in rural parts of China. As Dan Ewing reported early in 2002 "…the most restrictive aspect of the Chinese labour market is the jukou, the system that binds rural residents to their birthpace and prevents them from finding jobs elsewhere". This would appear to be a humane concern with freeing people to fully express their dreams wherever they wish to be. It is an argument presented in terms of its opposition to the cruel and restrictive practices of communism (and far be it for us to suggest that Chinese communism was a pleasant alternative). However, the nub of the matter becomes clear:

> China's competitive advantage is its vast supply of cheap labour and that has attracted billions of dollars in foreign investment. Yet to fully capture the gains from its labour surplus, China must efficiently match labour with capital. A fluid labour market would boost productivity and wages ('China Needs Labour Flexibility', Far Eastern Economic Review, March 14th 2002).

Although the author of the article makes reference to the problem of 120 million migrant workers flooding into the cities and searching for employment, he is critical of policies carried out by the Beijing government to minimize the likely social fallout of free-labour market creation.

Political and social destablisation occur alongside privatisation, placing, as we shall see, new pressures on indigenous and international government agencies dealing with the political instabilities of the Middle East, Asia or Africa and relying on aid and development to protect rich nations and to build international stability (Mallaby, 2002). The inter-meshing of economic dynamics associated with neoliberalism and growing political instability is a marker of a post Cold War world. The Financial Times reports that 'conflict is now more frequent within states than between them' while 'war and political instability undermines poor countries' (economic) prospects' (Financial Times World Desk Reference, 2002, p.60).

Of course, as we shall see in a moment, there are countervailing political pressures which take extreme forms in acts of terrorism (something now understood to be related to unjust policies and poverty) and the almost anarchic anti-globalisation protests which now accompany world trade summits that focus upon reducing poverty and stimulating international trade. Even so, in spite of the apparently enlightened policies associated with foreign aid to poorer countries, Fidel Castro was recently reported to have said that the neoliberal economic policies which ride on the back of such aid projects are "turning the world into a huge casino" (cited on BBC News 24, 22nd March, 2002).

If indeed the global economy is becoming a casino, then the odds are heavily weighted towards those who have vast resources to begin with. In this view of the global economy, the term economic globalisation as it is popularly understood is a bit of a misnomer. According to Thompson (2001), it in fact represents overwhelmingly quite narrow institutional interests aimed at continuing de-regulation of capital, investment activity and trade. This view can be supported once a range of possible indices for measuring 'globalisation' (which the European Commission understand to mean greater porosity of markets) is considered. The argument that economic globalisation is spreading throughout the world, reaching newly industrialising and poorer countries, rests upon quite dubious calculations (Hirst and Thompson, 1996; Thompson, 2001). Thompson argues that there has been very little change over this century, but that:

> on a range of measures, even after extensive adjustments, the international economy did not seem to be as globalized in the mid 1990s as it was on the eve of the First World War in 1913 (Thompson, 2001).

These measures of globalisation include calculating the ratio of trade to GDP and comparing figures for different countries over a number of years. This method of estimating the degree of globalisation takes into consideration the economy's productive capacity, and the relationship between this and actual exports. Thompson also argues that however one chooses to calculate economic progress, whether one uses measurements of trade to GDP or financial investment, there has been little change in terms of global economic openness over the twentieth century.

Take, for example, another index by which globalisation can be estimated: capital flows which provide indications of levels of borrowing and lending between economies. Lending takes the form of Foreign Direct Investment (FDI) and is usually associated with the global expansion of multinational corporations. These, as Thompson points out, retain a specific national base while also operating overseas. Trans-national corporations, on the other hand, are far more fluid, representing what is commonly understood in terms of foot-loose capital. Such companies will move around the globe to exploit the most favourable economic, social and political conditions but they are few and far between. Internationalisation of business activity has been occurring since the 1850s (Thompson cites the American Singer Sewing machine company as one of the first) and many companies are extending their overseas activities but this cannot be equated with globalisation.

Usually, the complex production and organisational activities of a multinational company may give the appearance of greater levels of internationalisation than do actually exist. Further complicating the picture are levels of diversification of production activities and a related proliferation of complex organisational designs and structures. Any one company may integrate these complex structures across countries. Thompson refers to Honda as a typical example of an extremely large, integrated company which has subsidiaries in a number of European countries that supply Honda with components which are then assembled in Japan, Brazil and the USA. Even so, it is still a Japanese entity with two thirds of its assets and sales going back to country of origin (Thompson, 2001).

Inequalities between countries remain high (see Gray, 1998). Ninety percent of multi-national headquarters are in the richest parts of the world, while 70 percent are home-based. This implies that nation states still remain an important presence in global economic activity. In addition, 70 percent of world trade is managed by just 500 corporations, while a miniscule 1 percent of multi-nationals own half the stock of foreign direct investment (Elliot and Atkinson, 1998, p.223). Trade blocks set up by richer countries with common vested political and economic interests act exclusively in the interests of their regions. Examples of these organisations include the EU, NAFTA and ASEAN. As the Financial Times put it recently: "They join together to offer mutually preferential terms of trade for both imports and exports." Even here, interdependencies may be overstated according to Micklethwaite and Woodridge, who regard globalisation as a kind of utopia whose emergence will depend upon the outcome of:

> a horrifically complicated and contradictory (process)...Canada and the United States are parts of the same free-trade zone, but the average Canadian province does 12 times as much trade in goods and 40 times as much in services with another Canadian province as it does with a comparable American state (Micklethwaite and Wooldridge, The Economist Special Issue).

Foreign direct investment remains concentrated heavily in key parts of the world, especially Europe, the Far East and the USA. Approximately 80 percent of trade conducted by the United States is conducted by multi-national corporations which are still reliant, (unlike trans-national globe-trotters) upon their home countries (Hirst and Thompson, 1996). Even within the richest parts of the world, large companies have a tendency to relocate production and service sites and engage in take-over activities to better exploit the talents, skills and training of local labour which may have the additional advantage of being cheaper and easier to deploy. Lind refers to this as 'plantation production', where an estimated one-fifth of imports to America are actually manufactured by American subsidiaries. These very activities are also bound up with the creation of a pool of economically and socially excluded at the global level; those who, for instance, make up what Castells (1998) refers to as a 'fourth world'. The fourth world is not confined to particular areas of the globe but is present as much in American and European ghettos as it is in poorer countries.

Social divisions

Earlier on, we made reference to the feelings of chaos and confusion which are experienced at individual, social and political levels. Some of these experiences may be accounted for by the fact that social distress is being made invisible by policies which consign the under-employed and unemployed to economic, social and political wastelands. The schizophrenic nature of economic, social and international policies depict such groups as scroungers, parasites, potential terrorists and outsiders (in the modern terminology of the economics of labour markets) one minute and then they are urged by officials and politicians to vocalise their stakeholding interests in a range of opinion polls and focus groups held by local authorities, local business and non-governmental organisations, the next. Of course, as we shall see, these apparently contradictory aims are really two sides of the same coin as far as emerging forms of governance go. Behind the discourses of integration and empowerment that characterise the governance strategies of a neoliberal order, the facts of wealth distribution and social, political and economic opportunities make the voicing of individual need (since it is individuals who are appealed to) nigh on impossible.

Any armchair sociologist or psychologist knows that the expression of ideas requires certain levels of self-esteem which in turn rely, fundamentally, on having suitable levels of recognition, validation and material security. As the Financial Times indicates, although wealthy countries dominate the world, other parts of the world are characterised by extreme levels of poverty and are 'locked into a cycle of unpayable debt, rising populations, and unemployment' (Financial Times World Desk Reference, 2002, p.58).

According to a United Nations Report in 1995, 5.4 billion people live either on low incomes or no incomes at all and some 1.3 billion people (approximately 30% of the world population) are living in absolute poverty. In more precise terms, according to World Trade Organisation statistics, 1.3 billion people survive on less than one dollar per day and a further 1.6 billion, more than a quarter of the world's population, exist on between one and two dollars per day. Some two-thirds of these absolute poor live in sub-Sahara Africa and South Asia. In a world where trade is crucial in generating wealth, at the start of the new millennium, some 48 of the least developed countries contributed less than half of one percent to a global trade total of about $7 trillions.

Seventy-three out of every thousand babies born in low income countries do not live until their first birthday. Women in these countries tend to be poorer and more deprived of opportunities than men; they are paid lower wages than men throughout the world and many women continue to perform work which is unpaid and unrecognised. Approximately one third of adults in the developing world are illiterate, two-thirds of whom are women. In terms of purchasing power parity (this takes into account different price levels in different countries) the poorest fifth of the world's population earns less than one twentieth of the richest fifth. Since 1980, economic decline or stagnation has affected over 100 countries and reduced the income of 1.6 billion people. In 70 of these countries, average income in 1996 was lower than in 1980 and, in 43 of them, lower than in 1970. In 1996, around:

> four hundred of the richest people listed in Forbes magazine owned the equivalent of the combined GDP of India, Bangladesh, Nepal and Sri Lanka, these having a combined population of 1 billion (Elliot and Atkinson, 1998, p. 223).

Furthermore, the United Nations Development Programme revealed in 1996 that the assets of the world's 358 billionaires exceeded the combined income of 45% of the world's population. UN figures show that:

since 1995, the world's richest people have doubled their wealth to more than $1trillion ($1,000bn). The number of people living on less than a dollar a day has remained unchanged at 1.3 bn (Denny and Brittain, The Guardian, 12th July, 1999).

Citing a UN Human Development Report of July, 1999, the authors of this article state that global inequalities in income and living standards have now reached 'grotesque proportions'. Thirty years ago, the gap between the richest fifth of the world's people and the poorest stood at 30 to 1. By 1990, it had widened to 60 to1 and today it stands at 74 to 1. The report is careful to highlight the fact that globalisation amounts to more than just flows of money and trade. Growing interdependence of countries is significant in the context of reductions in available time and space but it is market profitability with its tendency to generate income inequalities of gargantuan proportions that ultimately determines these inter-relationships. It is no wonder that, according to Strange (1996) growing inequalities are not just occurring between 'rich' and 'poor' countries but are felt within even the more advanced economies.

Extreme poverty and income inequality is growing in rich countries such as Australia that, in recent years, has pursued free-market policies. Brazil has one of the most skewed income distribution patterns in the world. Fifty percent of the country's income is owned by the richest ten percent, while the poorest 50% own only ten percent of their nations wealth. A few Mexican billionaires enjoy lavish lifestyles while much of the population has had to deal with a drop in real wages by over 70% in a ten year period and 13% live in extreme poverty. Income inequality has grown in Turkey since its economic expansion in the 1980s. The same goes for countries like the Philippines, while 44% of people living in Nicaragua have to survive on the equivalent of one American dollar a day. Egypt too is characterised by very uneven levels of wealth distribution where poverty is a common feature for those living in rural areas. Economic liberalisation has generated further inequalities in Mozambique (a third of the population live below the poverty line) and Mongolia (where, again, one third of the population live below the poverty line). The textiles industries of Cambodia provide only very low wages for their workers and there is extensive poverty among those living in the rural areas.

Of course cultural and political factors play their part as well. A whole history of apartheid in South Africa has contributed to the disproportionate incomes of blacks and whites living there. Sanctions imposed on the former Yugoslavia and conflicts within Kosovo, for example, have resulted in extreme levels of poverty, affecting up to two thirds of the population. Sanctions have seriously affected the declining economy of Iraq which has restrictions placed upon its ability to sell oil (notwithstanding its informal economic ties with some trading partners).

In the UK, income inequality in the mid-1990s was greater than at any other time since World War II. The top tenth of male earners earned over 3.2 times as much as the bottom tenth. A TUC survey (1996) of approximately 1000 companies, comparing performance in the mid-1980s and mid-1990s, found that the average ratio between highest paid director salary (excluding share options) and average employee salary grew from 7.8 in 1984 to 12.5 in 1994, a differential increase of 61%. During the same period, while the pay of the highest paid director increased by 115% in real terms (10.5% per annum) average pay increased by just 34% (3.1% per annum). On average, the highest paid directors enjoyed pay some 62 times that of their average employees. The more modest estimate of top pay rises of 26% has been identified in a Guardian survey (19.7.99) a rise that represents 'five times the growth in average earnings and 10 times the rate of inflation'.

In similar vein, the United Nations Development Programme in 1996 noted that, whereas in the 1960s the ratio of the most senior global corporate chief executive officers pay to that of the average production worker was 39:1, by 1997 this had changed dramatically to 254:1. As the Guardian reported:

> the UK's top companies last year managed to increase their average trading profits by just 6.9 percent....of the 13 companies which gave their boards rises of more than 30 percent last year, only six recorded an increase in trading profit.... After two years of New Labour, senior directors are still enjoying pay rises of 26 percent compared to an average of 3 percent for their employees (The Guardian, 19th July, 1999).

The UN is recommending that business should work with trade unions and environmental and development groups to counter global inequalities and corporate greed.

The experience of poverty impacts on health, education and life-expectancy. While the richer parts of the world enjoy relatively good health and social care systems, others are left to die from malnutrition or suffer diseases which could be eliminated by simple vaccination programmes. If you live in rural parts of South Africa, you have a high chance of contracting tuberculosis, HIV or AIDS. In this part of the world, the incidence of TB is 60% higher than the US and 20% of the adult population are carriers of HIV or AIDs. Again, in these countries, wars and internal conflicts have their impact as do UN sanctions which, directly or indirectly, obstruct access to medical supplies by those most in need.

Cultural factors

Although economic inequalities have immediate effects in terms of life experience and opportunity, globalisation is clearly a cultural as well as an economic phenomenon which is felt on a variety of institutional and personal levels involving the reconfiguration and stretching of social as well as economic relations; the growing fusion of social with economic practices and the increasing influence and spread of communication networks. All of these developments are having some impact on the power and autonomy of individual nation states whose formal authority to make decisions about policy affecting their own territorial and legal boundaries is being, to some degree at least, undermined.

The inter-relationship of global and local experiences are the result of a contradictory and dynamic process (Hall, 1991). Responses to international developments may take a local and global form and they may also involve local cultural identities, mediated by Westernised discourses and universal ideals. There have been a variety of political movements which bear some witness to this, including the secessionist movements of the former Eastern bloc and the unresolved tensions between and within advanced capitalist countries and the resurgence of activities of 'repressed' peoples. The Kurds, Palestinians, Irish Republicans or the Basques draw upon traditional cultures while demanding their equal treatment through appeal to the right for national self-determination established by the United Nations (Smith, 1995). Clearly, cultural flows are not simply one way and regional as well as local processes need to be heeded. There may even be some positive political developments, for example the European legislation on Human Rights which came into effect in the UK during Autumn, 2000. However, when protesters feel their voices are not heard through the usual formal channels, extra-parliamentary action is necessary. The number of people who comprise a variety of social and political groups joining direct action protests against the excesses of neo-liberal capitalism are growing. In some ways these groups are clearly perceived to be a threat to current policies and there has been a consequent rise in security to deal with them.

Globalisation and 'the transformation of democracy'

"Stop the New World Order, they want to get off" mocked a headline in the Sunday Times (13th August, 2000). Taking an ironic stab at the apparently naïve and self-indulgent protesters who mark the 'new barbarism', the authors (writers for the Economist, John Micklethwait and Adrian Wooldridge) argue that such political orientations to globalisation are a danger to a liberating, economically thriving free world. Their equation of globalisation with international free trade means that local responses, including also a growing trend towards regionalism, are marked out for their potential to obstruct historical progress by encouraging protectionism, the pre-cursor of closed authoritarian regimes which marked the earlier part of the twentieth century.

An attempt to highlight the positive social potential of globalisation, the article serves to emphasise the highly political and dynamic nature of what is clearly less than a foregone conclusion. Writing in The Economist, Micklethwait and Wooldridge argue that:

> Activists have already seized the initiative on global trade. They succeeded in scuttling both the OECD's planned Mulitlateral Agreement on Investment in 1998 and the launch of the WTO's new global trade talks a year later. They have also influenced the behaviour of firms and organisations. Global Exchange, a pesky outfit of some 40 people based in San Francisco, claims that it has bullied Starbucks into selling only fair-trade coffee beans in its cafes. A coalition of NGOs, student groups and UNITE, a textile workers' union, has sued a bunch of clothing importers, including Calvin Klein and Gap, over working conditions in the American commonwealth of Saipan in the Pacific. Seventeen companies caved in (Micklethwait and Wooldridge: 'Global warriors strike back', Economist Special Issue, Nov. 2000).

According to the authors:

> Multinational institutions such as the IMF and the World Bank are doing all they can to appease the protestors. Oxfam was heavily involved in designing the World Bank's debt-relief strategies. The IMF teaches NGOs the nuts and bolts of country-programme design, so that they can monitor what the Fund is doing. The result is that the international organisations not only embolden their critics to get more extreme, but also give them the tools to make their criticisms more effective (The Economist, Special Issue, Nov.2000).

Sociologists are equivocal about the democratic potential of globalisation. On the one hand, responsiveness on the part of governments and large corporations to new social pressures and demands is said to comprise a 'reflexive' or 'advanced modernity' (Bauman, 1998; Beck, 1992; Giddens, 1994). The potential this offers for the democratisation of social, political and economic systems is considered to be strong (Held, 1995, Hutton, 1999, Giddens, 2000). Basing their analysis upon the distinctive features of institutional structures like Europe or the sheer scope of the multi-national corporation (Thompson, 1997), others are more tentative in their claims. Generally, it is recognised that the often partial and contradictory developments characterising the new international order do provide some potential for positive change (see, for example, McGrew, 1997). Others are more pessimistic, arguing that globalisation really amounts to the internationalisation of oppressive ideological and organisational practices, a kind of cultural imperialism led largely by America, Western Europe and Japan (see, for example, Chomsky, 1998).

Some authors have referred to these different perspectives on globalisation as, respectively, the 'positive globalists', the 'transformationalists' and the 'pessimistic globalists' (Held, 2000). Pessimists question the existence of reflexivity which suggests a degree of active institutional or personal engagement with the problems of modernity. Pessimists emphasise the impotence of the public, baffled by global events whose causal underpinnings are no longer clearly intelligible, thus rendering them beyond individual or collective control. In this sense, globalisation does not refer to what the most resourceful and enterprising amongst us wish or hope to achieve. Rather, it is about what is happening to us all as we live with, or react to, the effects of mobile capital, corporate restructuring and a growing emphasis upon flexible employment. Any attempt to set long-term goals or to engage in debates about the substantive purposes of collective action are subordinated to pragmatism and the management of social relations as they arise in particular contexts, both at local and international levels.

A more positive approach is one that, while not necessarily embracing the globalisation thesis, recognises the responsive role which may be played by international non-governmental organisation (INGOs) whose higher political profile enables them to act as alternative vehicles of opinion in civil society. Cox (1997) highlights international non-party alignments and organisations targeting policies drawn up by formal governments, (for example, the non-party mobilization in Canada, the USA and Mexico against the North America Free Trade Area [NAFTA]). The

Zapatista revolt in Mexico was organised against the discourse and practices of global free trade. The successful timing of such revolts was associated with the reduced power of the Mexican state (Cox, 1997, p.65).

As noted earlier, a more recent example was the dramatic protest around the Seattle free trade talks, where internationally co-ordinated direct-action protesters, communicating with each through the internet, staged a highly organised series of demonstrations against the perceived injustices and inhumane policies of global capital. Another example was the well-publicised series of protests outside the World Bank and International Monetary Fund immediately prior to Easter, 2000. Those participating represented a coalition of pressure groups concerned with global poverty, environmental issues and social justice who were calling upon the World Bank and International Monetary Fund to abolish third world debts and to re-evaluate social values. These new social movements are fast replacing those organised around the industrialised working class, particularly given the extent to which the latter has become de-unionised and reconfigured in white collar or high-tech jobs.

Unlike their trade unionist forebears whose very functioning was bound up with the legislative machinery of government, the new social movements are distinguished by their emphasis upon direct action. Indeed, they are in one commentator's words 'sceptical of parliamentary and party politics, mainstream and marginal' (Davey, 1996). It has been argued that it is precisely the emergence of such direct-action groups that represent a challenge to liberal, representative democracy. The demands of new social and personal identities would be better catered for by a politics grounded in civil society (see, for example, Giddens, 2000; Bauman, 1997; Beck, 1992). This approach would widen input into decision-making and allow policies to emerge from daily, lived experiences.

In his introduction to 'The Transformation of Democracy?', Anthony McGrew (1997) argues that nothing is left untouched by globalisation but all areas of life are affected *differentially*. Integration *and* differentiation should be regarded as twin developments. As such, globalisation does not represent so much the weakened power of the nation state but its *transformation*, along with ideas of democracy on which the nation state depends. This way of looking at globalisation allows some scope for human agency and its potential to alter existing conditions. This is due in particular to the interaction of top-down and bottom-up pressures as twin developments of globalisation. Interacting dialectically, democracy is circumscribed both by the responses of groups affected and by the relative power balance of key global players. According to Robert Cox:

> Dominant forces, internal or external to the territorial or social setting in question, constitute the initial limits of the possible. These stimulate and configure a critical response. The response changes the power relations that once circumscribed what was thought possible. These changed power relations in turn create new limits and new challenges (Cox, 1997, in McGrew, 1997. p.50).

Citing Karl Polyani (1944, p.51), Cox suggests that this has been the case throughout the better part of the twentieth century, with various measures and counter measures being taken to secure conditions for social and political stability throughout Europe, America and Japan. Each strategy was only as good as the environment it was attempting to manage. This applied to, for example, the economic policies of the 1930s (which created the Great Depression and set in place the conditions for the rise of Fascism and were thus radically reformed); the demand management techniques of Keynesian welfare systems (which were an attempt to build a consensus between workers, their employers, politicians and the newly-emerging global institutions following the Bretton Woods Agreement of 1944) and its later transformation as a result of problems associated with international financial liquidity in the early 1970s; the OPEC oil crisis of 1973 and the financial burdens of the Vietnam war. As a long-term consequence of this, the business community has pressured governments to reduce the power of trade unions and to cut social expenditure (Cox, 1997, p.55). This latest development has served the interests of those who were most privileged in their integration into the global economy, including managers and highly skilled workers in the knowledge and finance sectors. The same policies, as we have already seen, were also responsible for the creation of a large mass of socially and politically excluded.

According to Held (1995), governments are being urged to rethink the role of the nation state and institutional structures of democracy. The nation state's relationship with civil society requires particular attention. Held notes a number of dis-junctures that limit the scope of existing institutional arrangements, operating at national and international levels. Of particular note in the current global context are the powers of political parties, military institutions, bureaucratic organisations, corporations and networks of corporatist influence; a variety of forces which put pressure on the range of decisions that can be made within a nation state. Operating both above and below the level of the nation state, such entities serve to shape and constrain the options of individual nation states (see Held, 1995, p.99).

Clearly, we need to be sensitive to the relative balance of power which any one country or region may hold at any one time, especially given existing inequalities and the different places from which different global players start. For example, the organisation of poor countries around campaigns for a New International Economic Order (NIEO) which would better reflect their own interests (indeed, incorporate them into the decision-making processes affecting the world economy) was demolished by the force of the 1970s economic crises and the resurrection of neo-liberalism. Conditions for workers and local communities had to deteriorate in order to attract multi-national companies and foreign direct investment.

Even here, the outcome of such endeavours is not necessarily certain due to countervailing political and social pressures which need to be acknowledged if governments are to retain their popularity (see Giddens, 1998). These twin bottom-up and top-down pressures are *international* in scope influencing, for example, the policies of other European states. What has diminished the liberal democratic state is the growth and intensification of a dynamic relationship between regions and the global economy (Held, 1995, p.121). New types of governance are being pursued to harmonise global and regional interests.

Some commentators have argued that organs of international governance lead to the overwhelming influence of both technocrats and sophisticated technology over political and individual decision-making. This tendency is reinforced by contemporary developments in, for example, the administration of markets by collectivist legal entities (e.g. mergers, cartels, corporate alliances) in association with powerful states and by new international bureaucracies, which regulate and support private power and 'free markets'. More specifically, Elliot and Atkinson argue the economic de-regulation and political authoritarianism go hand-in-hand:

> our mini George Soros may be free as a bird when acting as a financial entity, but stepping outside this role puts his relationships with the state in an entirely different light. Video-taped by closed-circuit television (by spring, 1997, government grants had paid for 4,500 such cameras in public places, with official hopes that 11,000 would be in operation by 1999), his house liable under 1997 legal changes to search without warrant, his child-rearing scrutinized by an army of public employees, tested at work for drugs and alcohol, psycho-analysed by dubious 'counsellors' on corporate 'team-building' weekends, hounded by national 'days/weeks of action' against smoking and drinking, our share-owning citizen may justly feel far more tightly circumscribed in his non-financial actions than he would have done in the 1970s...Not only is he under strict control outside the financial realm, but also within it. And at this point the ghastly truth may dawn: it is not he who has been set free, but his money. It is controls on capital that have been reduced, and controls on people that have multiplied (Elliot and Atkinson, 1998, p.89).

'Flexible' organisational structures and management approaches rely on the utilisation and instillation of appropriate cultural values through managerial discourses while intensifying labour processes. Even here, this rather bleak interpretation is countered by arguments which suggest that the discourse of flexibility has potential to 'empower' groups and individuals. This possibility has already been noted by politicians attempting to control the conditions attaching to devolution as, for example, in the creation of the Welsh Assembly in the UK context.

In this chapter we have identified a range of interconnected trends that vitiate against the genuine expression of stakeholder diversity. These include a) the prevailing neo-liberal orthodoxy which states that 'free-markets' are the only viable means of justly allocating societal resources and rewards; b) the growing integration of the global economy which remains unbalanced in terms of multinational investment practices, global market relations, differential life-chances, income and opportunity and c) a highly consumerist culture which saturates leisure, personal and political life in ways which prioritise marketing and opinion gathering of citizens over and above fully informed political engagement.

All of these trends coincide with the decline of parliamentary politics as a vehicle of political expression this being marked by understandable voter apathy in recognition of the increasing intervention of corporate interests in government and civil society. If this is the picture that presents itself to us now, what were the insights that economic models of stakeholding were attempting to provide? In the

Chapter 3

Economic theory and the stakeholding alternative

The economic foundations of the stakeholding approach can be found in a variant of the competitive market model known as 'Rhenish' capitalism. To appreciate fully the meaning and implications of the Rhenish model and its relevance to both business decision-making and, more broadly, the process of generating economic progress, an understanding of the essentials of conventional market analysis, sometimes referred to as the reduced form model, is first required. This is particularly important since the Rhenish model is but one contribution to a 'competition of paradigms' (Lachmann, 1986) that have dominated much of the literature of market economics in recent years.

It may be appropriate to acknowledge the diversity of models of market economics. Particular models of the market process may be both relevant and valuable as frameworks to help us explore outcomes in markets for different kinds of goods and services, under a variety of economic conditions and at different times in economic history. As Lachmann comments:

> To ignore such phenomena causing the diversity of market processes would blind us to the variety of circumstances that may shape market processes and prevent us from taking due account of the very forces that impel them and lend them shape (Lachmann, 1986, p.3).

An apparent strength of the model of Rhenish capitalism, according to the Lachmann perpsective, is its capacity to incorporate a much more extensive 'variety of circumstances', more reflective of the realities of the dynamic global economy than more conventional approaches have been able to achieve. Indeed, in examining a variety of approaches to market theory, Lachmann makes the critically important point that:

> Economists must learn to surmount the artificial barriers which today separate them from historians as well as students of other social sciences. This is an urgent task made no easier by the circumstance that, since the darkness of the age of the reduced form fell upon us, several generations of economists have grown up who do not even know what they are separated from (Lachmann, 1986, p.xii).

Market orthodoxy

The doctrine of free enterprise and the analysis of unfettered market dynamics that underpins it has played an important part in conventional economic thinking over the last two centuries. Dominant as the principal economic approach in the laissez-faire world of the classical age, economists and politicians came gradually to develop theories and strategies to contain, control and, on occasions, directly subvert market forces under the guise of Keynesian economic thought in the UK, the social democratic 'partnership' approach in Scandinavia, indicative planning in France and central planning in the command economies.

For free market economists, however, the essential 'truth' of the market mechanism has never been entirely vanquished and their influence has been great indeed; the concepts of the free market and free trade have frequently captured the minds of politicians and business decision-makers. From the initial seminal contributions of the 'classical' economists Adam Smith and David Ricardo, through the work of the neo-classicists and the Austrian School, to the more recent economic and political agendas set by influential 'monetarist' and 'new classical' economists such as Milton Friedman, Robert Lucas and Patrick Minford, a modern market-based analytical framework has been forged that has withstood not only socialist critique but also survived apparent emasculation by the 'state interventionism' of the Keynesian revolution.

In practice, economic decision-makers in government (particularly in the US and Britain) have returned, sooner or later, to some variant of free-market ideology in their approach to the management of economic affairs. The essence of market capitalism comprises a set of central beliefs and observations, proposed as being essentially 'fundamental truths'. A market left genuinely free to determine economic outcomes would be expected to deliver an optimal allocation of resources. With free markets in place and individual economic actors motivated purely by well-informed self-interest, each individual, acting rationally in a genuinely competitive environment, would actively pursue the maximisation of personal gain. As a result, however, the invisible hand of the market would secure for society the best possible economic outcome as long as competitive pressures were genuine. For the economy as a whole, market economists argued that the capacity of market forces to attain natural equilibrium at full employment in a free market environment would be sufficiently powerful to prevent the problem of unemployment appearing. Market freedom was the key. All markets in the economy - the labour market, the product market and the money market - would operate along free market lines so that genuine equilibrium prices would be established in each case. At equilibrium, everything supplied would be consumed - labour, land and capital - and there would be no resulting unemployment.

If unemployment did occur from time to time, as history suggested that it would, market failure could be the only explanation. Such failure could be attributed to either excessive power held by monopolists or trade unions or to excessive government economic activity that would inevitably distort the market. In an intellectual framework that allowed little scope for government intervention, governments would nonetheless have the mandate to eliminate excessive market power, wherever it resided, but would also be expected to keep its economic role (and associated budget) to a minimum. In this classical world, government would have to 'balance the books' and not allow a budget deficit to occur except in wartime, following which it would have to be immediately repaid through a succession of budget surpluses.

Free market classical economists saw the producer as the key component in the economy. Utilising the logic of Say's Law (in essence, 'supply creates its own demand'), they argued that as long as suppliers wished to produce for the market, then people and other resources would be employed. Inflation would only occur where the government allowed or facilitated an excess supply of money to circulate in the economy. Finally, since at a time of economic recession money often lies idle in the economy, to ensure that these idle resources were put to work, it was necessary for savings and investment to be equal at all times. Through free market forces, the classical economists believed this could be achieved. They believed that both savings and investment were determined by the interest rate that, under free market forces, adjustments in this rate (effectively the price of money) would inevitably achieve equilibrium. The fundamental ingredient for economic success in the classical world was for individuals to be free to make the most effective use of any comparative advantage they might possess, unfettered by government through excessive taxation, import restrictions or other forms of economic protection.

Exploring the concept of the market a little further, the conventional approach of the so-called Walrasian general equilibrium model of the market economy brings buyers and sellers together through the intermediary of a market auctioneer. The auctioneer receives offers and bids from market players and then conducts a process of tatonnement or price bargaining to ensure rapid and efficient adjustment to an eventual equilibrium in a smooth, apparently co-ordinated way. Excess demand and excess supply are gradually eliminated by this 'recontracting' process until genuine and stable equilibrium in attained with all relevant consumers and suppliers willing to transact at the equilibrium price.

This recontracting process allows for gradual adjustment to price changes and, with its focus on incremental change, is often referred to in economics as the 'marginal revolution'. In essence, this approach to market economics proposes that, given the important assumptions outlined above, free markets and free trade will lead to an allocation of resources which will be optimal from the point of view of every individual and every company in an economy. According to conventional market theory, it does not matter if, in reality, no such auctioneer actually exists to conduct the crucial bargaining process in a smooth and rapid manner. All that matters is for buyers and sellers in the market to behave as if an auctioneer was active in the market. The equilibrium process is the magic ingredient in the orthodox free market model and, without it, economies, left essentially to their own devices, are likely to founder.

The model of general competitive equilibrium that evolved from these ideas - and the political strategies that accompany it - moved back to the centre of the political stage after 1975 as politicians sought answers to the growing economic problems that seemed to be a long-term consequence of their more interventionist policy stance after 1945. Indeed, a rather naïve belief in the efficacy of market forces lies behind much of the political rhetoric of the last 25 years in the US and the UK. As Ormerod comments:

> The theoretical constructs introduced to economics over a century ago continue to pervade discussions of policy. They provide both a strong bias towards - and an apparently strong rationale for - policies which move towards the creation of a free, competitive market. For example, the political and social agendas of Ronald Reagan and Margaret Thatcher were powerfully motivated by the logic of free market economics (Ormerod, 1994).

The appeal of the competitive general equilibrium model to economists and political decision-makers, ideologically committed to minimising the role of government in economic life, was profound since it appeared to demonstrate, with mathematical precision, that:

> business should be left as much as possible to its own devices, without help or hindrance from the state (Ormerod, 1994, p. 46).

As long ago as 1937, the work of Ronald Coase on 'transaction costs' posed a challenge to the orthodox classical view of market behaviour. Coase identified two co-ordination mechanisms within the market, one outside the boundaries of the firm (i.e. market transactions) and the other within it. While normal market exchange transactions will determine the allocation of resources external to the firm, within the firm such market transactions cease to function and are replaced by an "entrepreneur-coordinator" who determines resource allocation within the firm and, therefore, the eventual production outcome. For the first time, the firm (and its internal functions and processes) became a key feature of the economy, worthy of study in its own right.

Williamson later extended this analysis to include the nature of the corporate environment and also the behaviour of decision-makers, providing a more inclusive and systematic theory of the organisation (see, for example, Williamson, 1981). Central to Williamson's analysis is the identification of two primary characteristics of human behaviour, the characterisation of which in terms of bounded rationality and opportunism are pivotal to his approach. Bounded rationality implies that there are finite limits on the degree to which human beings can make rational decisions, limits due partly to the mental power of the individual decision-maker but also due in part to the practical impossibility of being able to take into account every eventuality that may flow from a decision. Logically, then, the normal market process would be most effective for once-only transactions and quite inappropriate for more complex real-world transactions.

Smooth, natural adjustment from one equilibrium situation to another without the assistance of government intervention may well be possible where changes within the economy are minimal and infrequent and occur against the background of prosperity and full employment. The situation is very different, however, where the economic changes to be absorbed and corrected by the economy are profound and deep-rooted and markets are distinctly not free to adjust to equilibrium. Market forces can and do fail abysmally where the scale of change required and the associated expectations and responses of consumers and producers extend beyond what would normally be experienced in the 'corridor' around full-employment. In such circumstances, the equilibrating mechanism of the market cannot cope efficiently with major and sustained deviations from full-employment or even from an equilibrium level of national income below full-employment (Leijonhufvud (1967); Coddington (1976).

The forces that drive markets towards equilibrium are at odds with situations where uncertainty and extreme risk prevail. Such forces are likely to become even more unstable in an environment where the established 'modus operandi' of economic and, perhaps, political life has changed fundamentally. Significant movements away from equilibrium tend not to be reversible through minor price adjustments and, indeed, may generate substantial and enduring adverse adjustments in output and employment, long before the price mechanism can respond. Although the market mechanism will still attempt to secure equilibrium, prices are unable to genuinely reflect economic conditions and/or evolving social structures. As a result, the market's supposedly unique co-ordinating role is impaired and false signals will be transmitted to the economy with potentially devastating results.

As Coddington explained, a new market equilibrium may be achieved after a considerable period of time but at much lower levels of income and employment. More likely, a state of long-term disequilibrium will prevail, generating deeper economic instability and, potentially, weakening the economic base until it confronts the possibility of critical mass collapse. In this way, without countervailing intervention by government to correct disequilibrium tendencies in the economy, recession become economic depression. An obvious example is the Great Depression of the 1930s. This proved to be catastrophic both for the major industrial economies (especially the USA and UK) and also for classical economic orthodoxy which was unable to explain the origin and indeed the persistence of the disastrous economic conditions being experienced.

The Keynesian interlude

The work of John Maynard Keynes (1936) offered an alternative explanation for the Great Depression, identifying both natural processes within the business cycle as being *responsible* for the emergence and persistence of economic depression and the inadequacy of market economics in offering an effective solution. The Keynesian approach allowed the market mechanism and government to work in partnership to maintain economic prosperity and prevent sudden, devastating economic collapse.

Keynesians argue that natural business cycle behaviour results from perfectly natural individual responses to unexpected shocks experienced by the economy due to sudden changes in aggregate demand (i.e. anything which affects consumption, investment, exports etc). Such changes could include variations in investment levels resulting from changing expectations about potential return on that investment or could be attributed to changes in consumers' confidence in the future that will cause them to adjust their desired level of saving (and therefore consumption). Where these changes become significant, Keynesians would argue that government intervention may be required to help absorb and correct them, thereby maintaining equilibrium, and that such behavioural adjustments cannot be dealt with effectively by the market mechanism alone. In the Keynesian world, then, government intervention becomes necessary to overcome such behavioural deviations, so smoothing out the worst excesses of the business cycle but without preventing the market mechanism from performing its essential allocative role.

Keynes revealed the in-built tendency for markets to self-destruct in a particular set of circumstances and postulated that a free market economy with no government intervention would eventually and inevitably generate a situation in which prolonged and significant unemployment would become the natural state. The Keynesian approach required governments to maintain an effective set of policy tools, both fiscal and monetary in nature, which could be readily deployed when economic conditions worsened, designed to ensure that aggregate demand remained close to the level at which full employment equilibrium would persist. Through appropriate tax changes and/or variations in government expenditure programmes, in particular, incorporating multiplier and accelerator concepts where necessary, the Keynesian approach created a stabilising force in the economy, allowing governments the opportunity for the first time to 'guarantee' full employment and prosperity. This approach brought the annual government Budget statement into the economic spotlight for the first time as, from around 1944 in the USA and ten years later in the UK, it became the centrepiece of the demand management strategies designed to eliminate forever the scourge of economic depression.

However, despite the powerful Keynesian attack on orthodox market economics, a strange compromise was reached in the 1950s after Keynes' death. Belief in the power of market forces remained strong but - to avoid a repeat of the 1930's experience - governments began to use Keynesian intervention policies to secure and maintain full employment. The brief Keynesian interlude, most prominently observed in Britain between the mid-1950s and the mid-1970s, allowed governments a temporary and ultimately ill-fated opportunity to influence economic outcomes through the macroeconomic techniques of aggregate demand management. This phase of economic experience, however, where individual economic action was, from time to time, over-ruled by government-led intervention coincided with an unprecedented period of affluence in the UK and those countries that adopted Keynesian-type intervention measures to over-rule market forces. While income inequality and social problems remained within these countries, the Keynesian economic approach enabled governments to alleviate much of the mass unemployment, poverty and deprivation of the Depression years. In the 1960s and early 1970s, rising living standards and growing expectations of a better, more secure economic future replaced the grim economic collapse of the 1930s. As David Smith noted in the Sunday Times (21st January, 2001):

> Economists are used to describing the 1950s and 1960s as the golden age for the British economy. The emergence of the world economy from wartime dislocation and post-war controls gave full employment alongside stable prices.

Yet even those who led the "Keynesian revolution" in terms of practical policy-making at the time recognise that 'the picture that emerges is one of considerable success mixed with near disaster'. Smith quotes the memoirs of Sir Alec Cairncross, chief economic adviser to the government in the 1960s:

> Governments....took extraordinary risks with the balance of payments. As they were bailed out one after another with foreign credits, the impression of disastrous mismanagement deepened. Yet the credits were repaid, the standard of living rose faster than ever before and unemployment remained remarkably low.

However, with reference to Prime Minister Macmillan's claim to the British electorate in 1957 that 'you've never had it so good' , Smith comments that:

> What now looks like a vainglorious boast from Macmillan in 1957 was an attempt to convince the public, most of whom were far from convinced they were living in a golden age.

Born-again market economics

Despite the dominance of the Keynesian approach in the late 1950s and 1960s, market economists never fully accepted the defeat of the orthodox view. What some saw as a Keynesian 'revolution' was viewed by the classical economists primarily as a necessary amendment to orthodox theory in special circumstances which posed no real challenge to the fundamental truths. What evolved was an analytical framework known as 'neo-classical' economics which, while allowing Keynesian ideas to be accepted and implemented in practical policy-making, reinforced both with its name and graphical depiction the supremacy of the classical mode of thinking about economic issues in a market system.

Significantly, those who constructed the post-1945 global economy built an international economic framework comprising such key elements as the mixed economy, global integration through a fixed exchange rate regime and the guarantee of full employment while maintaining a formal commitment to free markets and free trade. Essentially, this represented a compromise between the orthodox classical approach and that of its Keynesian critics.

From 1944 onwards, the establishment of the International Monetary Fund and its parity value system to oversee international balance of payments problems; the creation of the World Bank to stimulate and facilitate investment-based aid programmes; and the introduction of the General Agreement on Tariffs and Trade international negotiations to stimulate and foster trade became the framework for the redevelopment of the post-war world economy. While these institutions were certainly responsible for improving the stability of post-1945 global trading relationships, they were very much designed to facilitate the expansion of business and the affluence their activities created was enjoyed principally by those engaged in business within the major industrial nations. Less-developed economies and the less well-off in industrial nations remained socially and economically excluded.

Furthermore, some analysts argue that the so-called 'golden age' contained within itself the seeds of its own destruction. As Smith noted:

> The golden age of the 1950s and 1960s came to an end for many reasons. People's aspirations ran ahead of the underlying economic reality - at a time of full employment, pay demands, marshalled by powerful trade unions, helped create an inflationary wage-price spiral. Britain's devaluation of 1967 proved to be an early warning of the collapse of the Bretton Woods system that had sustained the world through the golden age.

Smith adds that:

> The years of growth ran into the buffers when a surge in oil and commodity prices, a reflection of the pressures on global capacity, produced the stagflation (economic stagnation and high inflation) of the 1970s.

Over the decades since the reconstitution of the international monetary system following the collapse of the Bretton Woods system in 1971, the International Monetary Fund, in particular, has been criticised for its ideological, market-based, frequently monetarist approach to the resolution of global economic problems. For debtor nations requiring its support, its policy approach has tended to favour economic contraction, essentially reducing still further the living standards of the economically deprived, rather than the facilitation of growth-inducing policies in the poorer countries. Only recently has the Fund yielded to pressure from developing nations to encourage rather than obstruct economic growth and to recognise the damaging social impact of its former strategies. Such agencies are widely perceived to be the agents of western industrial nations and are greatly mistrusted in many of the developing countries.

Overall, then, during the Keynesian years, through the application of demand management strategies, utilising the theoretical and policy-related insights of the Phillips Curve trade-off between unemployment and inflation, governments were able to manage individual economies to near full employment levels of output on the back of a flood tide of international trade which initially expanded dramatically under the stabilising influence of the Bretton Woods exchange rate regime.

Yet, throughout the entire period and beyond, the market and its supposed efficacy in resource allocation remained a central core of mainstream economic thinking and practical policy-making. Interestingly, this suggests that there is a kind of continuity of ideas in the progression from neo-liberalism through Keynesianism (as it was understood and applied at the time, rather than in its more modern re-interpretations) to the conventional view of stakeholding.

During the 1970s, with the collapse of the apparently stable economic relationship that formed the cornerstone of the Keynesian approach, Keynesian economics was accused of being responsible for the creation of an 'inflation psychology', where the public gradually become used to inflation at ever higher levels and had begun to adjust their economic behaviour patterns in such a way that inflation was pushed to ever higher (and more damaging) levels.

Critics of Keynesian economics, for example, Milton Friedman in the United States, led the Monetarist attack on the Keynesian school and precipitated the renewed emphasis on market liberalisation. As Wheeler et al (1996) comment:

> It has been the central belief of American academic Milton Friedman ... that increasing shareholder value is the over-riding moral obligation for the corporation. Indeed exercising any other act of social responsibility is in effect a tax on the wealth of the owners and is therefore akin to a socialist doctrine .....it is at least arguable that Adam Smith's iron rules lie at the heart of Friedman's argument and the so-called Chicago school of ... economics (Wheeler et al, 1996, p. 34).

Friedman attacked the Keynesian policy of stimulating aggregate demand to attain full employment arguing that, while it might have the desired effect in the short-term, it simply generated inflation in the longer-term (see, for example, Friedman, 1963) In the view of the Monetarists, Keynesian intervention amounted to a recipe for inflation with, ultimately, no real gains in terms of employment or output. Worse still, they argued that consumers, wage-earners, indeed all economic actors, would adjust gradually their expectations of inflation, eventually coming to expect the trend towards higher price levels over time and, as a result, acting in such a way as to prevent the economic damage that results from adversely affecting their own economic situation. In this way, they suggested, inflationary expectations become gradually absorbed and self-fulfilling over time.

In the late 1970s and 1980s however, another group of economists, building upon the Monetarist critique, offered an even more powerful challenge to Keynesian economics. Importantly, their intellectual framework was essentially founded in classical economics (i.e. believing in the power of free markets and equilibrium adjustment) but adding a completely new view of what determines the reaction of the public to economic policy. This view - known as the "rational expectations" approach - had a profound influence on economic thinking for most of the 1980s in the UK and USA and, consequently, had a dramatic effect on political ideology and policy. Unlike the Monetarists, new classical economists [such as Lucas (1981) and Minford (1983) disputed even the short-term beneficial impact of demand management on output and employment.

Rather than inflationary expectations adjusting gradually over time, these economists contended that the public would immediately 'see through' any government attempt to stimulate demand and would anticipate the inflationary consequences. Their instant response to protect themselves from higher inflation levels would effectively eliminate the short-term benefits for the economy and the impact on inflation would be immediate and highly damaging. By focusing upon concepts such as the 'natural' rate of unemployment and stressing the inability of governments through demand management intervention policies to influence beneficially either the short or long run economic outcome, new classical economics provided the theoretical momentum for the restoration of the market mechanism to the core of economic decision-making.

Around the same time, however, the attention of academics and policy-makers was captured by another school of thought that also acknowledged the power of the market as the primary resource allocator but identified a new role for government in helping to enhance the efficacy of market dynamics. While recognising that markets worked best when left to their own devices, scope was seen for governments to offer incentives to individuals in their roles as workers, savers, decision-makers and risk-takers to behave in a particular, economically beneficial way. In a sense, this school of thought viewed the purpose of economic policy as being the bolstering of a deteriorating work ethic damaged by high taxation and government-inspired, market failure disincentives. Instead of implementing policies in a Keynesian sense to manage aggregate demand, policies would switch to creating incentives to increase supply, motivating individuals or groups to respond and generating improvements in critical economic parameters such as investment, work effort, business risk-tasking and suchlike.

The supply-side school, as their name implies, believed that government could play a valuable role in stimulating output by encouraging suppliers rather than consumers. Supply-side economists advocated government intervention to encourage supply-supporting activities such as savings, investment and business risk-taking, all of which were perceived to be crucial to the cause of economic progress. Specific incentive mechanisms (e.g. lower marginal taxes on high incomes) were recommended as vital stimulants to economic growth. In his book, The Share Economy, Martin Weitzman (1984) suggested that the process of economic growth could be better fostered by harnessing the sense of purpose and communal efforts of employees to the cause of corporate expansion and profit through widening share ownership. Arthur Laffer, one of the leading supply-side economists in the US, developed the Laffer Curve to indicate the disincentive impact of high tax rates on income (see Laffer et al, 1983).

The Monetarists, new classical economists and the supply-side school all constructed their various theories and policy recommendations around one central belief - that the market mechanism should be the supreme resource allocator in the economy with government reduced to a supporting role, facilitating its smooth operation where possible. The re-born market orthodoxy of the 1980's proved to be extremely powerful at the political level, particularly in the UK and USA, carrying with it a sense of moral correctness. In moral terms, individual freedom, choice and opportunity were paraded as the "right" things for government's to pursue. The Reagan plea, so central to his Presidential campaign in 1979-80, to 'get government off the backs of the people' clearly struck a chord with many electors on both sides of the Atlantic and, viewed in terms of defending the freedom of the individual, became a new kind of populist movement. UK Prime Minister Callaghan, fighting to remain in government in the UK in 1979, had already noted a 'sea change' in British public opinion, similar to that which had already revealed itself in the US. As Wheeler et al note:

> In the 1980s, belief in the essential morality of Smith-Friedmanite economics led first Margaret Thatcher, and then Ronald Reagan, to articulate extremely compelling, populist, political doctrines which virtually laid to rest the notion of interventionist economics as far as business and wealth creation in the English-speaking countries were concerned (Wheeler et al, p.34).

During the 1980s, the policy of privatisation provided the first real opportunity for releasing the power of the market more widely. Such a perspective was not confined to the New Right, but was, in part, promoted by the Left throughout Europe which shifted its attention from public ownership and collectivism to working with markets and trying to combine employment with social justice. It was also associated with what Callaghan (2000) refers to as the ideology of 'post-Fordism', whose influence was most notable in Sweden. This has significant impact upon the restructuring of welfare states to enhance 'flexible working'. By the late 1980s, the Social Democratic party (PvdA) of the Netherlands, (a country usually associated with Rhineland capitalism) was also focused on making markets work by appealing to the idea of the globalisation of the economy. By late 1983, Neil Kinnock, then leader of the British Labour party, introduced a 'modernising agenda' that was translated into 'supply side socialism' (Callaghan, 2000) later to be taken forward by Blair. Issues of 'electability' were a prime consideration here. As Callaghan argues:

> The leadership's project was to catch up with these modernisation trends which Thatcher's government had harvested and encouraged. If the Labour leadership thought that the future of any form of social democracy was uncertain in Britain, there was not much change of the party championing the idea of transferring the old programme, or a modernised version of it into the European Community...the European Community in any case seemed to be dominated by the right (Callaghan, 2000, p.111).

Throughout the decade, governments everywhere were under attack; concepts of deregulation, contracting-out, market testing and the like, increasingly exposed public sector organisations to the force of the market. By the late 1980s, such was the ideological grip of the market and supply-side economists on the political process, throughout Europe, but particularly in the UK, that leading government politicians were able to publicly herald the achievement of turning the UK not just into a home-owning democracy but also into a share-owning democracy. The wave of economic and political liberalisation that swept central and eastern Europe after 1989 brought market economics further into prominence. Government interventionists were in retreat and the neo-liberal economic approach appeared to have won the day. As Callaghan notes:

> Parties confined to opposition were also inclined to adapt to the reigning hegemony of neo-liberalism in one way or another - though the SPD began programmatic renewal in 1984 by giving more emphasis to gender equality and was significantly less complacent than it had been about the prospect of economic growth dissolving distributional conflicts (Callaghan, 2000, p.101).

Callaghan is careful here to note the specifically political responsibilities of the Left in abandoning some of the key principles of social democracy. This was due, largely to a general lack of confidence in pursuing their traditional agendas in the face of what they perceived to be declining electoral support.

What has gone wrong: global economics or neoliberalism?

In the modern global market economy, it is the essential framework of a competitive, open, fully informed society and economic system that is notable by its absence. To win in the modern global economic game, corporate players have no choice but to employ every possible legal device to secure and expand market share, attract customers from their competitors and establish market dominance to yield enhanced profits. In this world, it is not the 'invisible hand' of Adam Smith working naturally to achieve an optimum economic outcome; it has been replaced by 'the invisible elbow' (Jacobs, 1991), employed to good corporate or governmental effect by the powerful on the economic stage, leading to the conclusion that:

> what the iron rules of free enterprise miss is the human element (Wheeler, 1996, p. 15).

Furthermore, companies, governments and individual economic actors now operate in a turbulent, ultra-competitive and increasingly unpredictable global system. The age of relative stability and gradual change where marginal adjustment might have been thought of as approximating reality has vanished.

What are the key features of the new dynamic global economy? We may identify and define at least four important features. First, we observe a dramatic increase in the role and power of giant private trans-national corporations that influence and control so much of global business and often argue persuasively for market freedom, while then adopting market behaviour practices that creates markets that are anything but free. The process of globalising business has created gigantic corporations that exhibit little allegiance to the country of their origin but which bring immense political and economic influence to bear on the countries in which they choose to operate. It has been estimated, for example, that the top 500 corporations in the world now control 70% of world trade and 30% of global gross domestic product (GDP). Of the largest 100 'economies' in the world, 51 are corporations. In recent years, Mitsubishi's turnover exceeded the GDP of Indonesia; General Motors' that of Denmark; Toyota's that of Norway; Ford's that of Hong Kong and Turkey combined (see Wheeler et al, 1996).

The corporate merger phenomenon that continues to sweep through the global economy represents, for some, nothing less than a 'third industrial revolution', vastly exceeding in value, scope and market impact earlier examples of mergers and cartel formation. A major feature of global change during the 1980s and 1990s, this revolution has been driven by a variety of factors including technological change, corporate restructuring and rationalisation, government deregulation and the elimination of excess capacity.

Today, mergers are seen as an opportunity to transform firms and stimulate corporate renewal; to seize global market leadership (e.g. AOL/Time Warner); to enhance corporate assets and their capability (e.g. Volkswagen's acquisition of Spain's Seat); to capture assets and extend the product range not possible by other means (e.g. Sony's capture of CBS Records and Columbia Pictures). The aim now is to pursue business consolidation and geographic market diversification through mergers with the objective of becoming a global leader in core business areas. Again reflecting the core-periphery approach of so much of current management strategy, these companies divest themselves of profitable but nonetheless peripheral business activities in order to concentrate resources on their chosen core business.

Under the immense pressure of global competition, entire industries are being transformed in such a way that power is being concentrated to an extraordinary degree in very few corporate hands. In the pharmaceutical industry, for example, mergers have created giant concerns with multi-billion dollar turnover. Examples include the merger of Astra of Sweden with Britain's Zeneca (a $70 billion enterprise); Hoechst of Germany and Rhone Poulenc of France merging to form Aventis (a $47 billion venture) and Sanofi of France joining forces with Synthelabo also of France (a $26 billion merger). As a result, other large pharmaceutical companies have announced proposals to merge with or acquire partners. These include a proposed merger between Warner-Lambert of the US and American Home Products (a potential $135 billion combined); a hostile bid for Warner-Lambert by Pfizer of the US (a merger worth $218 billion) and that between Glaxo Welcome and SmithKline Beecham, both of the UK, currently worth some $170 billion.

The implication for large numbers of stakeholders is clear. Many people have suffered and will suffer loss of employment, income and livelihood as a result of corporate transformation. Ironically, in the US, tax system support for aerospace companies undergoing corporate transformation of this kind means that, with rationalisation and restructuring financed in part from taxpayer proceeds, it is probable that those employed in the industry will have paid through their tax contributions for their own economic demise.

Secondly, and contrary to popular discourses surrounding 'free-markets', the increasing influence of large global corporations has been paralleled by a remarkable expansion of the role of government in the economies of the major industrial nations since 1945, both in terms of employee numbers and expenditure. The growth of the public sector has been one of the real phenomena of the post-1945 period and government economic activity has been only modestly restrained by the post-1979 advent of Monetarist ideology. The expansion of the welfare state with its huge public expenditure commitments to education, pensions, social provision and health (which in some nations appear to have reached unsustainable levels of public funding) and the remarkable extension of higher education, often seen as the major determinant of human capital enhancement, to include an unprecedented proportion of the relevant age-group, have all served to change fundamentally traditional modes of economic behaviour. As a result, governments in recent years have had to implement welfare state restructuring measures designed to reduce budgets and erode perceived disincentives in the existing system.

Third, a number of other key features form the defining characteristics of this new dynamic global economy and its associated social structures. These include a remarkable enhancement of overall living standards in the rich industrial nations coincident with a widening gap between them and the developing nations; growing income differentials within developed nations; the increased significance of the service sector in the industrial economies as mature economic systems switch resources from agriculture and industry to the tertiary sector; the transformation of social structures from narrowly class-based to broadly hierarchical, with professional and bureaucratic organisations operating with clear career paths; the evolution of a 'skewed meritocracy' in which recruitment is nominally merit-based but where birth, school, and wealth can still influence career opportunity and progress; and the enhancement of women's role in the workforce coupled with a significant change in gender relationships.

Fourth - and perhaps of greatest significance - is the most crucial feature of the new global economy that we return to frequently throughout this book: the unbridled power of financial markets. Of all recent economic phenomena, the explosion of global capital, flowing freely at a moment's notice around the world, represents one of the most potent and dangerous elements within the new global economy. Castells (1999) argues that this feature of the new global economy really began in October, 1987 with the deregulation of the London capital and securities markets (the so-called 'Big Bang') which helped to accelerate the process of capital globalisation. It started the trend that has since allowed capital to be fully mobile around the globe and permitted a global view of investment opportunities to develop. The rise and spread of financial power is associated with new technologies which both allowed 'quasi-instantaneous trading' worldwide to occur and, at the same time, provided the technological tools to manage such complex systems.

As indicated in chapter one, deregulation and liberalisation helped to give rise to this explosion of global financial trading in recent years. In 1998, for example, the average amount of global currency exchanged around the world on a *daily* basis amounted to some $1.5 trillion or an amount 110% higher than the entire UK GDP for that year. Hedge funds (non-conventional investment funds which exclude bonds, equities and money market funds) enjoyed spectacular growth (by a factor of 12) between 1990 and 1997. At present, there are over 3,500 such hedge funds, nominally worth over $200 billion. Unregulated, these hedge funds are used extensively by banks and pension funds to circumvent regulatory limits.

In that part of the global financial markets that relies, above all, on advanced mathematical modelling conducted by powerful computers, the derivatives market, estimated market value in 1997, for example, exceeded $360 trillion. The enormous scale of this volatile and unstable market - and the potential for economic catastrophe contained within it - becomes clear when, as Castells (1999) notes, this market value represents an amount approximately 12 times the entire global GDP. In addition, cross-border transactions in bonds and equities as a share of GDP increased between 1970 and 1996 by a factor of 54 for the US, 55 for Japan and 60 for Germany. In comparative terms, between 1983 and 1995, the annual average rate of increase in world GDP was 3.4%, world exports 6%, the global issue of loans and bonds 8.2% and stocks of outstanding loans and bonds 9.8% (amounting to some $7.6 trillion in 1998 which is over 5 times the UK GDP for the same year).

At the corporate level, the volatility of capital movements can have dramatic consequences. For example, in December, 1998, the $25.4 billion market capitalisation value of on-line book trader (and market leader in its field) Amazon.com exceeded twice the value of all Russian stocks, which then had a combined value of $12 billion. In 2000, however, the same company was experiencing serious volatility in its share price and market valuation. On June 22nd, 2000, the Amazon.com share price fell by 24% in one day and again by another 17% on July, 26th, 2000. Despite these difficulties, the enormous market presence of internet-based companies such as Amazon.com which attempt to dominate business in their market sectors (known as the 'Amazon effect') bodes ill for other corporate players and is likely to concentrate business power in increasingly fewer hands. Peter Bradshaw, a Merrill Lynch analyst, interviewed in the Financial Mail on Sunday, 30th July, 2000 made the point succinctly:

> There will be very few winners in any field. If you're number one, you'll control the market; if you're number two, you'll make a fair bit of money; if you're number three, you'll just about hang in there. And if you're numbers four through to 20, you might as well forget it and go home.

In the modern economy, then, these financial flows display extremely unstable characteristics and can trigger off economic consequences far beyond the limit of their trading market, at times changing fundamentally economic conditions throughout the global economy. As Castells notes:

> Movements in financial markets are induced by a mixture of market rules, business and political strategies, crowd psychology, rational expectations, irrational behaviour, speculative manoeuvres and information turbulences of all sorts. All of these elements

are recombined in increasingly unpredictable patterns whose future modelling occupies would-be Nobel Prize recipients and addicted financial gambler, sometimes embodied in the same persons (Castells, 1999, p.57).

As a result:

Random forces rather than economic calculations seem to be the primary forces shaping market trends (Castells, 1999, p.59).

In the new 'invisible continent', as Ohmae (1999) terms the linkages between cyberspace and the evolving global economy, these 'random forces' induce massive financial flows which have the capacity to completely undermine government or corporate strategies, weakening again the power of self-determination for nation states, with sometimes dire consequences:

policy-makers in business or government are still, all too often, basing their decisions on ..... an earlier geopolitical environment that has already become defunct. They are unprepared for the catastrophes of the invisible continent; for example, millions of dollars might gush in or out of a local economy in nano-seconds, with the impact of a typhoon or hurricane on the population (Ohmae, 1999, p.9).

Castells (1999) highlights the unique feature of the 'invisible continent' of modern global capitalism that distinguishes it from its predecessors:

For the first time in history, the whole planet is either capitalist or highly dependent on capitalist economic processes. But it is a new brand of capitalism. Productivity and competitiveness are, by and large, a function of knowledge generation and information processing; firms and territories are organised in networks of production, management and distribution; the core economic activities are global - that is, they have the capacity to work as a unit in real time, or chosen time, on a planetary scale (Castells, 1999, p.52).

Ohmae extends this view of modern capitalism, suggesting that:

People today live in an 'information climate'.....electronic commerce inherently transcends national borders, tariffs, and trade restrictions. And distinctions and barriers (and the competitiveness that goes with them) are fading, not just among nations and regions, but between corporations, between for-profit and non-profit endeavours and between government bodies and non-governmental concerns (Ohmae, 1999, p.8).

Castells argues that global companies persist with and thrive upon the "endlessly variable geometry of value-searching." (Castells, 1999, p.53). In addition, the global inter-connections of the new economy mean that: "Networks, rather than countries or economic areas, are the true architectures of the new global economy." (Castells, 1999, p.61). What determines economic outcomes in the modern age, more and more, are intricate inter-connections between companies, developed and extended through cross-border mergers, takeovers, strategic alliances, joint ventures, technology partnerships, 'rainbow teaming' and notions of the 'virtual' corporation. With industrial supply chains globally becoming ever more interdependent, economic outcomes are influenced now as never before by an intensely complex matrix of corporate inter-connectedness across the globe, concentrating power and potentially exacerbating inequality.

Runaway capital, the growth of huge corporations, employment insecurity and growing inequalities all point to a turbulent global economic system. Clearly, the failure of markets to attain natural equilibrium in the modern global business environment as noted above is scarcely surprising, given the complexities and hitherto unexplored dimensions of the new 'invisible continent'. Ohmae defines three distinct dimensions to this new 'continent'. First, there is the real economy which is, in effect, the traditional economic system where economic actors engage in working, consuming, investing and so on within the recognised local and national economic boundaries of their company or nation. Secondly, there is what Ohmae termed 'the borderless world' in which business and finance develop inter-connections that go well beyond traditional borders, from corporate linkages that transcend those previously experienced and which may be all but invisible to the average economic actor going about her or his daily business.

Finally, Ohmae suggests that there is a new dimension in the modern business age which few economic actors would recognise as being part of their world at all, yet the influence of which hangs heavily upon their lives and fortunes. This third dimension might be termed 'economic cyberspace' - a new continent of its own where business transactions are conducted on a massive scale at a moment's notice, completely changing economic outcomes, although those affected by the fallout may never have played any part in the process or even realised it was happening. Not only are the implications for economic analysis and economic policy immense but the consequences for global economic stability must also be a cause for concern. For example, Ohmae notes that:

> For at least a century, economists have tried to use mathematics to model the real economy - the first dimension of the invisible continent. There is no good economic model for the second dimension, or the borderless economy, even today......then came the third dimension (Ohmae, 1999, p.8).

Within this third dimension, economists are experiencing problems explaining the behaviour of economic variables, movements in which often appear to contradict the predictions of conventional economic theory. More crucially, Ohmae comments that:

> While Paul Romer and others are trying to explain the productivity gains in the real economy, no one has even attempted to develop a mathematical model of the cyber-economy and how it interacts with the real-world economy of the first two dimensions (Ohmae, 1999, p.8).

This additional third dimension undoubtedly takes the complexity of modelling global economic behaviour into uncharted territory, but there is even worse to come as Ohmae contends:

> An even greater challenge for mathematical models comes from......high
> multiples.....Ironically, these mathematical multiples are the greatest factor making
> the mathematical modelling of the new economy impractical (if not
> impossible)...multiples reshape the global balance of power and redefine the real
> economy (Ohmae, 1999, p.8).

In a phrase destined to shake the very foundations of the mathematical modelling
school so central to the neo-liberal economic approach of recent years, Ohmae
concludes that "it is time for us to leave the mathematics and modelling behind".

Ohmae is not alone in expressing disillusion with the mechanical,
mathematical modelling approach of many who operate in the neo-classical
economic school. In a recent book, Ormerod (1998) continues the attack on
conventional market theory which he first outlined in 'the Death of economics' in
1994. Ormerod explains that:

> Conventional approaches to the analysis of the economy and society must be
> altered fundamentally if we are to make progress in understanding both how the
> world operates, and how we might try to change it for the better. they are more
> like living organisms......The behaviour of the system as a whole can never be
> understood by mechanistically adding together its component parts: just as a living
> creature is more than the sum of the individual cells which make up its body; so
> the economy and society are more than the sum of the individuals who inhabit it
> (Ormerod, 1998, p.x).

In response to the critical changes in economic, financial and social structure over
the last few decades, outlined above, a new economic system has developed,
incorporating a very different set of values and structures to that which preceded it.
Today, economic integration across different parts of the world is achieved
primarily through the interactions of business and not, as before, through a fixed
exchange rate regime. Growth and prosperity are pursued within self-protective
trade blocs with global negotiation through the World Trade Organisation to
stimulate 'global' business and economic development by reducing or removing
impediments to trade. In part, this development is identified with financial
deregulation whose greater autonomy in pursuing viable or cheap investment
opportunities wherever conditions allow - serves to render national macroeconomic
management somewhat out-dated and ineffective. Yet it has proved difficult to
replace national with co-ordinated international, macroeconomic management,
especially in times of serious economic recession. Ironically, the involvement of
governments in the developed world, (but most notably the UK and the US) in the
pursuit of clear-cut policies designed to liberalise finance in the furthering of
'market freedom' and 'consumer choice', are presented as a feature of forces
beyond government control. Policies borne out of previous governmental decisions
are presented as a necessary response to an independent, complex and largely
technologically driven 'global' arena. Ultimately the growing power of large
corporate entities that have most benefited from prevailing economic policy,
acquire additional impetus as a result of governments pursuing industrial and

financial policies that further encourage radical changes in business organisation and management with unfortunate outcomes for many people.

The new economy and the 'new economics'

In sum, the applicability of the neo-liberal approach to global economic issues and problems may be far more limited than might be expected. In particular, the reformulated neo-classical economic framework, which in various guises has continued to dominate much of mainstream economic literature in recent years, offering analysis of a neat, mathematically precise world, seems increasingly to sit uneasily with the turbulent global trading arena that currently confronts business decision-makers in all industries. More to the point, perhaps, in the last few years there is additional evidence that the global economy, once again, confronts an economic malaise that conventional market-based economic theory cannot adequately resolve. Ormerod, for example, noted in 1994 that:

> The world economy is in crisis. Twenty million people are unemployed in Western Europe .... and vast tracts of the former Soviet empire are on the brink of economic collapse. In this grim context, orthodox economics seems powerless to help. Teams of economists descend on the former Soviet Union proclaiming the virtues and necessity of moving to a free market system as rapidly as possible: systems of greater purity than those contemplated by Ronald Reagan and Margaret Thatcher. But despite governments in the former Soviet bloc doing everything they are told, their economic situation worsens (Ormerod, 1994).

Why should this be? In an earlier analysis of the origins of recent economic problems, Lachmann (1986) focuses blame on the evolution of neo-liberal, market-based economic models:

> In looking at most of the models that have been devised by economic theorists in the last two decades we find little endeavour to depict traits of reality and less effort to accentuate them. Most of them are designed to reflect a network of relationships between variables, the parameters of which, one hopes, will find a counterpart in the regression coefficients of statistical time series. But the methodology of impotence....which has come to dominate economics in the last few decades, has inspired its adherents with such a vivid fear of reality that they dare not touch it even at a few points of their own selection (Lachmann, 1986).

The problem is not simply that the neo-classical framework cannot adequately deal with the critical elements of time and uncertainty which many economists, for example Shackle (1972), identified as the crucial insight and principal lesson of the real Keynesian revolution. It has much more to do with the dramatic way in which the global economy has changed beyond recognition over recent decades and appears today, more often than not, to operate as if in a perpetual state of dis-equilibrium. Ormerod sees this as a central issue, suggesting that:

> For all its apparent mathematical sophistication, the core model of theoretical
> economics, that of competitive general equilibrium, is premised upon an entirely
> faulty view of the modern world (Ormerod, p. 208).

Ironically, the resurgence of neo-liberalism and market economics which underpinned the drive towards financial and market 'de-regulation' has presented governments with new challenges. Acceptance of the general assumptions surrounding markets as the natural mechanism for human development and the just allocation of economic resources continues to dominate policies drawn up by the EU, the IMF, and the World Bank. However, such is the turbulent and unpredictable nature of the international business environment that the orthodox framework of the Walrasian economic system with its simple notions of smooth and incremental market adjustment to economic change seems fundamentally inappropriate.

Individual economic actors and major trans-national corporations do not simply work within traditional markets, submitting their bids and requests to an unbiased co-ordinating auctioneer in the marketplace until a mutually satisfactory outcome is attained. In practice, of course, most major companies now address their principal corporate goals by adopting business strategies that favour constant pro-active radical change. It is their capacity to manage change that sets rather than responds to market conditions. To secure and retain sustainable competitive advantage in the intensely competitive global marketplace of the late 1990s, these companies constantly reshape their business operations and corporate structure, defining, researching and then accessing new markets.

To stay ahead in the competitive market, a range of techniques are employed by large corporations including: 'boundarylessness' (the ability to work efficiently both horizontally and vertically within the corporate hierarchy, bringing together many different business functions, sometimes in partnership with both customers and suppliers); speed in decision-making and strategy implementation (cutting back on unnecessary layers of management and thereby creating a flexible and responsive business organization which can target new market opportunities) and 'organisational stretch' (where ambitious, long-term corporate goals are set to push quality and efficiency standards to ever higher levels).

Large corporations recognise that, in a highly competitive market the time available for such strategic readjustment and corporate reconstruction is extremely limited which makes the need for rapid and flexible response that much more urgent. Corporate response now needs to encompass a much wider range of goals and be responsive to a far broader array of stimuli than ever before. Smith Ring and Van de Ven (1994) make the important point that:

> As the uncertainty, complexity and duration of economic transactions within and
> between firms increase, it becomes increasingly important for scholars and managers
> to understand developmental processes of how equity, trust, conflict-resolution and
> procedures and internal governance structures emerge, evolve and dissolve over time
> (Smith Ring and Van de Ven, 1994).

Key players in the modern global economy, both political and corporate, have come to recognise that there is an urgent need for the market-based approach to address not only the shareholder requirements of enhanced profits, market share and productivity but, more fundamentally, those of a significant number of economic, political and social agents with interests in securing broader environmental, ethical and other principally non-economic objectives. Responsiveness to wider interest groups than simply shareholders can have important public relations and marketing implications for the business organisation and requires redefining the market mechanism in a way which will both facilitate our understanding of economic events and outcomes and better enable decision-makers, both corporate and governmental, to respond effectively to dynamic global change.

Chapter 4

Challenging orthodoxy: new insights into capitalism and market behaviour

As identified earlier, countries throughout Europe and across the political spectrum began to embrace the idea that markets could be not just the most effective allocator of resources but also engaged with for a more 'realistic' and 'pragmatic' social democratic platform. All of this took place as a result of specific political parties responding to perceptions surrounding popular demand and taking issues of electability into account, (over and above 'ideologies' or philosophy), this serving to foreclose any radically alternative political programme (Callaghan, 2000). Particular attention has been given to supply side issues of workforce training, the fragmentation of industrial relations policies to provide greater flexibility of negotiations between employers and employees and the restructuring of welfare states. The industrial or business enterprise has taken on a new dimension in this changed political environment and market structure. Corporate conduct and behaviour has taken on a significant political dimension at a time in which corporate scandals, from excessive wage differentials to corrupt auditing practices and human rights abuses, continue to hit the headlines.

Some analysts have argued that the market behaviour of some firms, particularly in the Japanese context, may be analysed by utilising the concept of 'treaties', whereby contractual agreements exist within a long-term and stable inter-organisational relationship. In large Japanese firms, the information structure tends to be decentralised, enabling it to offer a more effective and faster response to shocks. These just-in-time methods of production have particular implications for employee relations, job security and pay – as we shall see in subsequent chapters. Nevertheless, from a managerial perspective, it was the organisational 'efficiencies' of this type of production which had appeal.   In the hierarchical corporate structures of Anglo-Saxon capitalism, an employee would have to notify his line-manager about a problem and wait for a management decision before taking action. In the Japanese case, however, information is shared as widely as possible from senior management to the lowest employee level so that problem-solving occurs rapidly and solutions can be implemented without delay. This effective response is enhanced by the absence of job demarcation and the widespread use of on-the-job training and job rotation.

An understanding of the production process therefore becomes deep-rooted at the level of the operating team with similar processes applying at the level of key departments, such as research and development. Another crucial element of the Japanese model is the quasi-integration of the firm with its sub-contractors. Sub-contracting relationships are built on long-term, stable partnerships which allows smaller firms in the supply chain to maintain the required level of investment, while also sharing knowledge and technology with the "anchor" firm, generating a formidably powerful and successful business. In many respects, then, there are some elements of a particular stakeholding model at work here with the wide-ranging involvement of the workforce and sub-contractors in the decision-making process. The phenomenal success of Japanese firms in the global economy in the 1990s suggested that, adjusted appropriately for the specific cultural and economic context, the effective harnessing of some of these key elements of stakeholding could enhance the potential for corporate success. Indeed, they were considered so important as a model for other countries to acknowledge and, where appropriate, emulate if they wished to re-conquer global markets from the Japanese that MIT economist Lester Thurow wrote in 1992:

> The communitarian Japanese business firms' modes of play are quite different from those of the Anglo-Saxons, and their success is going to put enormous economic pressure on the rest of the industrial world to change (Thurow, 1992).

Such optimism for the Japanese way ignored the importance of financial markets and their key players operating in the global economy. The dramatic slowdown in the Japanese economy in recent years is attributed primarily to issues of excessive debt and poor risk-management within Japanese financial organisations, leaving the new management and manufacturing techniques of 'Japanisation' very much still a powerful force in the global economy. Thurow's approach takes us right to the heart of the stakeholder debate in modern economics. He begins with a concept familiar to biologists but relatively new to the science of economics, 'punctuated equilibrium'. In the context of economics, punctuated equilibrium means that there will be long periods of economic stability which, due to sudden and often unexpected changes, will precipitate a period of destabilising and damaging economic chaos.

As an example, Thurow cites the transition from a world of mass production to one dominated by process technology. The disequilibrium created by this sudden and irresistible change, he asserts, confronts capitalism with a significant challenge. Such a change generates increased inequalities of income, wealth and opportunity everywhere as traditional skills become suddenly obsolete. The widening gap between rich and poor, between those in work and those unable to find employment, between those firms able to respond swiftly and effectively to market signals and those which cannot do so, all increase the anger and resentment felt by the dispossessed and pose a serious threat to a democratic society. As Thurow noted:

> How far can inequality widen and real wages fall before something snaps in a democracy? (Thurow, 1992).

And, indeed, inequality on a global scale has most certainly widened:

> In Latin America, the average Gini coefficient - the most commonly used measure of inequality, with 0 representing perfect equality and 1 representing total inequality - is almost 0.5. The average Gini coefficient in sub-Saharan Africa is slightly lower........In recent years, inequality has been increasing in a large number of countries. This increase has been most striking in the transition economies, where the average Gini coefficient had been around 0.25 until the late 1980's; by the mid-1990s, it had risen to more than 0.30. While this may not appear to be a large increase, it is quite significant for the short period being addressed (Finance and Development, 1998).

Given these developments, we can see why more attention became focused upon alternative economic models, such as that of Rhenish capitalism.

Rhenish capitalism

The essence of the development of what became known as 'Rhenish capitalism' was the need to pose a fundamental challenge to the age-old belief, so deeply entrenched in the writings of Adam Smith and central to the views of market economists ever since, that the pursuit of enlightened self-interest in a competitive environment inevitably achieves an optimum outcome through the 'invisible hand'. As Hutton notes:

> If information is held asymmetrically and your welfare depends in part on other people's strategies, the prosecution of undiluted competitive self-interest is often self-defeating (Hutton, 1996, p.251).

The Rhenish model appeared to offer an appropriate escape route from this 'self-defeating' outcome. As Ormerod suggests:

> by the rejection of the concepts of orthodox economics, of 'rational' behaviour in a mechanical, linear world of equilibrium, progress can begin to be made to a more powerful understanding of how economies behave (Ormerod, 1994, p.211).

The Rhenish model of the market economy starts from the assumption that, in a modern industrial society, economic efficiency can be enhanced by the establishment and development of a set of specific institutions designed to facilitate market interaction. The ideas which formed the intellectual basis of Rhenish capitalism have been applied in a policy setting in Austria, Switzerland, Germany, Scandinavia and the Benelux countries and elements can also be found in Japan (see, for example, Albert and Gonenc, 1996, p.184).

The Rhenish model has at its heart a unique contractual structure which determines how business corporations are governed. Such a model of the market economy relies upon:

continuous monitoring of managers by other stakeholders, who have a long-term relationship with the firm and engage permanently in important aspects of decision-making and, in cases of dissatisfaction, take action to correct management decisions through internal channels   (OECD Annual Economic Survey, 1995; Germany).

Whereas in the orthodox model of the market economy, decision-making is seen essentially as an individual process, conducted to maximise personal or corporate gain, in the Rhenish model, companies operate with a two-tier board with a supervisory dimension. This allows for a much more extensive representation at the corporate decision-making level of stakeholder interests and can be a powerful mechanism to integrate under- or un-represented interests. A focus upon the governance of firms, in terms of board composition, structure and process acquire additional importance.

In the Rhenish model, those who work for a particular company would have the right to contribute to corporate decision-making as much as those who act in a shareholder capacity on all matters where explicit contracts do not already exist. The extension of stakeholder rights to employees in this instance means that corporate decision-making - and hence economic outcomes - have to be on the basis of consensus, either formally as in Germany or less formally, but nonetheless adhered to, as in Japan.

It is important to note that such a consensual decision-making process does not completely over-ride the freedom of the individual (whether employee, manager or shareholder) to pursue his or her own individual gain. Nor does it imply that greater uncertainty about the company's economic objectives will result. Indeed, there is strong evidence that, in both cases, quite the reverse will occur. As Albert and Gonenc suggest:

> the sharing and joint exercise of residual management rights between investors and employees may enhance the firm's capacity to create wealth. In certain circumstances, such arrangements may provide a more productive basis for cooperation between rational wealth-maximising investors and employees - between investors and employees seeking to maximise their total income over the long term (Albert and Gonenc, 1996).

It is important to note here the inherent individualism and employment insecurity on which some apparently consensual agreements rely. Albert and Gonenc identify three kinds of contractual relationships:

> a) the indefinite labour contract, under which employees are granted contracts for an unlimited duration with guaranteed earnings. All business risks are assumed by the shareholders who can only agree such contracts where the company's market position is so strong, perhaps monopolistic, that risks are minimised. Such contractual arrangements can generate commitment, company loyalty and worker-manager trust but at the cost of significant business risk.

b) the 'spot' labour contract, under which employees are granted contracts which exist for very limited time periods and which are subject to continual renegotiation. In this instance, much of the business risk is transferred to the employee in the form of potential redundancy, often generating reduced commitment, more active labour market search and reduced trust.

and c) the incomplete or stakeholding contract, under which contracts are not formal or complete in themselves, either in terms of duration or projected reward. Such contracts recognise that both long term employability and potential earnings critically depend upon unknown future developments including not only market conditions and the efficacy of investment but also the abilities and productivity of employees. None of these factors can be adequately assessed in advance of real world outcomes. Instead of contractual commitments on duration of employment and/or earnings, stakeholding contracts allow employees co-decision rights regarding all of the critical matters that will affect their futures.

There has been a proliferation of spot or incomplete contracts which have led to increasing employment insecurity and a reduction of workers rights (see Sennett, 1999; Nichols 2001). From a business perspective a strength of the Rhenish capitalism approach to economic decision-making lies in the additional flexibility that this gives a company in a complex and intensely competitive trading world. In the entrepreneurial spirit of casualised labour and 'ownership of problems' the involvement of labour and capital in a joint strategic alliance is read as their *mutual* recognition of the need for flexible response to dynamic market pressures.

From the same perspective, a co-decision model of this kind, for example, enables a company to reduce temporarily its labour costs during a period of market decline, thus retaining its competitive edge. The long-standing practice in Japan for some wages agreements to be flexible, with bonuses only paid in times of corporate success, provides a good example of this point. Such a strategy is likely to generate positive market outcomes, enabling the company to restore and perhaps enhance employee earnings after the recovery of the business is complete and profitability restored.

Furthermore, under such agreements, it would now be in the employee's interests to develop skills relevant to the requirement of the company rather than those that might facilitate their labour market search elsewhere. The disadvantages of the other two forms of contractual arrangements are avoided and the commitment of the company's labour force to market success is intensified. Albert and Gonenc are optimistic in their description of this outcome as:

> mutual dependence, creating a community of faith between different parties over time (Albert and Gonenc, 1996, p. 186).

To some degree, in the uncertain markets in which businesses operate, they are genuinely more reliant upon workforces providing 'quality' services and products. The Rhenish model may allow, indeed rely upon, such stakeholders having a real say in determining economic outcomes. This requires the incorporation into this 'community of faith' of parties beyond those directly involved in the day-to-day activities of the enterprise; for example, customers, suppliers and local communities. Whether or not all are equally rewarded for their efforts is another matter that depends upon the integrity of companies and the confidence of workers to negotiate from the basis of their somewhat insecure contracts.

One good example of this relates to the supply base of global industry where profound changes have occurred in recent years (see, for example, Braddon and Dowdall, 1996) which highlight the degree to which traditional or orthodox views of market behaviour have changed over time. In what has been termed a 'post-Fordist production paradigm' (Latham, 1993), buyers and sellers are experiencing significant, rapid and cumulative changes in their relationship across many industries. Central to these changes is an enormous expansion of manufacturing activities based on less rigid and more highly adaptable (i.e. flexible) technological and organisational structures. From the corporate perspective, flexibility and responsiveness are the key elements here. As a result, models of business interaction are diverging from the polar models of competitive multi-sourcing and vertical integration, towards a new middle ground.

This has had practical consequences for industry and the market. For example, the Department of Trade and Industry, the Confederation of British Industry, the Bank of England, the Institute of Directors and the Department of Employment have all supported the move towards what has been termed 'partnership sourcing', designed to develop a deeper and more co-operative relationship between companies and their suppliers in the form of a long term relationship which is seen as producing significant improvements in performance and cost reduction.

The post-fordist approach to production includes the adoption of total quality management techniques, "just-in-time" production, flexible manufacturing systems, and vendor certification. Most recently, global corporations have come to recognise that, as a result of the intense competitive pressures in the market, current perspectives on production and market access will need to be transformed and that one essential ingredient of this transformation will be a dramatic change in the nature, role and extent of their supplier network. Ultimately then the 'new economy' extends throughout the supply matrix underpinning industrial activity.

As a result, major sectors of industry have extensively reviewed their supplier lists with the result that the number of suppliers to any single client company has been reduced significantly, while at the same time extended geographically, both nationally and internationally, to capture the most efficient, reliable and flexible suppliers.

Clearly, in an orthodox market model such dramatic changes in the relationship between key market players could not easily be coordinated. No central 'auctioneer' could provide an adequate facilitating mechanism to ensure the smooth and rapid adjustment necessary to avoid severe market contraction or collapse in a situation where everything is changing so rapidly and where the outcome is far from predictable. The inevitable outcome of conventional market adjustment in such a setting would most likely be considerable dis-equilibrium, together with consequent reduction of output and employment.

Why does the Rhenish model and the associated stakeholding approach apparently offer an escape route from this economic impasse? In theory, the Rhenish model provides an important means to assist the market mechanism to overcome such a disequilibrium outcome. By explicitly including the views, preferences and behavioural patterns of relevant key actors, both internal and external to the organisation, in economic and business decision-making, a unanimity of purpose can emerge which will encourage employee commitment, customer-supplier loyalty and integration, with distinct benefits likely to be derived as a result, including higher internal productivity, improved internal and external efficiency and a crucial sharpening of the competitive edge of the business organisation and its component parts.

This element of economic partnership serving a common purpose represents the most important feature of the social market consensus that emerged in some countries in the post-war period. As Albert and Gonenc observe:

> In practice, social actors and policy-makers in different countries determine their corporate contracting arrangements in the light of a nationally accepted paradigm of what is economically optimal and socially desirable, and they shape the permitted 'boundaries' and 'routines' of national contractual arrangements accordingly (Albert and Gonenc, 1996).

Initially, two elements of the Rhenish approach were considered important indicators of its strength and relevance to the modern global economy. First, at least for a period of time, the structure and duration of shareholder involvement in organisations operating within this approach remained relatively stable, suggesting a degree of acceptance by key players in the financial markets. Secondly, senior management hierarchies developed from within these enterprises, were considered to comprise personnel equipped with good understanding of the technological, organisational and implicit contractual nature of the organisation that helped to sustain its progress and development.

Clearly, however, the degree to which a society or individual business can in practice maintain the Rhenish approach to capitalist organisation depends crucially on the view taken of the structure and modus operandi of organisations or firms; how far it can be integrated into the economy or society within which it operates; the nature of the organisation and its objectives; the structure of the industry of which it is a member; and the boundaries that limit its activities. In essence, it will depend critically on the precise form and structure that capitalism takes in a particular society, requiring us to consider the important role of infrastructures, histories and political systems.

Assessing the overall benefits and costs of approaches to capitalism such as that of the Rhenish model, Minford (1998) suggests that:

>There should be some gain in security, as measured by income variability and inequality, but there is also likely to be some loss in efficiency, showing up in reduced average living standards (Minford, 1998, p.189).

However, Minford asserts that, in Anglo-Saxon and Oriental systems, where government intervention in the labour market is minimal and welfare is provided either through the tax/transfer system in the first case and hardly at all in the second:

>It is striking that, among OECD countries faced with these common trends, the Anglo-Saxon and Oriental approaches have generated much less unemployment and lower taxes than those of Europe (Minford, 1998, p.190).

Of course, we cannot stress enough that these perceived economic gains usually are secured at the cost of employment security and/or decent wages, especially for those who are employed on the 'spot' or partial contracts identified above. We can see this more clearly when we look at the extensive usage of such contracts in recent years. What is clear is a notable lack of imagination in terms of pursuing ideas that lie beyond the scope of the rationality of capitalism. Capitalism has become associated with individual freedom and justice and is widely perceived to have 'triumphed', or even, as Minford notes:

>It is not so much that capitalism has triumphed or that people have mostly seen through the stakeholder fallacy, though both are true ..... what we have seen is in fact the extinction of communism and the eclipse of socialism because people have discovered that only under free markets are human energy and ingenuity properly released and harnessed. Since economic freedom is also an important component of political freedom, people choose this capitalist mixture because it provides both economic success and personal autonomy (Minford, 1998, p.235).

The economic problems encountered in countries employing elements of the Rhenish approach called into question the capacity for stakeholding to genuinely transform economic interaction and outcomes. Furthermore, the work of Minford and others of the new classical persuasion helped to recreate the cult of individual economic freedom and, as a result, restored market economics to the centre of the political policy-making stage.

As we noted earlier, in terms of dominant schools of economic thought, the decade of the 1990s was associated with the apparent victory of neo-liberalism. As a result economic strategies involving a significant degree of concerted action at the macro-level by government, companies and trade unions, acting in partnership for mutual gain, diminished in importance during the 1980s and, by the 1990s, had all but vanished. In the context of a neo-liberal re-awakening, economic decisions were now decided and implemented primarily with reference to the implementation of mechanisms designed to facilitate market freedom and flexibility. As a result, governments across Europe have played an important role in implementing market-based economic policies that have frequently worked to the detriment of trade unions and other social interest groups. This process was, in part, driven by the urgent need for governments within the European Union to conform as rapidly as possible to the terms of the Maastricht Agreement in the drive to achieve a single European currency.

Euro-zone and the influence of Maastricht on economies and welfare regimes

On the theoretical front, the reconstruction of neo-liberalism provided a rigorous, defendable intellectual justification for limiting the intervention role of governments. It provided a powerful intellectual barrier to reverse progress toward concerted economic policy-making and, by emphasising individualism, effectively eroded the case for the stakeholder economy.

In practical terms however, perhaps more than anything else, the decision of the European Union to move towards European Monetary Union and the introduction of a single currency has helped to consolidate the position of this kind of economic approach and locate it firmly within the policy-making agenda to the exclusion of stakeholding ideas. For all European states, the urgent need to meet the economic criteria set down in the Maastricht agreement has simply over-ridden other policy objectives and necessitated increasing conformity to a neo-liberal, market-driven standard model in which both government expenditure and intervention must be minimised. It has become the conventional wisdom that no EU country can afford to move radically out of step with the others if it is to ultimately attain Maastricht convergence. The imminence of European Monetary Union during the late 1990s itself put in place a major practical barrier to the exploration of more radical agendas.

Since then, of course, for many member countries of the EU, European Monetary Union has already arrived. Following a relatively smooth introduction of the new currency in January 1999, the new euro area states were able to trade in the euro as well as their own national currencies and, as this book was nearing completion, those national currencies were withdrawn, creating the 'euro-zone'.

Despite the UK being outside the euro-zone at the moment, there is little doubt that the euro already plays a significant role in this economy also. In terms of trade settlements externally (but also some of those within the British economy) the euro is now regularly employed as the currency unit, a phenomenon known as "euro-creep" to some in the British press. In Britain, the issue of European Monetary Union and the role of the euro as ultimately a single currency are now very much on the political agenda.

Eleven countries are currently within the euro-zone with four others (including Britain) considering future entry. Some 70-75% of British companies who trade into the euro-zone tend to use sterling and their customers on the continent have, until recently, been prepared to carry the exchange rate risk. Now, however, euro-zone members have just one currency and Britain, therefore, must expect to see the terms under which it trades with euro-zone members change significantly. Euro-zone customers will demand either payment in euros or that British products are price-discounted so that the risk is equalised.

Britain will find it difficult in the longer term to avoid the constraining requirements of euro-convergence in limiting policy-making. Already many British financial services companies are moving from sterling to the euro, in advance of any future formal British entry to the zone, thereby accelerating the "euro-creep" phenomenon.

For Britain, euro-zone membership appears inevitable in the longer term. It is crucial to recognise that, using Department of Trade and Industry figures, about 50.8% of our trade goes into the euro area with, for comparison, 13.5% going to the USA, Canada and Mexico. Few people realise that more British trade goes to Germany than to the whole of North America. As a result, the impact of the euro on the British economy is already being felt much sooner than most analysts expected and it appears inevitable that the drive towards economic convergence that underpins so much of euro-zone economic policy-making currently will also seriously constrain the UK government's opportunity for independent action. At present, the British government's timetable for euro entry, depending upon the result of a referendum, remains a matter for speculation. Currently, the signs are that British entry to the euro-zone will happen during the life of the current Parliament. Despite its initial problems, the euro is here and is establishing itself gradually as a major world currency.

As noted above, central to the process of achieving European Monetary Union were - and remain - the so-called Maastricht criteria. Meeting these economic criteria has emerged as the single most important policy objective for most countries in Western Europe over the last decade. Maintaining policies designed to ensure the genuine economic convergence required for meaningful EMU across Western Europe undoubtedly will be the principal challenge for the next decade. Crucially from our perspective here, the Maastricht criteria spell out the demanding macroeconomic targets that specific countries must achieve before they can be deemed appropriate members of the euro-zone group. These criteria include the requirement that:

- a currency is able to remain within the normal band around parity set by the European Exchange Rate Mechanism for at least 2 years without devaluation;

- an inflation rate not exceeding 1.5% above the average rate of the three lowest inflation member countries;

- general government deficits do not exceed 3% of GDP;

- gross public debt does not exceed 60% of GDP;

- interest rates (long term) do not exceed 2% more than the average of those in the three member countries with the lowest inflation.

Although critics of the Maastricht criteria contend either that they are unnecessary to achieve stable monetary union or that they ignore other, more important, real rather than nominal economic indicators such as employment and output levels there can be no doubt that governments across Europe have come to view the Maastricht criteria as essential targets for policy. In most cases, economic policy has been adjusted to seek the rapid attainment of Maastricht targets for exchange rate movement and interest rate, inflation and debt levels. Furthermore, at the political level, these targets have appeared almost sacrosanct despite their impact, often adverse, on the real variables mentioned above. As Teague notes:

> Meeting the Maastricht criteria for entry into a European Monetary Union is the top economic priority of virtually every member state in the EU...an almighty scramble has broken out among the member states to rein-in government deficits to keep inflation and interest rates low so that they will not be excluded from a monetary union (Teague, 1998).

Maastricht, fiscal constraints and restructured welfare regimes

The key point here is that EU member states have generally adopted strategies of fiscal contraction to reduce government deficits and thereby to ease the inflationary and interest rate pressures argued to be associated with 'excessive' public debt. To implement fiscal contraction, these governments have often had to reduce public expenditure in areas affecting welfare policy and social provision - precisely those areas of government which attempt to offer the disadvantaged or socially excluded an economic lifeline, recognising their stakeholder interests in the economy. During the period prior to the launch of the 'euro-zone', the degree to which individual EU members' fiscal stance actually led to convergence with the Maastricht criteria differed considerably. Some countries - Denmark, Ireland and Luxembourg - performed well in terms of approximation to the criteria; others - for example, Italy, Greece and Belgium - did not.

Those in closest proximity to the criteria have maintained a tight fiscal stance for many years and those who have previously diverged rather more from the targets due to the adoption of less stringent and painful fiscal policy have had to compensate for this in the last few years with an even harder fiscal contraction. The price of qualification for European Monetary Union membership can be seen to be extremely high therefore when measured in terms of the recessionary pressure from fiscal contraction (with its consequent negative impact on output and employment) and the deleterious consequences for government expenditure on social and welfare objectives.

Many desirable social objectives have been sacrificed in recent years in the pursuit of EMU and some would argue that the development of a genuine stakeholder society is one of them. Looking at individual cases of Maastricht-driven fiscal adjustment in the approach to the 1999 qualification deadline, we can see more clearly how EMU-focused economic policy-making is impacting adversely on stakeholder interests. In Germany, particularly severe fiscal contraction has been required in the attempt to achieve the desired EMU targets. As Teague noted:

> Its austerity programme (Sparpaket) is the biggest single fiscal retrenchment in economic history. Altogether, the authorities plan to slash public expenditure by £30bn. A wide number of social programmes are being cut back while unemployment benefits and other entitlements have been frozen (Teague, 1998).

Similarly, in Spain and Italy, drastic action to reduce fiscal deficits was taken in the late 1990s, mainly by a significant reduction in welfare expenditure. The welfare state, perhaps the most appropriate example of earlier attempts by governments to recognise stakeholder interests in society by ensuring that there was some degree of concertation in policy-making and that, to some extent at least, national resource allocation took into account the needs of those unable or less able to protect themselves in an economic sense, has itself endured a state of apparent crisis for several decades. Rhodes (1996) suggests that the process of globalisation (or at least internationalisation) has played an important role in extending this crisis.

> For while during the 'golden age' of 'embedded liberalism' the growth - and parallel internationalisation - of western capitalism had been dependent on domestic social compacts (i.e. the expansion of governments' domestic distributive roles), in the era of 'disembedded liberalism' (unrestricted trade, liberalised financial markets) the ability of governments to live up to their side of the bargain is wearing precariously thin (Rhodes, 1996).

Rhodes asserts that the decaying power of government to secure desired economic outcomes and thus deliver on 'their side of the bargain':

> can be attributed both to the fraying of social safety nets (due to the sheer weight of budget deficits and the discontent of tax-weary publics) and the loss of government control in a global economy over employment and other broad economic policy objectives (Rhodes, 1996, p. 307).

Rising welfare costs (which, for example, absorbed about one-third of GDP during the early years of the 1990s in Scandinavia) continue to pose the greatest challenge to the maintenance of an effective welfare state, particularly when set against the array of new social trends and problems confronting modern industrial societies and the new global economic forces which make the attainment and preservation of vitally important domestic economic pacts or 'social contracts' almost unattainable.

   Some observers would question the demise of the welfare state, arguing that, despite the pressures of globalisation and the neo-liberal resurgence that should both lead to its contraction, social welfare programmes have continued to expand to cover the cost of higher unemployment and industrial restructuring. This view, however, is simply based on observation of nominal budgets and fails to recognise that many welfare states are failing to deliver promised outcomes in a range of crucial areas. New social challenges are appearing all the time and the welfare state is found wanting, even with respect to the historic challenges, let alone the new. As Rhodes notes:

> among politicians of all parties there is a profound loss of confidence in 'collective', public sector solutions in favour of either privatised or 'marketised' social services. How far this loss of confidence will feed through into policies that question the fundamentals of European welfare systems depends on a host of factors, notably the institutional make-up of those systems and factors largely beyond the control of decision-makers - primarily levels of economic growth and the impact of changes in the global economy (Rhodes, 1996, p.308).

We can note some quite radical changes to European welfare regimes under the influence of Maastricht. These are being broadly restructured to meet the changing requirements of business and to meet the anti-inflationary, fiscal restrictions discussed above. Esping-Anderson (1990) identified four models of welfare provision within Europe, each displaying a different labour market/industrial relations structure and institutional framework for welfare provision. He termed these models the Scandinavian, Bismarkian, Southern European and Anglo-Saxon models.

The welfare systems established in Scandinavia, although varying between countries, were social democratic in nature and designed to meet the expectations of the middle classes with a combination of generous benefit payments and equal access to such benefits for all workers. In the original schemes, there was no market-driven element and equal entitlement ensured the acceptability of the welfare programme across all classes in Scandinavian society. Central to the model was a long-standing commitment to full employment matched by a further commitment to protect income levels when these are put at risk by adverse economic developments.

These commitments were viewed essentially as 'rights' to which all were entitled, rendering the model both popular and also extremely expensive to maintain with its viability and durability only called into question as economic problems arose and became severe. Rhodes contends that the Scandinavian model was essentially corporatist in nature, constructed around a consensus between unions, companies and the government on critical issues such as wage formation and adjustment, restructuring and technology impacts. The crucial requirement was to hold together the social democratic consensus as the core of the system, a stakeholder compromise which, should it crumble under pressures from the global economy, would be likely to demolish the Scandinavian model with it.

In recent years, these global pressures have necessitated significant changes within the model with both Sweden and Denmark having to move towards decentralised wage bargaining with reforms in industrial relations practices. Furthermore, the burden of excessively high taxation eventually drove both countries towards a tax reduction strategy, bringing with it elements of both privatisation and decentralisation. Rhodes suggests that the changes wrought by global pressures within these stakeholder-inclined nations has been considerable with Sweden, Norway and Finland all witnessing a sudden and significant rise in unemployment in the late 1980s and early in the following decade.

Having to adjust rapidly and appropriately to the shifting economic forces unleashed by the liberation of global financial markets and international capital flows was central to the explanation for their economic problems. In response to global financial market liberalisation, these three countries implemented similar and virtually simultaneous policies in the fields of financial deregulation, fiscal adjustment and exchange rate management; decisions which failed to prevent (and indeed may have contributed to) the economic crisis of the 1990s. That crisis, in turn, served to fracture and then fragment the vital social consensus at the heart of Scandinavian economic policy-making and revealed, with stark clarity, the limitations of the early attempts at designing and developing a stakeholder economy.

The 'Bismarkian' model has been identified with the welfare state systems of, for example, Austria, Belgium, the Netherlands, Luxemburg, Italy and Germany (where the term 'Rhenish' has also been applied to their brand of capitalism in the past). These nations are most notable for the way that 'status differentiation' determines the rights of citizens to welfare entitlements (income maintenance and health care) on the basis of employment and family status. Almost all insurance-determined benefits are earnings-related and are funded by employee and employer payments with different terms and conditions applying to different occupational groups. Rhodes notes that the social insurance fund in these countries is managed by employers and trades unions and that the social insurance system is strongly biased in support of the family. However, the system does impose high non-wage labour costs on employers and does not appear capable of responding quickly or effectively to rising unemployment.

Germany has struggled to maintain its high-wage, high productivity approach and has problems with the tax burden relating to income maintenance, constrained wage differentials and weakness in employment creation. Furthermore, Rhodes comments that:

> at the same time, while labour costs rule out an expansion of low-paid, service sector jobs, the country's innovation system is locked into a Fordist trajectory that also prevents the creation in large numbers of their high-technology, highly paid equivalents (Rhodes, 1996, p. 315).

The German economic success story was constructed on an agreed long-term industrial strategy, a powerful and centralised labour organisation, a long-term approach to capital investment unifying banks and industry, and a strong, well-funded vocational education system. As a result, however, wage and non-wage costs in Germany have become prohibitive and, with Fordist production processes relatively simple to duplicate in other low-wage economies, many German companies are choosing to relocate. Rhodes notes that the competitive challenge of global markets and associated corporate restructuring within Germany has created a large pool of unemployed people, both unskilled and skilled. As a result, what were once perceived to be the advantages and strengths of the German economic system have increasingly become seen as sources of weakness which obstruct the capacity for the system to adapt flexibly as required. In essence, the Fordist employee has secured a place as a 'privileged insider' in German labour markets, with the costs of adjustment borne by 'outsiders' (those who are the unemployed or precariously employed).

Rhodes also identifies the welfare programmes of southern Europe (Spain, Greece, Portugal and Italy) which have been minimalist in nature and have relied heavily upon Church, family or private charity provision. While these countries (Italy apart) have tended to have low welfare budgets, in recent years the costs of such provision has risen sharply and the distribution of welfare benefits has become uneven 'occupationally and territorially' (Rhodes, 1996, p.316).

Some groups are well-protected (public employees, white collar workers and full-time, permanent wage-earners in medium-and large-sized enterprises while others, the 'under-protected') receive little income support while unemployed. Rhodes noted that Spain, Italy and Greece have all experienced serious labour market problems in recent years, a problem aggravated by the low level of participation in education, weak and ineffective training systems and pervasive, growing structural unemployment. All countries in this group face problems adjusting to the pressures emanating from the global market. Rhodes comments that:

> We can no longer cling to the principles of the Fordist 'golden age', when a virtuous circle linked productivity growth and employment expansion, and rising income translated into higher demand for manufactured goods. Now, demand growth for manufactures will no longer create more employment...because the growth in demand for these products has not kept pace with productivity gains. The solution...is more post-industrial, service sector employment (Rhodes, 1996).

Unlike the corporatist, consensus-driven Scandinavian model, the Anglo-Saxon version thrives on individualism in the liberal sense. Stakeholding is here closely identified with individual property ownership and rights. As Ackerman and Alstott, writing from an American perspective argue under the heading 'The Individualist's Case for Stakeholding':

> In contrast to most public programs, this one does not restrict the rights of private property on behalf of some collective good. It is based on the opposite premise: property is so important to the free development of individual personality that everybody ought to have some (Ackerman and Alstott, 2000, p.191).

Such an argument is based upon a particular interpretation of human nature, one that also links individual identity and self-expression with consumer activity. Individual equal opportunity replaces a general preoccupation with the establishment of safety nets and there is an emphasis upon individual responsibility for pension and welfare provision. In Ackerman and Alstott's account we should be 'trustees' of our individual futures. It is up to the individual 'and not the state to decide how much insurance she needs', for protection against possible redundancy, accidents or illness (ibid, p.134).

Rhodes argues that the scaling-down of the welfare state in the UK under the Anglo-Saxon model may be very difficult to reverse given the tax-averse nature of an electorate which has become used to tax decreases in recent years, at least on incomes. Major structural deficiencies within the UK relating to innovation organisations, research and development levels, poor quality training, capital market flexibility and regional regeneration potential are all highlighted as damaging consequences of the Anglo-Saxon model which, Rhodes argues, will ultimately prevent the UK enjoying both 'progressive competitiveness' (the return to a high-wage, high-skills equilibrium) and the spin-off regional benefits that would otherwise flow from inward investment from the multinationals. In the case of the UK, the Anglo-Saxon model has created a two-tier economy, comprising a prosperous, efficient and value-generating service sector together with a manufacturing sector which is not only in crisis but has been described recently as approaching 'meltdown'. Without radical change to the Anglo-Saxon model, Rhodes contends that:

> Britain will be relegated permanently to a second rung of industrial nations ......
> (with) long-term difficulties in maintaining living standards across all social
> classes......social fragmentation and the further erosion of the Beveridge welfare
> model are the predictable outcome (Rhodes, 1996, p.314).

The nature and role of the state itself (and in particular its capacity to provide for its genuine stakeholders, through welfare policies and public goods provision) is rapidly changing. Following the principles of Thatcherism in the 1980s, the UK began to move quickly towards the US welfare system. Benefit payments are subject to more rigorous means-testing assessment and the better off groups in society have been encouraged to leave the compulsory state welfare system and either top-up or actually replace state benefits and transfers by joining private insurance schemes. The universal spread of the original Beveridge approach to welfare has now been replaced in the UK by a minimalist but less expensive welfare system with the state benefits that remain allocated to those defined as 'deserving' poor. In part, this is because international bodies such as the IMF and the OECD have rigorously pursued the objective of freely-moving international capital and, in such a world:

> Public goods-including *regulatory* goods (property rights, a stable currency, trade
> and production regulations), *productive/distributive* goods (public ownership,
> public services, direct or indirect involvement in finance capital) and
> *redistributive* goods (health and welfare services, employment policies, corporatist
> bargaining processes) - are all becoming steadily more difficult to provide and
> control (Rhodes, 1996, p.308).

The process of liberating global capital created, in effect, "the most powerful pressure group of all - international corporate capital" (Rhodes, 1996, p.309).

Welfare states across the globe are being restructured to meet the demands of global capital. Some have referred to the inter-linkage of welfare policies promoting labour flexibility in terms of a Schumpetarian or post-Fordist welfare state. The implications of this for shifts in the relationship between state and civil society are vast as increasingly, states have to reach into the informal organisations of civil society to carry out their objectives and to harmonise a range of social interests and economic demands.

In sum, under the influence of global financial market forces that tend to have a pronounced deflationary bias, macroeconomic policy becomes focused less on full-employment provision and more on anti-inflation strategies. The deflationary policy bias thereby created carries with it economic conditions that are hardly appropriate for the extension of a genuine stakeholder society. Particularly in those countries within Europe (such as the Scandinavian nations) which had become recognised for their expansive welfare provision and for the prevalence and prominence of the social and political coalitions, approaching real stakeholder communities, that helped maintain such provision, the impact of neo-liberal, market-liberating policies and their deflationary bias proved problematic in the extreme.

For example, at the start of the 1990s, countries such as Sweden, Norway and Finland confronted combinations of comparatively slow economic growth and financial instability. The adjustment price for these economies has been considerable with a combination of high unemployment levels, massive public debt and very high interest rates. As they became ever more immersed in the global economy, even these stakeholder-minded nations were unable to avoid powerful and invasive deflationary pressures, culminating in a significant reduction in public services and, ultimately, the unravelling of the very social coalitions on which the future of the stakeholder society in these countries so critically depended.

For critics of the stakeholding approach such as Minford (1998), their economic demise was all too predictable. For example, Minford noted that:

> We were told that Sweden was the middle way, with its taxes at 70% of national income and its cradle-to-grave socialism - no sooner admired by our fickle leftists than it too collapsed and Sweden is as a result in the process of far-reaching capitalist reforms. Now comes Germany....seen in its social charterism of the past two decades as pleasantly left-wing or 'middle way'.....alas, the curse of leftist admiration strikes again. Germany's labour costs are two-and-a-half times the UK's, six times Korea's, and twenty times Poland's. There is ....an unemployment crisis in Germany...low employment of women ...and....industry is relocating as much as it can outside Germany...into Poland and the Czech Republic (Minford, 1999, p. 7).

Minford draws the conclusion, so central to the proponents of 'radical Right' economics, that:

> 'Stakes' sound as cosy and caring as the 'middle way' (the same idea) once did. But such stakes are not only a violation of property rights but, unsurprisingly, do not work either. We just have to accept that capitalism, for all its 'unacceptable

faces', by giving people the fruits of their efforts and ingenuity, delivers the results. Whenever tyrants, planners or social do-gooders take over, the economy suffers in the end (Minford, 1999, p.8). .

This is an interesting point of view given the dramatic influence of corporate power over peoples' everyday lives (Mombiot, 2001). Aided by governments pursuing neo-liberal economic policies with their vigorous activities focused on creating 'free-markets', (by for example, cutting corporation tax, reducing business interest rates, challenging labour legislation and legislation on health and welfare (see Nichols 2001)), it can hardly be said that the invisible hand of the market exists. Indeed a sizeable share in a company (companies being a key beneficiary of governmental and state policies) is the easiest way to become a member of the wealthy (Novak 2001). Nor have markets been responsible for allocating according to the efforts and ingenuity of all society's members. While certain sections who have benefited from the economy have been given a huge, highly visible, helping hand, others have been left to struggle with poverty, long working hours associated stress and ill health (Nichols 2001) as social bonds become broken by the neo-Taylorist rationality of the modern business world.

To 'have a stake' surely requires open debate about the desires and needs of particular groups, desires and needs which are out of keeping with dominant sectional interests. As we shall see later, this partly explains why there has been a growing interest in communitarian political agendas, emerging from the lived experiences of social collectivities. In the absence of a thriving public space, there is an inherent tendency for vested interests to manipulate and control the terms of debate. Participation then becomes tyrannical due to the narrow terms set down by corporate and financial lobbying groups.

The power of global finance

As the above outline of converging welfare states and work practices suggests, pressures on the state to deal with conflicting demands and interests are bound up with its role to preserve conditions appropriate for capital accumulation. To focus only upon the activities of national states is to ignore the global dynamics of capitalism in which nation states are immersed and are responsive to, as a means of 'managing' the global circuit of capital (Burnham, 2001). As noted earlier, there are a range of international organisations committed to the neoliberal agenda, including the IMF and the World Bank. Andrew Gamble, citing Coates (2000), refers to the ways in which the 'competitive pressures of capital accumulation…force the convergence of all capitalist models and all national economies towards neo-liberal institutions and policies, such as privatisation, deregulation, shareholder value, flexible labour markets and residual welfare'.

Governments will tend to promote ideas *only* if they are in keeping with the *general* interests of modern capital forms (notwithstanding the important influence of 'local' and 'global' cultural and political processes). A broader, truly humane approach is unrealistic in this context. Hugo Radice argues that anybody expecting the state to 'tame' capitalism for the benefit of all is seriously deluded. The state is a capitalist state and will only make modifications if these are seen to be in keeping with business interests. France, often referenced for its resistance to globalising economic forces, provides a good example of this:

> The Jospin government in France has just barely managed to introduce the 35 hour week for two reasons: first, that big business can easily afford it and is more concerned right now about restructuring corporate ownership, governance and finance; and secondly, because it can strong-arm the very weak French unions into making concessions on 'flexibility' that will ensure that the burden falls on wages, not profits (Radice, 2001).

The limits to effective capital accumulation have to be acknowledged by key players in the global economy which is why some concessions may be made to a broader civil society. Ideological processes play a pivotal role here. According to Gamble, neoliberalism can be thought of in terms of a 'new hegemonic creed' facilitated by its 'assimilation with globalisation' (p. 132). The prevalence of employment in "the *reductio ad absurdum* of the triumph of business values: everyone is now a business" (Elliot and Atkinson, 1998, p.76). Paradoxically, the individualisation of social problems on which neoliberalism relies; may contribute to anarchic and atomised social responses which are less predictable and manageable outside the safe parameters of a more stable economy and solid welfare institutions. For this reason Gray argues that neoliberalism is limited by the character of its own aspirations:

> economic globalisation does not strengthen the current regime of global laissez faire. It works to undermine it...There is nothing in today's global market that buffers it against the social strains arising from highly uneven economic development (Gray. 1998, p.7).

National and international governance structures may perceive and respond to such dangers but following the points already made about the inherently capitalist nature of the state, any concessions to countervailing social and political pressures are likely to be relatively limited and piecemeal. We would argue that this is most clearly witnessed in the UK by New Labour's treatment of the ideas of the stakeholding economy, originally promoted by Will Hutton.

Broadly, the dangers for the economy of reduced co-operation and commitment of workers, in addition to a blind ignorance of the needs of local communities on the part of investors and shareholders, was signalled by Will Hutton's 'The State We're In' (Hutton, 1995). Referencing the important lessons offered by Bismarkian, Rhenish and Scandinavian models, Hutton made a passionate plea for policies which could help to overcome the 'narcissistic culture' (Lasch, 1980) generated by international neo-liberal policies. He argued that these adversely affect the community or the sense of civic responsibility upon which welfare restructuring and reduced public expenditure, key components of neo-liberal economic policy, rely.

Moreover, uneven global development necessarily produces poverty and social, political and economic disenfranchisement for significant proportions of the population. In addition to demographic changes, these place further burdens on welfare states. Nor are welfare states benefiting from transfers associated with the long-anticipated 'caring-sharing' peace dividend of the post-cold war world. The effects of foot-loose capitalism on the social body are perceived to have ramifications for the long-term interests of capitalism and economic growth itself. In addition, a large proportion of unemployed people and under-paid labour results, ultimately, in increased welfare, policing and social security spending:

> marginalisation, deprivation and exclusion follow. All of these developments have proved unsustainable economically. ...Market rule has recoiled on the state's finances; as the polarisation of society has worsened, public spending on crime, health and specialist education has increased and social security spending itself, even though the rates are meaner in relation to average earnings, has ballooned as poverty drives millions through the drab waiting rooms of the rump welfare state (Hutton, 1996, p.175).

Both the demand and supply dimensions of the economy become increasingly erratic, according to Hutton, largely as a consequence of short-term investment strategies on the part of banks and government and a widespread acceptance of stock market 'rule'. The whim of the stock market, trading shares on the basis of unstable expectations, results in fluctuating share prices based upon inflated forecasts of a company's short-term performance and encourages capital flight whenever performance, measured in terms of the share price is deteriorating. Recent revelations about - and consequent legal action against – Enron and some other leading companies in the United States and the dire failures revealed in the account auditing process have served to highlight stock market volatility and impact, coming as they did at a time when stock market indexes around the world were already falling steeply.

As companies engage in aggressive merger activities in order to gain the highest returns for investors, redundancies and possible plant or business closures often follow. The creation of a large number of unemployed personnel and the anxiety regarding future employment insecurity which ensues for those who are fortunate enough to remain employed impacts upon welfare spending in its various forms, as already mentioned, but also affects consumption activities. As a result, firms may experience a fall in demand (Hutton, 1995, p.181). In line with the Keynesian explanation for economic recession, a vicious cycle of under-investment, unemployment, and reduced demand over-rides the free market principle that enterprises, in such market conditions, will become dynamic and innovative, creating additional revenues to feed back into society. Markets, in essence, can self-destruct.

Hutton (1996) argued that one of the key problems associated with the British economy is its distinctive reliance upon the City for corporate investment, a situation not exactly replicated in the US, Germany, Scandinavian countries or Japan for example. All of the latter, although varying in business and financial culture and practices, are regarded as normally enjoying corporate financing which incorporates a longer-term view of company performance which is encouraged either by enlightened employment legislation (where all affected by company employment practices are regarded as 'stakeholders'), or which has strong national and local commitment to business performance with banking services and enterprises working closely together and taking a long-term view.

Stable long-term investment, according to Hutton, will necessarily result in high potential returns for everyone as the economy continues to grow and as more and more enterprises, learning from the knowledge and technological innovations of their predecessors, enter into the market. The solution, according to Hutton, is to curtail the excessive autonomy of financial markets that need to be managed according to the needs of business, not the other way around. It is argued that it is easier for financial markets to adapt to business than it is for business to adapt to changing financial activities; moreover:

> a market-based financial system is itself a source of uncertainty in unsettling the relationship between savers and investors (Hutton, 1995, p.246).

A particularly interesting point is made by Meltzer and summarised by Hutton:

> showing that the rate of return on private investment is necessarily lower than the wider economic and social benefits which it brings, and which the price mechanism....
> ..cannot capture; as a result there needs to be some form of government intervention to lift investment to its socially optimal level (Hutton, 1995, p.246).

Without an appropriate economic dimension to policy, stakeholding becomes meaningless and ineffectual (Plender, 1997, p.16). A coherent stakeholding approach would involve government intervention against City short-termism, commitments to reducing poverty and inequality through re-distributive taxation, and 'promoting union-employer 'partnership' in the workplace'. A free-market interpretation of stakeholding amounts to little more than wider share-holding which is why in America the term 'stakeholder' is often used interchangeably with 'stockholder' (Preston and Sapienza, 1990). Stripped off any radical connotations, stakeholding has acquired a fudged ideological quality, leading Maltby and Wilkinson (1998, p.197) to argue that:

> stakeholder governance is a concept which owes its appeal to its imprecision and is unworkable in practice...its deployment, rather than imposing accountability on capitalism, merely represents an attempt to make free market capitalism look more acceptable.

Stakeholding, diluted somewhat by the rhetoric of 'social inclusion', together with partnership and teamwork, was promoted by Gordon Brown, the incoming Chancellor of the Exchequer in 1997. He made reference to a '*socially just and economically efficient*' country where people are '*empowered with new opportunities to succeed*'. The individualistic orientation of policies that place great stress upon the building of the skills and knowledge base for competitive edge in a modern global economy is difficult to overlook. It is one that is in keeping with classical liberal versions of stakeholding based upon 'economic citizenship' (see for example Ackerman and Alstott, 1999, p.154 and p.191). In addition, stakeholding rapidly lost its economic dimensions to become one of the vocabularies (along with 'empowerment', and 'partnership') associated with the 'modernisation' of the welfare state (Clarke and Newman, 1999, Newman, 1999) and the reconstitution of citizenship. Just six years after Blair's 1996 Singapore speech, it appears that the stakeholding approach had been all but abandoned by the New Labour government in the UK. This led Naughton (1999) to comment that:

> Will Hutton defends those slippery concepts, the 'Third Way' and 'stakeholding', in equal measure through his columns in the Observer. But now he admits his good friend, the Prime Minister, no longer shares the same vision of what that actually means in practice.

The international dimension

Held (1997, p. 131) argues that:

> government economic policy must to a large degree be compatible with regional and global movements of capital, unless a national government wishes to risk serious dislocation between its policy objectives and the flows of the wider international economy. A country needs to be extremely well protected economically and politically…to risk such dislocation.

While Held refers to the underlying structural dynamics of anonymous global capital movements, Kelly (1997) points to underlying vested political interests and active exertion of influence by more powerful nation states:

> These forces will include pressure from other states to conform to acceptable 'norms' of behaviour in the economic sphere; and processes of social, economic, technological and even environmental interaction for which national borders simply do not exist… (Kelly, 1997, p.54).

Recognition of the power of different countries to impose their own models on others is fundamental to the stakeholding debate. As we have seen there are clear attempts on the part of international agencies promoting free market economic perspectives, including various drives to establish   harmonisation of financial, security, labour legislation and regulatory systems throughout OECD countries (through Maastricht and European Monetary Union at the European level; through the World Bank, the International Monetary Fund and the World Trade Organisation at a broader international level).

There is clear evidence of this from recent UK experience. Ramsay (1998) has argued that the Labour government (under a strategy initially launched by John

Smith) has gone out of its way to court the City and has worked closely with representatives of American business interests. Ideas associated with the latter have been disseminated and articulated through organs like the Trade Union Committee for Transatlantic Understanding (LCTU) and the British-American Project for a Successor Generation (BAP). The election of New Labour in May 1997 was heralded as a coup for these American interests (see Ramsay, 1998, p.113). According to Ramsay:

> the people around Blair, the key New Labour 'project' personnel, are linked to the United States, or the British foreign policy establishment, whose chief aim, since the end of the Second World War, has been to preserve the Anglo-American 'special relationship' to compensate for long-term economic decline (Ramsay, 1998, p.114).

Analysts also suggest that the 'welfare to work' policies, of which the Anglo-Saxon approach to stakeholding is a part, are essentially US 'ideological exports', promulgated by bodies such as the Manhattan Institute, the Heritage Foundation and the Hudson Institute. This has clearly also influenced industrial relations policies in the UK with the government opting out of key elements of the EU Social Chapter. By 1998, it had become clear that the government's approach to employment relations reform was designed to go with the grain of the free market and not against it. Characteristically, Britain has supported the neoliberal approaches pursed by big business lobbying groups in Europe (which have been actively promoting the principles of free-trade, economic expansion, the de-regulation of labour markets, world trade and investment liberalisation since the mid 1980s [see, for example, Balanya, Doherty, Hoedeman, Ma'anit and Wesselius, (2000)]. Furthermore, in common with the US, the UK has shown itself reluctant to intervene in the free-floating outcomes of global finance.

It is, however, not only the British government which is partial to big business interests: the UK's stance on policies which favour, overwhelmingly, multinational and transnational corporate interests simply reflects, aside from a few exceptions (notably France), a range of OECD and European orientations to the 'global economy'. Through a range of informal and formal networks and personal invitations, representatives of the top companies throughout Europe are able to access politicians working in Brussels. Balanya et al (2000) have documented the influence of such elite groupings through for example, the European Roundtable of Industrialists, (ERT) and the Transatlantic Business Dialogue (TABD). The implications of such networks of influence for democracy, are vast. This is something we come back to discuss in the final two chapters. For the moment, it is important to register Balanya et al's conclusion that, as far as foreign economic policy goes:

> The European Commission regards TNCs as a natural constituency that supports its quest for power in exchange for a say in policy matters (2000, p.178).

If the economic status quo was to remain in place, then something else had to be done to alleviate the glaringly obvious social malaise so well documented in the literature of the1990s. A moral agenda was to fill the vacuum, one which became so pronounced that Jonathan Friedland writing in *The Guardian* (8/11/99) remarked of the ascendant Republican Presidential contender, George W. Bush that he "talks less like a politician and more like an evangelical pastor". No doubt Bush was emulating his predecessor who, along with UK Prime Minister Blair, had already adopted a moral stance on problems which are clearly, if not wholly, associated with the new economic order.

This moralistic posturing with its preoccupation with control of individual human behaviour and responsibility was a detraction from other more important economic issues. The focus upon individual behaviour and action took place in a political vacuum which was itself bound up with the presentation of the economy as globally self-evident, anarchic and uncontrollable. Within this context it is not surprising that, as Elliot and Atkinson highlighted:

> Blair and Clinton wanted to create the 'good society' but without the controls on capital which existed during the 1950s and 1960s and which even conservatives like Eisenhower and Macmillan saw as necessary ...Instead, they took the 1960s mixture of economic intervention and social liberalism and turned it on its head, pushing social authoritarianism into the vacuum left by the surrender of economic policy to the dictates of global capitalism.......but Clinton was happy as Arkansas governor to withdraw driving licences from high-school dropouts, and Blair was keen on curbs on drinking, bans on cigarette advertising, a campaign for children to inform on shops that sold alcohol to under-age customers, and contracts in which parents would pledge to provide twenty minutes of reading practice with their children every night (Elliot and Atkinson, 1998, p.155).

Tony Blair and Bill Clinton tended to target new scapegoats - welfare dependents and the criminalised poor for example - to smooth the way for policies which continued to ignore the social impact of financial de-regulation. Even a UK newspaper like the Daily Express, not known for its socialist sentiments, was sensitive to British Chancellor Gordon Brown's attack on benefit cheats and casualised workers evading tax. As Simon Hine ('Why don't we hit the rich tax avoiders?' The Express, March 10th, 2000) noted, Gordon Brown's assault on the 'black economy' has won predictable plaudits from predictable sources. "Scroungers, illegal immigrants and criminals are sucking this country dry" screamed one right-wing newspaper which applauded the Chancellor's intention to get tough with people who claim the dole while working or get paid cash for casual employment to avoid paying tax. The message is clear: this is a moral crusade. In the run-up to the US Presidential elections of 2000, the electorate were urged to soldier on 'in the army of compassion'. Meanwhile, in the UK, Prime Minister Blair attempted to re-assure us in 1999 by stating 'I am my brother's keeper'.

While the poor were being targeted for their bad behaviour, George W. Bush's campaign picked up a growing concern among wealthy, if alienated, Americans as they wondered how to buy 'meaning', creating his own web page aptly titled 'Prosperity with a Purpose'. In stark contrast to the reality of increasing pay differentials and growing relative poverty, feature articles in the Sunday Times highlighted the apparently imponderable issue of growing dissatisfaction among members of a wealthier nation (see, for example, the *Sunday Times*, 18.7.99). It is assumed that dissatisfaction is less about social class inequalities than it is about competition and rivalry with the person sitting at the next office desk. The Increasing social fallout, rising levels of anxiety, alienation, depression and poverty are understood as overwhelmingly *cultural* phenomena, a development which has been associated specifically with economic globalisation and weakened nation states (Lorenz, 1999). As an example of this Giddens (1994) states:

> Material poverty appears less crucial in explaining untold levels of crime and depression which affect affluent societies than *interpretations* of it, according to different *lifestyles* and *values* (our italics).

Such revisionism occurred in the context of increasing concentration of wealth and the growing insecurities of the middle classes, who were no longer prepared to be the liberal minded champions of a social and education system on which their own success had relied. Even though Britain has the poorest record for welfare spending in Europe, Polly Toynbee writing in *The Independent* was quick to admonish her readers:

> It is no good whingeing about welfare state promises made 50 years ago. The state can't pay and that's that (The Independent, 31.1.96).

Commentators across the political spectrum have pointed to an increasing fiscal burden and its associated pressures on the welfare system, despite the efforts of successive Conservative administrations to curtail it. According to Byrne (2001) however, those who are popularly represented as an expanding middle England (actually the top fifth of post tax income) have enjoyed vast increases in income and they could well afford to pay extra taxes to fund public services. In this Byrne is quick to point to three major factors that represent a reversal of fortunes for the mass of the population but especially for the poor who are worse off than in 1978 in terms of their share of total income:

> the massive reduction in the taxation of higher incomes with the maximum rate of direct income tax now being set at 40% only. Second, there have been large increases in indirect taxation, and especially VAT, which has a disproportionate effect on people on low incomes. Third, top salaries have risen much faster and further than wages and salaries in general (Byrne, 2001).

Still, in the ideological context of debates highlighting the conundrums of a post-industrial, middle class, global economic order, the moral inflection of welfare state restructuring with its associated onus on individual responsibility is, according to Gamble and Kelly, both a low cost strategy (in keeping with welfare cuts) and viable in an electoral sense. The restructuring of society and culture can proceed through the vehicle of individual duty and active involvement in the institutional structures of state and civil society.

Blair's moral vision of 'New Labour' was reflected in recommendations on social policy published by Frank Field. According to Field (1997), notions of welfare often draw on misguided assumptions about human nature. The collectivist principles of social democracy, in particular its emphasis upon redistribution of societal resources to the poor have, according to Field, misunderstood altruism as something existing outside of human self-interest. Collectivism and the goals of redistribution undermine or 'disempower' the poor who are patronised by being 'done good to'. Moreover, based upon means tests, benefits tend to encourage the worst aspects of human behaviour (i.e. fraud and cheating) and penalise effort by attacking savings.

Self-interest, according to Field, should be respected in social policies that place an emphasis upon personal development and self-expression as well as 'rights with responsibilities'. These would form the fundamental requirements of social inclusion and citizenship in which all could engage in the direction and control of new localised institutions (Field, 1997, pp.9-10). Welfare provision is seen as a major influence of social behaviour since it 'bestows rewards (benefits) and allots punishments (loss of benefits)' to reflect societies basic 'ground rules of societal behaviour' (Field, 1997). It therefore follows, according to Field, that 'good behaviour should be rewarded', and attention should be given to the relationship between a desire to be good to the wider community and simple self-interest. Making everybody responsible for themselves and for each other is one way of achieving this goal. This approach could include, to take a topical example, revisions to personal and company pension schemes so that they are more accountable to individuals buying into them or perhaps a new national insurance scheme which could pay for the training and benefits of those who have paid into the scheme.

Such revisions are one way of encouraging people to recognise that their interests coincide with those of the wider community and to appreciate that national insurance payments are precisely that, insurance against the risks we as individuals bear in the face of less certain employment patterns and changing demography. In such an approach, stakeholder welfare policies would be increasingly insurance-based with the payment of benefits much more closely linked to the payment of contributions and, in the context of pension schemes, individuals would effectively own their own capital. Moreover, given the likelihood of continued high public spending in the future, it is important to create a stakeholders welfare state since 'voters will support schemes costing more only if they are their own schemes'.

In an important sense, following the abandonment of the Keynesian welfare state during the 1980s, the incoming Labour Prime Minister in 1997 felt compelled to redefine the meaning of socialism. The stakeholding ideas offered by Hutton, according to Campen, (1995) were more than timely in replacing the vacuum left by the abandonment of clause 4 (the commitment to state control of key enterprises), the globalisation phenomenon and the need to appeal to what has come to be known as the 'two-thirds/one-third' society. Thatcherism had fundamentally changed the social structure in the UK: the rank and file, strongly unionised, blue-collar working class had been severely reduced in number. New Labour had to be much more broad-based electorally than it had in the past. As a result, in Campen's words:

> New Labour has embraced Thatcherism, accepting a market-driven economic strategy. Blair, having abolished the old clause 4 and replacing it with a new one,

ripped out the heart of the party but at the same time gave him a clean sheet to write on. The new clause 4 starts 'The Labour Party is a democratic socialist party'....As reported on March 14th 1995 in the Guardian, the day after the new clause 4 was revealed, Blair stated...I believe this is a defining moment in our history (Campen, 1999, p.5).

Training for flexible working practices is a key plank of the new social welfare. Field's attention to training and skill enhancement has focused on the supply side of labour markets (Alcock, 1997). This has been criticised by backbenchers in the Labour Government for ignoring questions of poverty and inequality. In addition, they argue that the piecemeal and pragmatic response to the needs of business limits critical debate and the scope for radically rethinking welfare provision. While the nation's work-forces are being urged to take responsibility for Britain's economic well-being as it competes in the global economy, it is largely wealthy business executives and shareholders who are enjoying the highest returns of 'greater productivity'. Flexible working, longer working hours and relatively low pay for their employees is resulting in disproportionately higher salaries for executives (see The Guardian 22nd August, 2000). Hutton had called for a closer partnership between trade unions and managers but members of the TUC are increasingly disenchanted with New Labour's position on employee relations since it continues to undermine the power of trade unions (see The Independent, 19th July, 1999). As Gamble and Kelly (1999) suggest:

> New Labour is no more likely to impose radical changes on firms in the name of the stakeholder society than Old Labour was in the support of industrial democracy (Gamble and Kelly, 1999).

Key elements of Hutton's argument concerning the need for business, finance and government to invest in social capital - and for businesses to be more sensitive to the external environments in which they operate - have been adopted piecemeal as a way of overcoming some of the problems associated with societal fragmentation. While critical issues relating to the revised role of finance have been hurriedly dropped, Hutton's observations about social capital have proved popular in the training of tomorrow's globally oriented knowledge workers. Highlighting what has now become some of the standard tenets of the global corporation, Blair outlines his 'vision of a young country' in the following terms:

- embracing flexibility;
- attracting foreign investment;
- building up workplace skills (where universities are to become 'universities of industry');
- a long-term framework for fiscal and monetary policy;
- restraints on public spending;
- 'social cohesion' through an emphasis upon 'social capital' (Blair, 1996).

This 'vision' is particularly significant for our discussion of stakeholding in terms of the emphasis placed on 'partnership' between work-forces and managers and it is to this element of the stakeholding approach that we now turn.

Chapter 5

The business process revolution: workers, producers, consumers

So far we have looked at the fundamental characteristics of the global economy which includes the rise of giant corporations and corporate interests; the de-regulation of finance (resulting in greater economic instability) with a consequent reaction on the part of businesses to pursue aggressive 'flexible' strategies, (often through the use of spot or impartial labour contracts); the implementation of fiscal controls and policies focused upon the reduction of public expenditure. As we have seen, these pressures have impacted on welfare regimes across Europe. Stripped of any grounding in more inclusive economic and welfare policies, stakeholding appears as a free-floating, quite arbitrary concept within managerial rhetoric. The distinction between rhetoric and reality is sometimes stark.

For many people, decision-making in the modern global economy seems remote, complex and liable to impact upon lifestyle and expectations in a sudden, unpredictable way. While she or he continues to play a part in local economic activity, deriving employment and income from so doing, it is becoming apparent that the key economic and business decisions that affect future prosperity are being taken by relatively few corporate, financial or political leaders located elsewhere in the global economy. Not surprisingly, the average person, employed or not, begins to feel like a pawn in an increasingly incomprehensible global economic game.

This, of course, is very much in contrast to the perception that would have been held during the three decades after the Second World War. Against expectations at the time, post-war reconstruction and development, founded upon the demand management framework of the Keynesian approach to economic policy-making, ultimately generated an unprecedented wave of employment and affluence. As the Keynesian boom spread across the world, industrial nations were perceived as not only economically powerful but able, perhaps for the first time, to pursue their own economic destiny. Full employment and rising living standards became the prime objective of government economic policy.

In contrast to the pre-war years, the years of unbridled prosperity associated with the 1960s and early 1970s instilled a general sense of confidence in terms of relatively secure employment, and social stability. The downside of this period was an over-reliance on the unpaid, undervalued domestic labour of women whose restricted career or workplace opportunities were fed by the ideology of the 'family'. It was also a period bound up with post-colonial struggles; the inherent racism of the post-war settlement was associated, in turn, with colonialism (see

Clarke and Newman, 1998). Internationally, an excessive super-power arms race took place in an ideologically split world order while welfare systems often drew upon an unequal division of labour between men and women.

Nevertheless, while we should resist constructing perhaps too romantic a view of the period, it is true to say that there was a degree of stability that has been lost in recent years. In the transition from that period, a range of new opportunities have been gained, especially for women and more generally in terms of the movement towards more democratic and equal relationships and growing acceptance of new ethnic, national and sexual identities (Giddens, 1994; 1999).

Post-war prosperity owed much to the trading certainties engendered by the Bretton Woods agreement on a exchange rate parity system, signed in 1944, and to the trade-stimulating effect of the General Agreement on Tariffs and Trade which followed soon after. Together with the application of what may be termed 'global Keynesianism' and the economic stability and development generated, at least initially, by the activities of the International Monetary Fund and the World Bank, a unique set of forces were unleashed almost simultaneously, designed to generate wealth and ensure its transfer particularly to and between the industrial nations. For real economic recovery after 1945, the post-war international economy required a powerful economic 'locomotive' that could power the system towards recovery and prosperity. The United States, through the Bretton Woods gold price agreement, massive overseas business investment and the financing of overseas military operations, performed the role of 'locomotive' to great effect, further strengthening its hegemonic power in the process.

During the 1970s, however, the post-war economic miracle began to fall apart. Exchange rate instability became endemic; inflation accelerated to new, dangerously high levels partly as a result of the 1973 oil shock; and the (by now) orthodox Keynesian policy solutions appeared to be incapable of the task set for them. Many governments turned reluctantly to Monetarism after 1975 to try to restore inflation control and renew economic stability and, as a result, the Monetarists' free market ideology moved to the centre of the policy-making stage. The phenomenal wave of market liberalisation policies that followed over the next two decades helped to unleash a range of turbulent, volatile and unpredictable economic forces that frequently bedevil the global economy today. The global economic problem is, in essence, now one attributable to rapid and unco-ordinated economic change taking place at an unprecedented rate, fuelled by the global adoption of a laissez-faire ideology, limiting government intervention and creating consequences that the world's under-resourced economic and financial institutions both promote yet also struggle to manage.

The demise of 'concertation'

Across Europe in particular the era of 'concertation' (economic management based upon attempts at achieving consensus between government, employers and trade unions) began to disintegrate as Monetarist ideology and market economics recaptured the political stage. The trade union movement, so central to the process and development of concertation in economic policy-making in the middle years of the 20th century, became seriously weakened by the political and legislative onslaught unleashed against them in the 1980s. Compston (1998) notes that the trade union movement was also fractured by:

> the emergence of a large and well-educated middle class and a broadening of the range of issues on the political agenda; new social movements such as the environmental and peace movements competed for the allegiance of union members; trade union unity was weakened by the decline of working-class subcultures based on mass manufacturing…. The feminization of the workforce; the emergence of large and growing service sector unions….and the formation of productivity coalitions between individual employers and their workforces (Compston, 1998, p. 513).

According to Compston, the crucial dimension of the move towards liberalization is its apparent irreversibility, undermining, in turn, the concertation process in countries where it previously had policy-making relevance and eliminating its future role in those countries where previously it had not.

To test the extent to which policy concertation has been undermined in practice, Compston (1998) focused attention on the period 1985 - 1996. The passage of the Single European Act, a cornerstone in the policy construct of the new liberalism, marks the starting point for the investigation and the fate of the concertation process in eleven West European countries is explored. These eleven nations are divided into categories of low concertation (Britain, Ireland, Germany and Italy), high concertation (Sweden, Austria and Switzerland) and intermediate cases (Denmark, Norway and the Netherlands). Examples are drawn from this analysis below to illustrate the range of levels of policy concertation that still exist within Western Europe.

In the case of the low concertation countries, Compston found mixed evidence of genuine concertation in the policy-making process over the period. In Britain, the experience of policy failure with the demise of the Social Contract approach in the 1970s and the diminution after the 1979 election by the Thatcher government of long-standing national consultative mechanisms (such as the National Economic Development Council) effectively terminated the concertation approach.

Despite the theoretical support given to the concertation process in France under the national indicative planning approach that was a central feature of French economic management during the 1960s and 1970s, Compston found scant evidence of such an approach actually being put into practice over the decade up to 1996. Existing formal mechanisms (such as the Economic and Social Council) were effectively disconnected from the actual policy-making process and, while informal contact between state and corporations within France continues, the formal consultative structures which underpinned the strategy of indicative planning, argues to be so important in generating and sustaining economic growth and an 'economie concertee' in earlier decades, now plays little role in the economic policy-making process.

In Germany, consultation over economic policy-making has always been more prominent although, crucially for debates on stakeholding, the actual co-determination of policy has not. With an emphasis on the containment of industrial disputes, concertation - particularly in the industrial relations area - has traditionally been viewed as a key contributory element of Germany's economic miracle. However, government interest in concertation was eventually undermined in Germany by the fact that both employers and trade unions were totally opposed to government involvement in wage-setting decisions.

However, the unusual economic circumstances surrounding the reunification of Germany in 1992 did create the need for a response that comprised a significant concertation element with Chancellor Kohl entering into wide-ranging negotiations with companies, trade unions, the Lander, other political parties and trade associations which culminated in March 1993 in the Solidarity Pact, setting in place a consensus-based economic strategy to facilitate the reunification process. This explicit example of concertation in the policy-making process in Germany, however, can be viewed more as an emergency response to a complex and unique economic and political situation rather than as the standard agenda for policy formulation on a more widespread basis.

More recently, renewed concertation has been abandoned as Germany has had little choice but to respond to the demands of integration into both EMU and the wider global market. Germany's economy is the world's third most technologically powerful after the US and Japan but its overall flexibility has been hampered by structural market rigidities (which include significant non-wage costs associated with hiring new workers) which have contributed to unemployment becoming a long-term, not just a cyclical, problem. Germany's aging population and its high unemployment level have driven social security outlays well beyond the capacity of its workforce to fund. Furthermore, the continuing modernization and integration of the eastern German economy remains a significant financial burden with western Germany still providing annual subsidies of about $70 billion. (CIA World Factbook, Germany, 2000).

In Austria and Switzerland, however, despite pressures from the intensely competitive global economy, the role of economic policy concertation remains prominent and relatively undiminished in importance over the period. In both cases, it is doubtful whether government legislation that lacked a full consensus could succeed. However, as economic problems have become more severe over the period, so the tensions and disagreements within the social partnerships in these two countries have undoubtedly intensified. Nevertheless, policy concertation still retains some credibility and the concept of a social partnership remains a recognised central pillar of the political system.

Much has changed, however, in one of the nations that has consistently displayed a high level of concertation in economic policy-making, Sweden. With a powerful trade union structure and employer federation both locked formally into the government decision-making process, Sweden has long operated a form of concertation where the representatives of labour, capital, consumers and other interest groups had genuine influence over policy outcomes. In many respects, at least at the macro-level, Sweden during the early 1970s could be said to have approximated a kind of stakeholder economy with genuine access to and influence on government and its policy outcomes. Confrontation between the key union and employer groups participating in the concertation process over the issue of future business ownership after 1976 seriously disrupted the process of smooth, consensual Swedish policy-making and additional pressures such as a sharp increase surge in welfare costs and the need to ensure that Sweden did not move out of line with the requirements of the global economy ultimately sowed the seeds for the eventual retreat of concertation within the Swedish economy.

The adoption of a more focused neo-liberal economic policy approach made concertation more difficult to pursue and the government began to scale down the number and range of interest groups represented on commissions and terminated the requirements for unanimous agreement before policy-related commission reports could be published. During the 1990s, concertation as the central pillar of Swedish policy-making effectively collapsed with, first, the decision in 1991 to withdraw employer representatives from the boards of all government agencies and, secondly, the election of a conservative, pro-liberal policy government in 1992, replacing the Social Democrats in office, with a distinctly anti-concertation political agenda.

As a result, union representatives were removed from executive boards and, despite a temporary and much more limited phase of concertation after 1994 with the re-election of the Social Democrats, the consensual approach to Swedish policy-making was much reduced. Sweden, perhaps, is the best example of a country that has seen its concertation approach ravaged by the pressures of globalisation and the rebirth of liberalism. Yet, concertation in Sweden's near neighbours - Denmark and Norway - appeared to have increased during the period up to 1996 and still remains a powerful force in the policy-making process, although how much longer this can be maintained must be questionable as the struggle to compete in the global economy, so dominated today by neo-liberalism, continues to intensify.

Corporate response

Against such a background, many modern corporations are changing fundamentally the way their business operates and the manner in which individual employees are treated. Companies have adopted far more radical, fundamental changes in the way their organisations are structured and operate in order to enhance productivity. From a classical economic perspective, the driving forces behind such changes are understood to include, on the demand side, a more highly competitive global market in which consumers demand better quality and variety from a more innovative product range; and, on the supply side, the recent revolution in information and communication technologies together with unprecedented improvements in the education and training of workforces.

As we are constantly being told by management gurus, competitive edge and market success depends upon a firm's capacity to innovate, continuously improve its product and, crucially, adjusting the production process and harnessing new technologies and highly trained labour to the requirements of the flexible firm in a global market. In a sense, these corporations have set in motion a new styled workplace regime that subordinate the individual to the *global market* needs of the company. Beck has argued that such processes are responsible for creating 'The Brave New World of Work' (2000). It involves the transfer of insecure employment from the third world and newly industrialising countries, to the first world – a process encapsulated by the phrase 'The Brazilianization of the West':

> ...remarkable is the new similarity in how paid work itself is shaping up in the so-called first world and the so-called third world; the spread of temporary and insecure employment, discontinuity and loose informality into Western societies that have hitherto been the bastions of full employment. The social structure in the heartlands of the West is thus coming to resemble the patchwork quilt of the South, characterised by diversity, unclarity and insecurity in people's work and life (Beck 2000, p.1).

Of course, such observations reflect a long-standing perception of the decline of employment security and the growth of so called flexible working practices, all of which are presumed to be associated with the rise of information technology and impact of flexible manufacturing systems (Toffler, 1980). Although, there are many conflicting accounts of the extensiveness of such production systems (Aglietta 1979; Amin 1983; Piore and Sabel 1984) with many arguing against the birth of the new and enlightened post-Fordist culture, it would appear that everything that can be done will be done to assist the implementation of this 'lean manufacturing' revolution, regardless of the impact on the individual employee, customer or supplier.

Such changes include the introduction of teaming arrangements between firms; partnership sourcing; purchasing and supply chain reforms; and the sub-contracting of non-core business activities. For some industries, for example defence production, what has been variously defined in terms of a post-industrial or 'third wave' revolution is scarcely under way [Toffler (1982) and see, for example, Braddon and Dowdall (1996)] In the global restructuring process currently under way, it is multinational and transnational corporations which are determining the business practices (and often the peformance) of smaller companies. Even though different strategies will be pursued by individual countries and companies aiming to achieve competitive advantage (Thompson and McHugh, 1995), Thompson et al suggest that production and management systems are:

...subject much more directly to dominance effects from perceived 'best practices' and the need of trans-national corporations to integrate their diverse activities and structures (Thompson et al, 1995, cited in Thompson and McHugh, 1995, p 102).

Localised and institutional national frameworks tend to operate as a constraint upon universal tendencies, resulting in twin processes of harmonisation and differentiation, although both movements are bound up with the creation of more flexible workforces. The latter is also associated with the ways in which a society defines 'the common good' (Sennet, 1998).

Such notions are in turn influenced by different types of capitalism. Entering into the recently fashionable debates surrounding stakeholding already referred to, Sennet describes capitalism in terms of different "terms of power on which markets and production are allowed to operate":

> The Anglo-American regime has few political restraints on wealth inequality but full employment, while the welfare networks of the Rhenish states, which are more sensitive to ordinary workers, are a drag on job creation (Sennet, 1998, p. 55).

As we have already identified however, there are clear movements towards implementing legislation which undercuts collectivist forms of decision-making throughout Europe, this having direct consequences for the restructuring of both states and welfare states associated with the kinds of regimes identified by Sennet (see also Chamberlayne et al (eds), 1999) Thompson and McHugh also argue that in such a context:

> the space for national and local is squeezed as organisational forms and practices demonstrate convergent tendencies (Thompson and McHugh, 1995).

As far as 'best practice' is concerned, the application of modern approaches to industrial manufacture and management are seen as an integral part of a new approach to corporate strategy by many large companies seeking to succeed in the global market of the 21st century. First, such companies are restructuring to enhance the speed with which decisions can be made and implemented and to improve their flexibility and adaptability to the changing needs of the market. Corporate hierarchies are being flattened in order to cut reaction times and accelerate the flow of ideas within the organisation. Global joint ventures and alliances are sought to share capital risk, acquire information and technology and facilitate access to new markets. Cross-functional management teams chase new business opportunities and stimulate the cross-fertilisation of ideas within the corporation.

Additionally, these companies are refocusing their businesses both locally and globally. Components are standardised wherever possible to achieve scale and scope economies and management teams comb both the world and their own corporate operations for new ideas with global potential. Although the tendency to relocate production and production systems to different parts of the world is not a recent development, the organisation and co-ordination processes of large trans-national corporations which compete through a range of networked activities across the world is new (see Porte, 1990, cited in Thompson and McHugh, 1995). Central to these processes is the subsuming of:

> national economies...into the system by essentially international processes and transactions (Hirst and Thompson, 1992, p.360).

The authors argue that:

> New countries (eg. China), regions or social formations, notably the new post-Communist economies of Eastern Europe, are gradually brought into the financial and corporate workings of the global economy and pressurised to specialise in the provision of certain goods or services as cheap labour (Thompson and McHugh, 1995, p.98).

Moreover, the internationalisation of financial markets and their closer integration with production facilitates the activities of trans- and multi-national corporations. The liquidity of banking system has been affected by 'runaway capital', a focus of concern in the writings of Will Hutton (1996 and 2000); this also making for a much more volatile global economic market. Within such a scenario, flexible production helps to equip modern corporations with the technological means to compete powerfully in the global market. At the same time, however, it can also exert a profound influence on societies in which it is implemented (Hughes and Lewis, 1998), raising a number of key issues for governments and corporations including, as we have already noted in relation to the restructuring of welfare regimes:

- amending social legislation to incorporate new employment trends;
- facilitating training and retraining to enhance skills and competences;
- restructuring wage systems to accommodate organisational change and emerging employment patterns;
- responding to the equal opportunity implications of employment restructuring;
- developing more flexible organisations in the public sector;
- providing appropriate support for smaller organisations and individuals disadvantaged by the drive towards the 'flexible firm' organisational structure.

The implications of emerging employment trends, driven by the needs of the global economy, have received much political attention. The de-regulation of labour relations is increasingly significant in shaping everyday lives throughout Europe. Non-standard forms of employment constitute 34 percent of labour in Argentina, 30 percent in Bolivia, 20 percent in Columbia and Mexico and more than 50 percent in Peru (Beck, 2000, p.98).

This has, on occasions, precipitated demands for greater attention to the employment-creating and sustaining dimensions of policy. The European Council meeting in 1994 in Essen, for example, demanded the increased employment intensity of future economic growth, stating that this should be fostered by a 'more flexible organisation of work in a way which fulfils both the wishes of employees and the requirements of competition'. Unfortunately, in practice, the emphasis thus far seems to have been on achieving greater flexibility in the labour market while frequently neglecting its impact in the actual workplace.

There have been a number of changes to labour contracts and working practices designed with the creation of flexible workforces in mind. These include, the simplification of pay structures and bargaining, a shift from industrial relations to human resource management; the introduction of round-the-clock shift systems; the greater use of subcontracting; self-employment and the use of temporary contracts; home-working, franchising and part-time contracts, in addition to legislative changes which have served to undermine trade unions (Millward, 1994). All of these developments serve to externalise uncertainty and risks onto external groups and individuals (Thompson and McHugh, 1995). Some commentators argue that the real meaning of the flexible firm involves a blurring of traditional distinctions between full and part-time work, being in and out of employment, between work, leisure and education, and between the formal and informal economies.

The notion of 'flexibility' in the business context is often presented in terms of allowing greater choice and control - enhanced personal choice between work and leisure and improved control over the individual's life, since workers are no longer tied to a 9-to-5 working mentality. Enhanced flexibility has in practice been achieved through mass redundancies, harsher working conditions and reduced real wages. Diminishing job security and lower real pay levels are the true characteristics of the 'flexible' nineties', (Millward, 1994), otherwise read as a 'Victorian version of employee relations' (Bassett, The Times, February 15th 1994).

The majority of flexible workers are now part-time staff who are much easier to 'hire and fire', creating a situation in the UK where about one-third of employees have no employment protection at all. Numerical and functional flexibility (Atkinson, 1984) - the buzz-words of modern management - involve a reduction in the workforce combined with demands that retained employees absorb other people's work as well as their own. Employment recruitment is often driven by the need to ensure that new employees are willing to subscribe to the flexibility requirements of their employers. As one critic put it:

> Being flexible- that is, willing to bend over backwards- is now widely seen as a prerequisite for being employed at all. Many companies at the forefront of bringing in flexible working undertake strenuous testing of job applicants, in order to establish that they have constructive attitudes as much as skills aptitude. If you are prepared to do whatever they tell you and earn whatever they give you, you might just get the job. Then you can enjoy the benefits of functional flexibility and earnings flexibility, at least until the next round of numerical flexibility catches up with you.

The 'feminisation' of the labour force has been seen as one of the more positive aspects of increased employment flexibility. Over 70% of women of working age are now in employment and women now constitute almost half of the active workforce in the UK. Furthermore, it is asserted that employment flexibility has also helped to ease the pressures of women working and raising a family, thereby removing an age-old barrier to the pursuit of careers for women in employment.

However, for powerful corporations, women represent cheap labour since women's average pay is still less than three-quarters that of their male counterparts (see Equal Opportunities Commission, 2000). In part, this is attributable to the fact that some 40% of women employees work part-time where wage rates tend to be much lower than for their full-time equivalents. All of this is not withstanding global and cultural differences where, for example, women working for trans and multinational corporations, perhaps as franchise or contract workers in third world countries are often heavily exploited.

Pressure of redundancy is a sure means of generating appropriate attitudes to the flexible workplace. Evidence from the Citizens Advice Bureau in 1993 suggested that, faced with redundancy, many employees were willing to accept pay cuts of between 10% and 35% with some retained labour working a 70 hour week for £140 pay. The threat of employment insecurity has clearly increased over the past decade. A survey of 400 companies in 17 countries cited in The Times, March 4, 2000 illustrates the point, showing that 'employment security' between 1989 and 1999 declined from 70% to 48% in the UK, in Germany from 83% to 55%, in France from 64% to 50% and in the Netherlands from 73% to 61%. The nature of employment, itself, has also changed significantly. Since 1980, the number of men working part-time in the UK has doubled, the number of people employed in firms of more than 500 employees has slumped to less than one-third of the employed population of the UK and nearly one in ten UK workers are self-employed.

In the US, industrial restructuring continues apace with Ford, a symbol of a more economically stable modernist culture, cutting 35,000 jobs (approximately 10 percent of Fords global workforces) as plants in New Jersey, Missouri and Ontario in Canada are closed to deal with losses of £1.4 billion. This adds to jobs already lost here in the UK with 2,300 workers at the Dagenham plant having been made redundant.

As a result of organisational 'streamlining', employment insecurity also features prominently among the concerns of the managerial sector. The UMIST/Institute of Management annual survey for 1999 lists the major concerns held by managers as being first, how to fund their retirement and second, how to ensure employability in future workforce. The skills listed by survey respondents as those likely to be required to ensure future employability included IT skills (54%), skills in managing information knowledge (42%), communications skills (25%) and marketing skills (23%). Interestingly, all of these skills are those appropriate for home-based tele-workers which suggests a continued drift towards this kind of fragmented, insular socio-economy in the future. Gradually, some leading edge, global business organisations are beginning to transform themselves into 'virtual' organisations where relatively few key staff form the core of the company and the majority of the labour force work on a flexible basis from home. There is disagreement as to the broader positive social implications of new technology (for an interesting critical discussion see Wyatt, Henwood, Miller and Senker (eds) 2000). However, Carey and Jackson have forecast continuing future trends where:

> most organisations will have only a small core of full-time permanent employees working from a conventional office. They will buy most of the skills they need on a contract basis, either from individuals working at home and linked to the company by computers and modems (teleworking) or by hiring people on short-term contracts to do specific jobs or carry out specific projects. In this way, companies will be able to maintain the flexibility they need to cope with a rapidly changing world (Carey and Jackson: Creating Tomorrow's Organisations, 2000).

Such observations, however, have to be placed within the context of variation in company product, size and market and the structural realities and constraints of global competition, and employment legislation.

In the context of neoliberal economic policies, so great is the magnetic force of the global market and so stringent its requirements for success that companies are urged to explore the flexibility option in reconstructing their global market strategies. In other words, the dynamics are overwhelmingly structural, related to specific economic policies. To dress this up in terms of a simple moral issue is to miss the point. This is structural as well as cultural. Europe has a market size of some 370 million consumers, the largest consumer group in the world, and is the home for about 16 million companies. Many of these companies have already implemented some key elements of the post-Fordist production paradigm although, according to the European Commission, the spread of the flexible firm approach within Europe has been notable for its relative tardiness.

Appeal to the consumer

New business practices do not only involve manipulating the average economic actor as a flexible producer. The new 'science' of consumer segmentation means that the corporate sector also seek to manipulate that same economic actor through her or his consumption. As Nick Gardner in the Sunday Times noted in May, 2000:

> Are you a clever capitalist, a rising materialist, a bijou homeowner or a member of the chattering classes? If you don't know, be assured, your bank does - as does your insurance company and even your local supermarket.

In the intensely competitive global economy of the early 21st century, a consumer's economic standing can affect their access to a wide range of products and services from mortgages and personal loans to special offers from retailers. Consumers are increasingly segmented and classified in terms of their potential value to the organisation attempting to sell to them. Consumer characteristics are researched and assessed and then employed to 'personalise' advertisements and other forms of product presentation. Ultimately, individual consumer profiles may be employed by, for example. call centre staff to improve product targeting. More importantly, perhaps, consumers who do not meet the specific requirements of the organisation (for example, a bank or insurance company) will effectively be de-selected, being defined as inferior consumers with higher risk profiles. In similar vein to the core and periphery strata in the flexible labour market, consumers, too, will be defined as core players with sound economic standing and peripheral with 'unsatisfactory' economic profiles. Gardner notes that:

> Cybase, which studies consumer behaviour, says that every person hits an average of eight touch points each day through which data about their behaviour is logged for marketing purposes. Use of telephones - the numbers we call and for how long - is monitored, so we can be targeted for special deals.......When we visit a supermarket and use a loyalty card, our basket of goods is analysed to determine our life-styles, whether we are single, have children and what products we may buy.

The use of post-codes and census data to segment consumers remains at the forefront of consumer monitoring and targeting. Gardner notes that Experian, a global information company, employs addresses to identify 19 different types of consumer. Social and expenditure trends by area can be determined and exploited by the enterprising organisation and likewise specific groups of consumers can be identified and targeted. As noted earlier, Gardner identifies some of these classifications of consumers:

- 'clever capitalists and gentrified villagers' which appear to be the most profitable group to target, especially for financial service companies;

- 'bijou homeowners', described as 'notoriously disloyal', who seize the best offers as soon as they can and readily switch between suppliers of the products and services they require;

- the 'chattering classes' with 'wallets thick with credit cards', large mortgages and little savings; and

- 'smokestack shift-workers', by far the most unappealing to companies and therefore the most vulnerable to blacklisting and effective consumer exclusion. Concentrated in declining industrial areas, living in cheap housing on relatively low incomes, these consumers are considered non-profitable customers for selling organisations, especially banks and other finance companies. Unemployment risk, low income and location means that these consumers are effectively defined as an underclass as far as the corporate sector is concerned.

Whether as a producer or a consumer, the average economic actor may feel today that she or he is little more than a pawn in the wider global economic game. Far from being recognised as a genuine stakeholder in the economic process, such individuals are effectively being manipulated by the corporate sector as part of the drive towards business survival and success in the global market. And as that individual struggles to maintain a degree of independence and self-fulfilment within the global economy, the forces of corporate power are continually gathering strength on all sides.

Social breakdown and the corporate saviour

As we have argued, governments throughout the western world are broadly supportive of neo-liberalism. Although there was flirtation with the alternative stakeholding models offered by Rhenish capitalism, we have seen that on a variety of political and economic levels, major institutions like the IMF, the World Bank and the OECD have tended to dominate debate and many countries formerly identified with concertation are shifting their policies to conform to a largely Anglo-American perspective (Balanya, Doherty, Hoedemann, Ma'anit and Wesselius, 2000).

These developments are further facilitated by Maastricht and global security frameworks, which although modified to take into account new dilemmas associated with the post-cold war order, remain dominated by America and by the requirements of American foreign policy. In relation to this, it appears that the concept of the 'military industrial complex' (Eisenhower, see Black and Black, 1994) still holds with the Pentagon's support of mega-mergers in the defence industry being firmly tied in with the requirements of US foreign and economic policies.

To reiterate, changes to economic policy that favour global finance and the establishment of free-markets, have had a significant impact upon business practices. These are affecting people's lives both within the context of increasing work pressures and longer working hours but also in terms of personal relationships and experiences of leisure. The latter is dominated by a consumer culture where pleasure is associated with buying things and services in overcrowded shops, restaurants and 'leisure centres'; often goods and services produced or supplied from third world factories with 'sweat shop' employment conditions.

Moreover, new security pressures, the growing political and social impact of religious fundamentalisms in addition to terrorist activities and secessionist movements no longer contained by the Cold War - add to a generalised sense of insecurity. Ironically, it is due to the free-market philosophy pursued by governments and business that social problems including increasing poverty, widening income differentials, and social alienation are proliferating. Within this framework, the economic impact of alienated, disenfranchised social groups from refugees to the long-term unemployed; and problems such as reduced workforce commitment and weakened national identity (in addition to a sceptical orientation to formal politics and worsening family breakdown) continue to present obstacles to the unproblematic continuation of neo-liberal economic policies (Gray, 1998; Elliot & Atkinson 1998; Plender 1997; Reich, 1991).

Having benefited greatly from the economic policies pursued by governments, big business represented in political rhetoric as 'flexible' and responsive to market fluctuations, is being made a *'partner'* in government policies. Ironically, it is now the business world that is seen to offer the best framework for dealing with many of the problems wrought by its own activities. This has particular implications for an economically diluted and anglicised deployment of the language of stakeholding. As we have argued throughout, new strategies on both the political and ideological plane are required to neutralise increasing economic, social and political tensions. However, the corporate and managerial framing of much political debate serves to limit the parameters in which genuine public debate, (representing the interests of a variety of so called stakeholders), can take place. Because of an overwhelming faith in big business to deliver solutions to social problems, political processes that should involve the generation of informed and open public debate at local and national levels, are being reduced to little more than opinion gathering exercises akin to market research (Maile and Hoggett, 2001). It might be argued that it would be naïve to expect governments to reflect wider social interests and the current corporate culture is only the latest of a long line of attempts by states to draw on business to legitimate the wrongs of capitalism when these are becoming too explicit for comfort. This was as true of the philanthropic face of capital in the nineteenth and early twentieth centuries when the capitalist world was faced with the threat of communism, as it is today. Having said that we need to be cognisant of the novel set of circumstances which, as already indicated, are leading to the redrawing of the boundaries between state and civil society, with increasing interventionism into areas formerly belonging to the private sphere on the part of the latter - and the incorporation of the latter into government strategy.

As an example of these trends, during the mid 1980s, it was management writers Hayes and Watts (1986) who, in their appropriately titled book 'Corporate Revolution', called upon industry to engage in public relations (PR) activities, designed:

> to demonstrate the common interests of industry and citizens in the face of public segmentation, the rise of legislative pressure groups, knowledge workers, ...public interest groups and terrorist groups (Hayes and Watts, 1986, p.142).

In the event, the PR exercises of individual companies were considered insufficient to re-integrate the fragmented social and political groups wrought by the end of the Cold War. The menace of the Soviet Union could no longer provide such a ready political foil for the free market and highlight the free market's purported qualities of light, goodness and freedom (see Chomsky, 1998). The *firm* was seen as occupying a special, intermediary space between government and civil society. In this sense it was considered to play an important role in the harmonisation of conflicting interests and potentially chaotic societal change.

Similarly, it was not long after President Bush's prescient speeches in the 1980s (which identified emerging social and political threats let loose by the imminent closure of Cold War international relations) that the United States began to pursue policies to encourage multinationals to adopt a more proactive stance on areas of social policy, once considered to have a more directly political remit (see, for example, Kuttner, 1997, p.32).

In this context the Stanford Research Institute in California was one of the first organisations to promote stakeholding as a dimension of social capital theory (Plender, 1997, p.17). Popular with both British and American governments, social capital theory is presented as an easy antidote to the aggressive 'hire and fire' policies of corporate downsizing which mistakenly treated employees as factors of production, rather than intelligent purveyors of quality products and services. In the face of the social fall-out of aggressive hire and fire policies associated with the earlier phases of neoliberalism, alternative managerial ideas, informed again by social scientific research, were expounded and deployed in an ad-hoc way in official policy documentation. In a strange inversion of what started as the implementation of private sector management techniques into the public sector, aggressive individualism and enterprise were later compared unfavourably with the more socially aware and humane ethics of the public and voluntary sectors (Mintzberg, 1996).

As already stated, business and social responsibility became equated with *managerial* responsibility much earlier in the century, long before the Thatcher and Reagan years. It was an approach adopted by major companies like the Ford Motor Company and IBM and practised at least until the late 1950s (McHugh, 1988, p.10). Indeed, Thomas Watson, the founder of IBM, foresaw a potential 'win-win situation' for all involved in ethical company activities, this resulting in reduced absenteeism, reduced misuse of company resources and higher profits. Ultimately and perhaps more significantly given our analysis of the rise and fall of 'stakeholding', management theories often had an ideological role and were drawn upon to promulgate the idea of world peace through world trade; the cohering of national interests in the name of social progress for *everybody,* aimed at diluting the threat of socialist politics (Bendix, 1963; Child, 1969; Clark, 1914).

Implications for the new governance

Ideas of managerial or corporate social responsibility which were particularly popular in the complex organisations of 1950s America have their counterparts in the growing inter- as well as intra-organisational relationships of the modern world, particularly as a means of dealing with potential organisational and social fragmentation noted earlier. The post-war creation of 'organisation man' was still a by-product of corporate collectivism couched within the dominant philosophy of liberal individualism. Today organisations have been flattened to the detriment of 'organisation man' or the regular lifestyles and social relationships that enhanced the male career. The closer interface of organisations, shareholders, customers, consumers and suppliers mean that 'corporate collectivism' is giving way to a more open and nebulous systems of communication. Complex organisational structures and dynamics are to some degree becoming externalised to wider working and business relationships. It is in recognition of this that the UK government is redefining the relationship between different sectors along the lines of a 'partnership' (Newman, 2000) this being understood in terms of a new type of governmentality with 'partnership' being a core conceptualisation of modern public sector management. The discourse of partnership which informs the new governmentality, amounts to an attempt to deal with increasing instability and fragmentation within the public sector (Ling, 2000) this requiring the incorporation of 'hard to reach groups' 'into compliant collaborators in creating a more inclusive society' (Ling, 2000, p.90). Social inclusion and authoritarianism sit side by side. In Ling's words:

> Governmentality... concerns the colonization of identity through which an obedient population and civil society is secured...in this context it is concerned with making the voluntary sector, user groups and others fit to be partners within a new strategic arena....prior to their participation in the partnership they must demonstrate their capacity to be good partners'... (Ling, 2000, p.89).

Jessop (2001) has argued that the constant reference to issues of 'good governance' has far broader global implications which are associated with the creation of a Shumpeterian economic and political culture. This entails a focus upon supply side issues for the continued survival of neoliberalism which must now broach new contradictions and pressures. The increasing popularity of the economic theories of Joseph Shumpeter are witnessed in a range of policies which deny the centrality of economic policies surrounding the promotion of neoliberalism and instead, highlight the significance of technological and human innovation, networks and communities working for the survival of a global technologically-driven order. Kleinman (2001) is one advocate of this perspective which rejects the argument that neoliberal policies and global trade are responsible for increasing unemployment, income differentials and poverty. He prefers to highlight productivity and technological factors and the consequent need to train workers in appropriate skills. A consequent focus on the creation of 'enterprising' and innovative individuals now held responsible for broader government and corporate failure is a characteristic feature of the technologically-driven globalising doctrine which informs much economic and social policy.

Welfare state restructuring pivots upon the creation of suitably flexible workforces – coached in appropriate cultural values and 'skills', to enable them to adapt to a fast paced global world. The growing emphasis upon individual and community responsibilities for political and economic failures is seen most clearly in the latest World Report which Jessop analyses for its 'good governance agenda'. In the face of growing conflicts, contradictions and pressures, Jessop concludes:

> Given its unstated acceptance of the global neo-liberal project, it is hardly surprising that the *World Report* also shares its agenda of promoting 'good governance' as a third way solution to market failure and state failure. In the eyes

of the international agencies that promote the 'good governance' agenda, this is essentially a technocratic fix that relies on the harmonizing powers of dialogue within appropriately structured and organized forums. It assumes the absence of contradictions, antagonisms, and conflicts that cannot be resolved through deliberation and it relies on good will to override bad faith (Jessop).

Governments face the tension between continued commitment to trade liberalisation, largely led by financial institutions (see Ramsay, 1998) and social stability. One of the most often cited areas of concern is the negative impact of growing poverty and perceived inequalities on the long-term interests of the global economy, since there is a perception that poor people are more likely to resist global economic change (OECD report, 1997) and to demand greater global stability.

Bound up with this perception is the now well-rehearsed argument about the detrimental effects of social exclusion to the economy. Social exclusion from the workplace tends to take priority for a variety of social groups and individuals whose experience of social exclusion contrary to prevailing political doctrine, are often complex and nuanced (see for example Levitas, 1999). Some have argued that neoliberal policies have served to increase poverty for some, while enhancing the wealth of others, (a universal and historic experience which has reached unprecedented levels on a global scale) (Novak, 2001). But business representatives and mainstream politicians prefer to highlight the relative impact of unemployment and reduced participation in world trade, a disjunction between technological and economic progress and individual capacities to adapt. Kleinman (2001), along with others, has argued that models of welfare remain influenced as much by national cultures, traditions and economic conditions. Such subtleties are lost on leading business representatives who simply point to the demands of a growing contingent of poor unemployed on welfare spending in general, this then being regarded as obstructing economic success:

> The problems of poverty and the distribution of employment and national income can have massive fiscal implications. If levels of welfare dependency are allowed to rise too high, then inevitably there will be a significant impact on business as well, particularly on taxes and incentives (Commission on Public Policy and British Business, 1997, p.29).

Of course, it is possible to interpret this quote as illustrative of the argument put forward by Kleinman: that lowering wages, for example, is not wholly in the interests of the advocates of neoliberalism. As we have seen, an alternative interpretation highlights the increasing pressures on welfare states to conform to economic policies, stressing adaptation, flexibility and change on the part of whole sections and sectors of society, this having consequences for public sector employment levels and experiences at the European level (Geddes, 2001). Geddes describes emerging welfare states as a "corporate welfare complex". He argues that this reflects a general assumption, promoted originally by the neoliberal New Right, that markets can provide better organisational, production and consumption models than the public sector (Geddes, 2001, p.498).

It is possible to recognise this in a range of policies promoted by international institutions subscribing to neoliberalism and uneven levels of conformity or innovations at national levels (see for example Bovaird, 2001). Indeed much research highlights the differential ways in which national governments have responded to the demands of globalisation. Re-conceptualising the relationship between society and economy has been a major strategy in approaching these problems. Such re-conceptualisations are behind ostensible attempts to integrate poorer countries into the global economy as a means '... to overcome social obstacles and rigidities, and to reform areas of major *economic dysfunction*' (OECD, 1997, p.112). In terms of growing political debates, strong civil societies and governance systems operating under the auspices of international law are regarded as paramount to global economic success. Part of this globalising quest involves attention to the development of *human capital* through enhanced education and health investment and by the greater participation of all people, especially women, in economic and political life. The call for people to change their skills, to change their personal behaviour, to change their lifestyles as a response to global economic change is a facet of the new governance (Newman, 2000).

More broadly, international organisations, comprised of a coalition of representatives from different countries, have assembled special bodies to deal with *'global'* problems associated with financial deregulation and unstable financial markets, the management of national and international political movements, secessionists, 'terrorists' and refugees. As we shall see later, attempts to extend Westernised governance structures to poor or under-developed parts of the world tends to coincide with military intervention, something often presented in terms of 'peace keeping' and 'containment'.

New interventionism

Fundamental to these developments are attempts on the part of governments and business (most notably in the US and the UK) to actively intervene in civil society with the aim of containing 'global social disorder'. Within the context of British welfare state restructuring, Clarke and Newman have indicated the dual process of the shrinking of the state and it's simultaneous prevalence and intervention in civil society. They refer to the various mechanisms by which this takes place in terms of 'managerialised dispersal' (Clarke and Newman, 1997, p.29). While not arguing for a complete or uniform outcome, managerialised dispersal involves a strategy, by which the state reconstructs itself. This in turn involves the reconfiguration of power structures which are vertically organised (e.g. central/local relations) these being 'overlaid with changes in the horizontal axes of inter-organisational relationships'. The latter entails a series of contractual relationships between the public and private sectors, and quasi marketised practices within the various organs and institutions of the welfare state. What is interesting about this analysis from a broader global governance perspective is the way in which:

The vertical axis aligns agencies as delegated authorities between the centralised power of the nation state and the 'consumer' power of the periphery, while subjecting them to more rigorous forms of financial and performance evaluation. The horizontal axis characteristically repostions them in a nexus of marketised or quasi-competitive relationships. Within this field of forces agencies are typically given the 'freedom to manage' ...This freedom is intended to recruit such agencies to the practice of 'self-discipline' through the internalisation of financial and performance targets (Clarke and Newman, 1997, p.30).

All of this represents a conscious strategy to overcome the fragmenting dynamics of neoliberalism. An important element of this type of incorporation is witnessed in a variety of international publications (for example, see OECD, 1997; Commission on Global Governance, 1995), where stress is placed upon a reassessment of *cultural* values (see Peters and Waterman, 1980). It is an interesting and notable fact that the manipulation of *'culture'* played a significant political role in the forging of national unity from disparate feudal elements and later played an important role in the rise of German Fascism. It is also notable that organs of civil society, particularly the voluntary sector became incorporated, along with 'culture', into state objectives (Chamberlayne, Cooper, Freeman and Rustin, 1999). Similar tendencies may be noted in contemporary society the increasing focus upon *'cultural'* and *'social'* matters, coincide with a state simultaneously weakened by the impact of economic globalisation and becoming more centralised and authoritarian (Maile and Hoggett 2001).

Associated with this is a shift of focus away from the bigger policy issues (this being much influenced by international organisations) to a preoccupation with intervention in matters personal and local. A related development is a concern with rethinking *'values'*, this being tied up with the abandonment of fundamental *political* principles (Plant, 2001, p.557). The most recent example of this in the UK was David Blunkett's call for immigrants to adopt British "norms" (see 'Loyalty oath urged for immigrants', The Daily Telegraph, December 12[th,] 2001). This is a development upon a more pervasive deployment of quasi-sociological and anthropological accounts of 'people management', itself being a corporation styled translation of *'society'* and 'social' process.

As already stated, the 'business community' (an interesting phrase which obscures differences of influence and interests of large, medium and small enterprises) has been called upon by international economic institutions and national governments to assist in a range of policy areas targeted at social cohesion, law, investment, trade and sustainable economic development. At a time in which the relationship between business and politics is becoming more than uncomfortably close (see for example the latest scandal surrounding the energy company Enron as reported in the Observer 3rd February, 2002). At both national and international levels, the maintenance *'of stable and prosperous communities but also countries'* (our italics) relies upon the design of *'foundations'* of rules of law while ultimately *'creating opportunities and outlets for self-expression and development'.*

Much is being done to shape appropriate attitudes to free-markets. *'Collective, international'* effort hinges upon the harmonisation of regulations and 'rules of conduct' and the strengthening of *'competition'* to stimulate economic growth, *'without weakening shared bonds and attachments of society and community'* (OECD, 1997, p.93). Across a range of disparate cultures and states, these *'global interests* in *cultural'* training and sensitivity occur via the transmission of international management practices. In addition, shared cultural bonds complement the transition from strong public sectors reliant upon *'acceptance for change'*, by creating *'acceptance of the necessity of competition'* (OECD, 1997, p.94). The extension of new work regimes to 'lifestyles' and personal habits, is focused upon the re-creation of social solidarities around acceptance of a competitive market economy. These objectives have become common currency in official policy documentation, as businesses become increasingly integrated at both a national and international level. The increasing reliance upon corporate initiatives and their business discourses appear 'non-ideological' by giving the impression of being *'beyond politics'*. The highly managerial inflection of Tony Blair's rhetoric reflects this shift when he argues that the role of government 'is not to command but to facilitate... in partnership *with industry*... not a matter of ideology but of *national interest'* [our italics] (Blair, 1996).

The managerial inflection of political rhetoric can be explained in terms of one observation that, in the context of a dynamic, sometimes unstable global economy, government has reduced autonomy and is fast becoming a matter of what Hirst and Thompson (1996) refer to as 'administration'. Business, as a kind of metaphor for neo-liberal economics, on the other hand, is still understood as operating in the sphere of civil society, outside the formal remit of the nation state and is, paradoxically, increasingly politicised in terms of it's role in the provision of social cohesion. 'Business' and the 'economy' are terms which are used interchangeably to refer to the ineluctable and natural dynamics of rational decision-making and daily practices of everyday life which appears to supersede and transcend the state and polity since it operates 'in the area of the non-political' (Bauman, 1998, p.66).

This development has ideological implications. In spite of appearances and claims to the contrary, narrow or sectional interests are universalised to *all citizens*, employed, unemployed, under-employed, overworked, well paid and poorly paid. The corporation casts large chunks of civil society in its own image - from the ways in which it shapes public space and consumerism, to the rationalities it introduces into both home and work life. In the context of a stakeholding agenda which plays upon the notion of universal rights to be represented and heard in political decision making, *'business'* stands out as universal, pragmatic, street-wise and representative of whole sections of society. Business is a universal category that obscures the differential political and economic power of large and small enterprises this being a significant omission when it is in fact the multi- and trans-national corporations that have benefited most from financial de-regulation. Big business is overwhelmingly represented in government and inter-governmental policies promoting 'free-trade' and de-regulation. This is documented in research pointing to the influence of corporate elites and networks on European policy (Balanya, Doherty, Hoedeman, Ma'anit and Wesselius, 2000), this reflecting similar dynamics influencing the IMF and World Bank (Monbiot, 2000).

In the UK, New Labour's recruitment of corporate leaders to key political positions (Draper, 1997, p.164) has been described in terms of the 'new corporatism' (see, for example, *The Economist,* 14th-20[th]August, 1999). Business is one of the largest 'social partners' working on specific tasks in this 'Task-Force Revolution'. Chief executives and chairmen of 28 of Britain's biggest 100 public companies act, part-time or otherwise, as government advisers in what are allegedly widened government networks (IPPR, 1997 p. 1/2).

The Commission for Public Policy was created in 1995 at the instigation of Baroness Blackstone and Lord Hollick. Their ostensible aim was to build on the success of John Smith's Commission on Social Justice. The Board of Commissioners included Bob Bauman (British Aerospace); Sir Christopher Harding (Chairman of Legal and General); Professor John Kay Director of the School of Management Studies (Oxford); David Sainsbury, Chairman, J. Sainsbury plc and John Monks, General Secretary of the TUC. The above expressed a concern to re-draw the boundaries between state and civil society as a means of dealing with problematic issues of 'social exclusion'. The re-conceptualisation of *economic success* as embodying *social* needs was an attempt to dilute the starker aspects of societal change left in the wake of neoliberalism.

It was argued that improved British economic performance would rely on a shift in welfare policy, in particular, the re-forging of state/business boundaries via the reconstitution of citizens as active (individual) participants in economic and welfare programmes. Although policy transfer from one country or even one area of a country to another is less than straightforward, due to institutional and cultural differences (Bovaird and Halachmi, 2001, Flynn 2000) welfare restructuring has tended to emulate American models of welfare or 'workfare'.

We would not tend to argue that emerging rationalities and discourses are in any sense uni-linear reflections of an underlying economic reality. Rather, what we have to address is a complex process that institutionalises structural power through the widespread adoption of *cultural values* (Gill and Law, 1997, p.138). These cultural values continue to hold a managerial quality, one which can quite easily accommodate current concerns with communities and local interest groups, which are in the process of being decimated by financial de-regulation (Gray, 1998, pp.110-113). While the OECD and World Bank stress the importance of learning 'skills' for work in the flexible global company, British policy pivots upon the concept of 'welfare to work' and 'the New Deals'. New Deals include benefits being matched to workplace 'training', with employers being paid subsidies for the effort. Similarly, managerialism itself has been shown to take quite distinctive forms according to different countries (Flynn, 2000).

Having said that, it would appear within the British context at least that, as Kuttner (1996) writes, political concerns are being over-ridden by issues surrounding the governance of the enterprise, a focus which is less threatening to the corporate world (see Gamble and Kelly, 1997, p.5). In the private sector these kinds of governance issues tend to be focused upon discussions surrounding the economic benefits that derive from good common-sense management practices. There is little or no concern with political or social direction, other than the prevention of the worst corporate excesses. Indeed, emphasis tends to be placed on reducing regulation by formulating 'codes of practice'.

This perspective is not too out of keeping with a fairly common perception among leading sections of the business community that long-term economic interests may be threatened by the ravaging effects of short-termism simply understood as bad management (see, for example, Roddick, 1996). Careful management strategy, eager to protect long-term *shareholder* interests would then be sensitive to the views and interests of 'direct' and 'indirect' or 'secondary' stakeholders. Direct stakeholders may be considered to include employees, investors, customers, suppliers and the local community. Secondary or indirect stakeholders may include civic institutions, academic and media commentators, regulators, pressure groups, trade bodies and competitors, all of whom form part of 'the social ecology of the free enterprise system'. Extending the concept, stakeholders could even be defined to include the environment, non-human species and future generations, since all of these presumably can be seen as 'having rights' and, indeed, are often represented, as such, by well-organised pressure groups (for example, Friends of the Earth, Greenpeace, Life and the League Against Cruel Sports) NGOs, voluntary organisations and welfare agencies all currently described as 'partners' in British social policy. How far such interests are fully expressed in corporate decision-making is another matter.

Some might argue that stakeholding, even from a fundamentally managerial perspective, would better encourage reflexivity on the part of strategic players, albeit in terms of continuing commitment to neo-liberalism. In this scenario the stake-holding issue is about how best to *create added-value beyond the business deal itself*, involving a switch in focus to highlight dimensions such as product and service quality, customer care and after-sales service, ecological protection, trust and integrity. All of these, properly incorporated in the decision-making process, deliver a 'best practice' outcome and may well enhance the economic value of a business activity for shareholders, while generating stronger employee and customer commitment, loyalty and trust, all of which can serve to strengthen a company's position in the market. These more conservative elements of stakeholding, according to Wheeler et al (1996), amount to a:

> sophisticated view of the company as a social vehicle whose speed and steering are dependent upon careful reading of the road signs and the behaviour of other road users. Meanwhile, the route is best determined by involving all passengers with knowledge to contribute to the map reading (Wheeler et al, 1996).

In Blair's words, it is 'one of the oldest strategies for creating value'. Within this context, if stakeholding has been taken seriously at all is *because* of its managerial inflection (Lister, 1997). The needs of 'The New Economy' characterised by the capital machinery and electronic technologies of global companies like Boeing and

Microsoft (see, for example, the Independent, 19th July, 1999) and the free-markets on which they rely are of pivotal concern for the new managerialism.

The recasting of sociological and other social scientific knowledge as managerial know-how is a key element of stakeholding. This revised conceptualisation of the company is one that recognises it, as Ed Mayo, Director of the New Economics Foundation notes, as a social institution. Here economic exchange is seen to rest on a bedrock of trust and co-operation. This perspective may account for the higher profile of a range of sociological treatises that call on governments to recognise the varied importance of culture, norms, values and the changing needs of advanced or post-modernity. The establishment of trust is regarded by many commentators as the precondition of success and survival in a post-industrial society (Fukuyama, 1995; Perkin, 1997) and is also regarded a key component of 'The Third Way' (Giddens, 2000).

A recognition that 'the market is more than the sum of its parts' (Hutton, 1999, p.89) is one thing, but it would appear that the whole tendency is to look to those cultural and social dynamics which are beyond the market, rather than addressing the market itself. Despite Hutton's concern that the 'economic' is our modern day guru, in political rhetoric at least, the 'economic' is increasingly diluted by the search for a 'socially inclusive society', rather than the necessary checks and balances to the economy which would result in greater fairness to all.

The ambiguities of stakeholding result in a variety of interpretations, dominated in the current political climate, by those who take as their starting point the needs of the flexible firm. While the British trade union movement remains loyal to collective bargaining, it has displayed some optimism for the possibilities of stakeholding believing that it may encourage information sharing and disclosure of executive pay. Perkin (1997) believes that professionals working within businesses themselves possess the greatest social vision especially as they challenge the old ruling elites:

> In the United States, big business men like Richard J Franke have called for a more responsible approach to democracy by business, 'to counter the excesses of greed and unfair advantage that threaten our concept of the just society' by means of a modern social contract' guaranteeing a fair and open system with a 'sense of general proportion between the haves and the have nots'. Tony Blair's call for a stakeholder society is catching an opportune tide that is beginning to flow around the world, *which even British and American businessmen are more aware of than their obsolescent politicians* (Perkin, 1997, p.47) (our italics).

In sum, there are range of pressures upon businesses which relate to the changes wrought by societal and institutional fragmentation, these themselves being related to earlier neoliberal policies which have favoured institutional and de-regulated finance to the detriment of local communities, livelihoods and lifestyles. Businesses are also facing greater competition in increasingly saturated markets. Larger businesses have the financial and political clout to enable them to be more proactive in responding to social and economic pressures. The most effective means of achieving this is through their active involvement in politics, to change the terms of engagement between state, business and civil society more broadly. Their influence has wrought significant changes in labour legislation, this serving to dilute the relative power of labour across Europe and America, to determine decent pay levels and job security within both private and public sectors.

As we have seen, the above developments extend into the international political and private arenas. Clearly, social and political threats associated with growing inequalities resulting from neoliberalism need to be managed by corporations and governments alike. The following chapter identifies some of the trends which mark what is now increasingly recognised to be a new world *disorder*, issues around military spending and international relations characterised by increasing intervention in poorer countries by the Western allies, being of great social, economic and politic significance for anybody interested in exploring the international potential of stakeholding.

Chapter 6

New world disorder

As we have already seen, it is not just at the national but also the international level that the state and business are encountering the pressures of social and political upheaval, as well as varying degrees of economic change. We have also noted the contradictory and aggravated nature of some of these developments, many of whose outcomes cannot be easily contained or predicted. It is perhaps not surprising that there should be an emphasis on the part of the various international bodies promoting neoliberalism on effective 'management', whether it is the management of conflict in Bosnia or the administration of 'aid' to war-torn developing countries in return for their subscription to western ways of doing things.

Modern managerial discourses enter into political strategies focused upon containment of civil and political unrest, drawing upon the insights offered by social science in the process. Similarly, managerial discourse is then generalised to the societal and political sphere. For example, the human resource management vocabularies of empowerment, self-help, equal opportunity and decentralised decision-making become entwined with attempts to re-conceptualise democratic processes. All of this amounts to the new governance witnessed in a range of developments, from the containment and processing of refugees from the mid-1980s onwards (Loescher, 1992) to the terms and conditions which attach to investment and aid in developing countries. Rules of conduct and the establishment of appropriate cultural values prevail in the strategies and publications of international bodies, including the UN, UNICEF, OECD, the IMF and the World Bank.

Due to the fact that international changes are often partial and contradictory, as noted in chapter one, it is possible for countervailing political and social pressures to utilise the more positive aspects of western foreign policies and discourses for alternative, albeit modified strategies. In this context, Lasch has identified the contradictory dynamics of globalisation, specifically as this relates to the combination of increasing centralisation of power in the developed economies with increasing social fragmentation:

> On the one hand (the world) is now united through the agency of the market, as it never was before. Capital and labour flow freely across political boundaries that seem increasingly artificial and unenforceable. Popular culture follows in their wake. On the other hand, tribal loyalties have seldom been so aggressively promoted. Religious and ethnic warfare breaks out in one country after another: in India and Sri Lanka; in large parts of Africa; in the former Soviet Union and the former Yugoslavia (Lasch, 1996, p.48).

The stakeholding agenda is one which must be located in the sensibilities and anxieties generated by the short-sightedness and greed of a neoliberal social, political as well as economic culture. Yet, while whole sections of the world's poor and socially excluded are being urged to revisit their moral values, as a means of reducing public expenditure (a central tenet of neoliberalism) and maintaining social order, it is what Christopher Lasch refers to as the new elites, those who have benefited from the economic status quo, who have reneged on their responsibilities.

Through their financial investment practices and their businesses and leisure activities, these elites it is argued, have effectively revolted against the constraints of time and place (Lasch, 1996). Their acknowledgement of civic obligations does not extend beyond their own immediate neighbourhood. Instead of supporting public services, the new elites put their money into the improvement of their own self-enclosed enclaves. They gladly pay for private and suburban schools, private security and private systems of garbage collection but they have also managed to relieve themselves, to a remarkable extent, of their obligation to contribute to the national treasury.

Within the developed world, for those who have 'made it', a sense of security relies increasingly on the purchase of sophisticated alarm systems and the building of high, possibly electrified, fencing to warn off the hungry and socially and economically excluded. It is a notable but perhaps unsurprising fact that the prison population of America alone tripled throughout the 1980s and 1990s (Bauman, 1997, p.60) and has grown by well in excess of 20% in many European countries. An increasing concern with security and surveillance systems testifies to heightened perceptions of personal *insecurity* (Elliot and Atkinson, 1998) this leading in turn to additional spending on policing and the privatisation of security systems which have become highly profitable enterprises. The 'poor' often share the material aspirations of their wealthier counterparts, regarding their own value in terms of their ability to purchase consumer goods. In turn, global poverty cannot be divorced from international policies serving to exclude and marginalise poor people through, for example, their subjection to relentless criminalisation and surveillance systems (Bauman, 1998). This has particular resonance given that much poverty is associated with the fact that the population of large areas of the world is economically inactive. In this sense the poor are:

> fully and truly *redundant*, useless, disposable and there is no 'rational reason' for their continuing presence...The sole rational response to that presence is the systematic effort to exclude from normal society, supply and consumer choice, mediated by allurement and seduction (Bauman, 1998, p.59).

Governments and business networks are obliged to manage the contradictory dynamics associated with 'free-trade' very carefully. Developments in media and satellite communications, for example, may be characterised (quite problematically according to Wyatt, Henwood, Miler and Senker, especially given the tendency for corporations to dominate information technology and networks) positively as informing the 'information society', but they also enable more of the world's poor and socially excluded to see - and compare themselves with - wealthier parts of the world. Inevitably, this puts intensified pressure on existing institutions and social arrangements as rising expectations lead people to demand more from their lives. Satellite communication has also been a successful channel for secessionist political movements, including that of the Kurdish diaspora and, more recently, the much publicised terrorist activities of Osama Bin Laden.

From the perspective of governments, the expression of social discontent in whatever form is *perceived* to be in perpetual danger of eroding the centres of political power (Chomsky, 1998; Bauman, 1998). From at least the time of the 'new world order' speech of former US President George Bush in 1990, the threat to the 'free world' has overflowed its traditional Cold War boundaries to occupy a new, ill-defined space within and between national territories.

In recognition of the greater permeability of national borders and the limited capacities of national governments to deal with the unexpected demands of globalisation, international bodies are now actively engaged in designing policies to better manage a fragmented civil society (see Cox, 1997). One way of managing the potential disruption wrought by a disaffected, socially excluded people is to provide humanitarian aid under the guise of poor relief (a top priority of the United Nations and a major activity of a vast range of non-governmental agencies). An alternative measure is to pursue different models of democracy to those we have come to associate with the classic, liberal democratic state. There is a concern among many leading specialists in the field that administrative structures are being designed primarily to act more as investment channels, rather than vehicles of political representation. At worst, such organisations may be involved in the shoring-up of what Susan Strange (1996) refers to as an 'international business civilisation'; one in which only the new elites have a real role to play.

For example 'regionalism' at first glance appears non-partisan but still favours the free market principles of economic globalization (see, for example, Hirst and Thompson, 1996). Apart from anything else, regional forms of governance may act as 'weak' or 'quasi-states', which, according to Bauman, are:

> easily reduced to the (useful) role of local police precincts, securing a modicum of order required for the conduct of business, but need not be feared as effective brakes on the global companies 'freedom' (Bauman, 1998, p.68).

In turn, 'pacts' between national and local and regional governments are drawn up to ensure political consensus on economic policy.

Meanwhile, the reconstitution of international security appears in the universal 'global' discourse of 'peace-keeping' and the upholding of human rights and democracy when in fact, as Ignatieff (1999) has noted, 'globalisation has split the world into two zones, a safe zone and a danger zone'. United peace-keeping forces support 'friends' of the Western world, (i.e. serious trading partners) while, in the process invading and interfering in the conflicts of those countries which are considered weak. Other countries, regions or indeed continents are largely ignored and systematically marginalised within the global news media.

Where poor relief is inadequate to prevent political destabilization then military force is evoked by the international community (Cox, 1997, p.58). In sum, the rationale and conditions for aid, along with military strategies have had to change to deal with a variety of economic, social and political complexities all of which are associated with the contradictory aims and effects of neoliberalism and the countervailing pressures and resistances they spawn. The end of the cold war also rendered almost completely inappropriate and ineffective established procedures and mechanisms for the maintenance of global peace, stability and security that had held together the international security framework for almost half a century.

At the start of the 1990s, even the world's most powerful nation, the United States, was struggling to maintain its global security role, hindered by massive internal and external debt problems, a weakened and increasingly uncompetitive economy and by uncertainty about the nature of the 'new world order', following the collapse of its former super-power rival, the Soviet Union. In due course, it was recognised that a different 'new world order' would evolve but, in the immediate aftermath of the 'outbreak of peace', it was not at all clear what the mechanisms and processes which would become its key elements would be. More importantly in the short term, the ultimate goal of the emerging security framework was anything but clear. Kuttner had aptly summarised the predominant sentiment at the time:

> it is undeniable that the post-war era is at last over, and its governing assumptions, long since dead, can now be properly buried. And it is high time to think seriously about the design of a new post-hegemonic world system (Kuttner, 1991).

As the new world order developed over the ensuing years, an optimistic assessment might have been that the apparent removal of the threat of self-destructive super-power conflict would not only necessitate a major reconstruction of the international order but, in doing so, allow a greater voice in evolving international relations to a range of formerly excluded groups and countries.

In the decade following the end of the Cold War, however, global security issues and the absence of the much-vaunted New World Order, properly structured to meet the changing requirements necessary to deal effectively with evolving global conflict, were forced onto the centre of the political stage. The invasion of Kuwait by Iraq and the subsequent Gulf War was first amongst a series of international 'humanitarian interventions' that characterised the 1990s. Somalia, Bosnia and later in the decade Kosovo, (Ignatieff, 1999) exposed only too clearly the gross inadequacy of the post-Cold War mechanisms for global security provision.

The sense of crisis and disharmony among the allies that pervaded the 'management' of these conflicts underlined the piecemeal nature of short-term solutions and their failure to incorporate any fundamental notion of broader 'stakeholder' involvement. This disharmony in global conflict management remained all too obvious until the unimaginable destruction and loss of life associated with the terrorist attacks on New York and Washington in September, 2001 appears to have precipitated a significant change in both US policy and in global geo-political relations.

The US, now led by a President not expected to exercise a cautious and considered response, was thought likely to revert to 'normal' behaviour and to launch massive bombing raids on those held to be responsible. Large-scale deployment of troops and military equipment followed. Early talk of "the first war of the 21st century", the "axis of evil" and a "crusade" against terrorism seemed to presage precisely such action. Yet, in the weeks that followed the US 'twin towers' catastrophe, caution seemed, initially, to be the watchword and immense effort at the diplomatic level was put into constructing a powerful and lasting coalition of nation states, all ranged together against terrorism.

The apparently contradictory aims of humanitarianism, the pursuit of democracy and military intervention were resulting in fudged, ill-thought out strategies to deal with a terrorist threats not easily identifiable or manageable. While some form of military action against defined targets (whether it be terrorist leader, Osama Bin Laden; the Al-Qaida terrorist network or the ruling Afghanistan regime, the Taliban, that offered support to such terrorists) was seen as inevitable, the idea was that it should be deployed in a focused, limited and somewhat surgical manner, designed to achieve only what the global coalition would sanction without fracturing and, in particular, taking care to minimise loss of civilian lives. It also, uniquely in modern military combat, featured an ad-hoc and poorly conceptualised humanitarian dimension.

The latter might, cynically, be seen in terms of legitimation for increased western intervention in poorer parts of the world. Part of the ostensible rationale that was given for the destruction of anti-aircraft sites in Afghanistan, for example, was to allow US aircraft unhindered access to the skies over the country in order to drop significant supplies of food and medical aid to isolated communities. The images which hit our television screens of poor, terrified people running to catch the parcels as they earlier dodged bombs - came under extensive public criticism. Governments and international agencies must deal with increasingly critical and better-informed publics who – as already indicated – are far less trusting of politicians and officials. Hence, although a similar coalition approach was employed in the Gulf War a decade earlier, the negotiations this time at least recognised and publicised the need for major issues of disenfranchisement, repression and poverty to be addressed in tandem with the eradication of terrorism. In a sense, to capture the support of the global coalition, the United States and its key partners have to accept that their foreign policy must in future address crucial issues such as the creation of a genuine Palestinian state. Winning the war against terrorism would ultimately involve more than military power; it would surely require the removal of the principal causes of terrorism themselves, poverty and political and social injustices. In so doing, even the most firmly established and enduring global geo-political relationships (such as that between the US and Israel) may be called into question.

It was interesting to note that, just a few weeks into the so-called "war on terrorism", pressure for the cessation of US and allied bombing of Afghanistan began to appear within the coalition while demands for action on these other issues became much more prominent. Analysts noted that:

> in this particular conflict, there can be 'no meaningful military victory unless the inescapably grim consequences for those already hard-pressed people who are caught up in it can be minimised and effectively addressed as winter begins' (The Guardian: 8/10/01).

Afghanistan, ravaged by the effects of war, already had the fourth worst under-five mortality rate in the world and the highest outside Africa. It also had the worst maternal mortality rate in the world after Sierra Leone; a life expectancy of between 40 and 45 years; with only 12% of the population of 21m having access to safe water and just 29% access to basic health services.

The experience of the Gulf War in the early 1990s suggested that a massive commitment of military personnel and equipment at enormous cost - and with tremendous effort on the diplomatic and military fronts - can secure a military victory of sorts but, at the same time, could still fail to achieve the real strategic objective behind the military campaign. For example, despite the remarkable scale of the resources deployed by the US and its allies at the time to resolve the crisis, the eventual outcome left the Iraqi regime of Saddam Hussein firmly in place and may even have served to strengthen its internal position. It is a strange 'new world order' where, despite the mass deployment of the most proficient, highly-trained troops; the most advanced weapons technology; and the world's most sophisticated leading-edge surveillance and information-gathering equipment, the most visible culprit responsible for invasion, terrorism and ethnic cleansing remains in political control of his country. The allied leaders (and apparent victors), Bush, Major and now Clinton, have all left the centre of the political stage.

The immense suffering of an oppressed and pauperised Iraqi population, crushed under the Hussain regime and years of allied economic and trade embargos, has not been resolved and occasional bombing by the US has been depicted necessary after more than a decade to enforce a 'no fly' zone over the Kurds in the north of Iraq. The outcome has meant that, through no fault of their own, much of the Iraqi population have been left to bear the personal, social and economic costs of sanctions and intermittent warfare with little real chance of removing the (once useful to the US and its allies) regime whose actions led to their implementation in the first place. Any ostensible humanitarian aims on the part of the western allies are increasingly undermined in the face of public perceptions that the US and the UK in particular have strategic political and economic interests of their own which inform their blind pursuit of a full-scale military attack on Iraq. The failure of America and Britain to respond to electoral dissent over the war and their attempts to manipulate the UN, suggests a less than effective and equitable global security system, let alone one which could hope to address real stakeholder interests in an enhanced new world order. At the moment, the apparent desire of the US to achieve a regime change in Baghdad has been constrained by the need to work closely with the United Nations in order to secure some kind of a coalition when it comes to war. UN strategy has been to agree to the re-deployment of weapons inspectors to Iraq to assess the extent of any Iraqi breach of UN resolution on the development of weapons of mass destruction and to compel Saddam Hussain's regime to complete a comprehensive dossier outlining Iraq's weapons programmes. At the time of writing, the inspectors continue their task, the dossier has been completed and submitted and the US and its key allies continue to prepare for what many political commentators see, in spite of great public dissent, as the inevitable conflict to come.

Soon after the Gulf War in the early 1990s, the political manoeuvrings among key global security players that preceded the humanitarian disaster in Bosnia confirmed that a solution to the problem of maintaining global security and stability in the post-Cold War world had barely been addressed and revealed both ineptitude and tardiness in the formation of allied strategy, particularly in Europe. The dreadful events that followed indicated in a striking manner that traditional global security mechanisms were out of date and that the piecemeal security framework that had replaced them was largely ineffective in delivering an equitable outcome for genuine stakeholders. Disagreements, on occasions, between Nato allies; the apparent inability of European governments to speak with one voice and deal quickly and effectively with what was initially perceived to be 'a European issue'; and problems at the level of the United Nations culminated in a horrific humanitarian catastrophe in Bosnia which has surely left in its wake the seeds of future conflicts to come.

To expose its inherent frailty further, the fledgling post-Cold War global security system was then exposed to the Kosovo crisis. Building upon centuries-old and highly complex historic roots, the Kosovo crisis began in the early part of 1998 initially with the displacement of over 300,000 refugees, principally Kosovan Albanians. A ceasefire was eventually agreed in October 1998, allowing these refugees to find shelter in order to avoid a major humanitarian disaster that winter. Although a verification mission was deployed in the region under the auspices of the Organisation for Security and Co-operation in Europe, the hostilities began again in January 1999. In March 1999, the Paris conference sought to secure a peaceful resolution to the conflict. However, the peace terms were rejected by the Yugoslav delegation and, in response, Nato threatened to commence an air-strike campaign against the Milosevic regime, should the conflict continue.

Once again, while the airstrike campaign eventually compelled Milosevic's government to accept defeat and withdraw from Kosovo (and while Milosevic himself remains on trial for war crimes at The Hague) the current conflict resolution framework of the United Nations (and Nato) appeared fragmented, cumbersome and often difficult to hold together for all allied participants. Although, unlike in the case of Iraq, the Milosevic regime was ultimately replaced, the population of the region - have suffered devastating economic, social and personal consequences over a protracted period of time. Clearly, the world does not yet have the kind of modern security framework that can successfully underpin a genuine democratic and effective new world order and ensure justice and equity as part of the resolution of conflict. Experiences such as the crisis in Kosovo underline only too starkly the present limitations on the capabilities of existing international organisations for swift and effective action to preserve global security, let alone create peace and harmony.

The position and role of Russia in the global security framework was a further problem highlighted by the Kosovo crisis. Still an immensely powerful military nation and a key actor in global security, Russia retained between 70% and 80% of the former Soviet defence industry following the dissolution of the USSR and, despite the economic rigours of the last decade, continues to combine devastating military power with widespread economic and political instability. The crucial requirement for Russia's voice to be heard in the evolving global decision-making procedures for conflict resolution was made abundantly clear during the Kosovo crisis with the allies eventually recognising that Russian concerns could not be ignored and their involvement in the resolution of the conflict became imperative.

Revising the global geo-political environment

From the discussion above, it is now clear that the processes and mechanisms required for successful global conflict resolution have changed fundamentally. A different set of 'global' risks must be addressed, including:

> regional conflict, weapons of mass destruction, terrorism, and the so-called 'asymmetric' threats like cyber-warfare (Vershbow, 1999).

Currently, those involved in global security management are more concerned with managing global risks and establishing a high level of preparedness for dealing with isolated but strategically significant regional conflicts and terrorist actions, rather than preparing to respond to perceived super-power threats. Until the late 1980s, Nato, for example, based its military strategy and associated defence budgets on expectations of:

> A relatively predictable high attrition, extended duration, Central European (military engagement), backed up with the threat of massive retaliation to deter nuclear-armed ballistic missile attack (Gansler, 1998).

After 1990, however, the strategy shifted to one where conflicts would be addressed by:

> more limited - but almost always, coalition - engagements. They will be fought with smaller, lighter, more mobile forces and equipment; with concentrated firepower precisely delivered from long range. Wars of attrition will be replaced by so-called 'reconnaissance strike' engagements (Gansler, 1998).

These crucial developments in modern military strategy will inevitably impact significantly upon future global military and strategic requirements. Reflecting the new mechanisms and discourses of governance discussed in chapter 5, Nato and the United Nations have been called upon to play new roles in the 1980s and 1990s which principally involve the deployment of United Nations (and/or Nato) forces in a 'peace-keeping' or 'humanitarian' role within 'crisis zones'. By 1998, the United Nations was maintaining some 16 major peace-keeping operations across the globe, deploying over 20,000 troops from 70 countries. The financial cost of maintaining such a peace-keeping role has varied over the decade from over $3 billion in 1993, 1994 and 1995 to over $1 billion in 1997 and in 1998. Included within this UN function are observer missions (such as those in Tajikistan, Liberia and Georgia); transition missions (such as that in Haiti); and stabilisation forces (such as that in Bosnia-Herzegovina).

In this post-Cold War setting, then, the evolution of military and security strategy internationally is driven by a regular re-evaluation of the risk of limited and regionally-focused conflict. In turn, this evaluation helps to determine, within tight budget constraints, the shape, content and distribution of future military provision and associated expenditures. Concern with East/West alliances which dominated so much of earlier NATO strategy has now been replaced by a military strategy focused upon the efficient provision of 'rapid response' units, trained and equipped to carry out swift and effective intervention globally to support peace keeping (James, 1995), to provide humanitarian aid and to carefully monitor and contain what are regarded by America and its allies as 'problem areas' - rather than the maintenance of huge military capability. 'Peace-keeping' and military intervention go hand-in-hand. This rationalised security strategy continues to reflect western or more specifically, US hegemony.

As part of the rationalisation of defence spending, each major arms-producing nation, operating within a range of international treaties and other agreements (UN, NATO, EU, CSCE, G7) will be continually re-assessing its overall military commitments within the evolving UN security structure, identifying the nature of the forces and weapons systems required to support the policy and deciding how, why and when to use them. To reiterate, slowly, the key nations with military power are beginning to construct a new doctrine for military engagement, focused ostensibly upon 'peace-keeping' and 'humanitarian action'. In the process they are seeking to put in place the kind of security architecture that places a greater emphasis upon disseminating (some might argue imposing) western informed models of democracy through the organs of civil society, aid workers, NGOs, development agencies and funding bodies. As we have already argued, this is a characteristic feature of the new international governance comprising a network of agencies and alliances working in tandem with the requirements of neo-liberalism, the protection of 'free-markets' for example, through the maintenance of social and political stability that favours western foreign investment practices.

The architecture of international security has yet to be sufficiently reconstructed to ensure that all relevant players in the resolution of global conflicts have a clear voice. At the moment, as we are witnessing in current US and UK policies on Iraq, issues of democracy, equity, and accountability in conflict resolution are being overlooked – this indicating a clear disjunction between the democratising and moralising rhetoric of the new governance - and actual practice.

The position of Russia in this reconstruction of the 'New World Order' is interesting. As we noted earlier with respect to the Kosovo crisis, Russia, ravaged by foreign debt and domestic economic collapse, still remains a potent force that cannot be ignored. What Russia lacks in economic power it now compensates for in terms of shrewd diplomatic strategy exercised by President Putin to ensure that Russia remains a powerful force in the emerging 'New World Order'. Burdened by over $130bn of debt, almost half of which is owed to Western industrialised nations and their banks, and with the value of its natural resources threatened by potential oil price reductions due to the recessionary impact of the terrorist attacks, Putin has assembled what amounts to his own "coalition within a coalition" to exert pressure on the US and its principal allies. Using his close personal association with Germany – Putin, a fluent German speaker and a former KGB officer in Dresden – has effectively gathered together those European states which are more reluctant than others to commit full support to military plans by the US and will use this 'nervousness' to exert influence on President Bush and the other coalition leaders. As Maddox commented in the Times, 26th September, 2001:

> Mr Putin is, if you like, assembling his own band of supporters, an alliance of the ambivalent, scooping it out of President Bush's grander coalition......Even before September 11, President Putin had used the German relationship to build up nervousness in continental Europe about Mr Bush's plans for a missile defence system. He used the pretext of missile defence to drag Mr Bush into Cold War-style armament talks to Russia's advantage.........Now he is about to see how much he can extract from the US for his support in allowing the US to use Central Asian states as bases.

The assembly of the 'grander coalition' that supported the Afghanistan strategy owed much to the diplomatic missions of the UK's Prime Minister, Tony Blair and the US Defence Secretary, Donald Rumsfeld. Without question, the coalition was assembled with, in certain cases, a considerable degree of 'arm-twisting' and diplomatic deals. It is here that we see key political players in this particular phase of the reconstruction of the 'New World Order' emerging. They include Russia, as discussed above, Pakistan, India, Iran, Uzbekistan and Saudi Arabia. Furthermore, it is no coincidence that Yasser Arafat arrived in London in mid-October 2001 to discuss the Palestinian issue with Blair at such a critical time.

Clearly, the role of these political entities - and their support for the US-led coalition as the conflict in Afghanistan evolved - served to fundamentally reshape both the emerging 'New World Order' and, more directly, the structure and direction of US foreign policy within it. It is also apparent that the deterioration in the Palestinian situation since 2001 has made the formation of an effective US-led coalition against Iraq now much more difficult. It is precisely the 'old' US foreign policy that lies at the heart of the current conflict and its origins.

Since the 1970s, there have been two principal elements of US foreign policy in the region; namely, its relationship with Saudi Arabia and that with Israel. In the case of Saudi Arabia oil money and US support have kept the Saudi royal family in power for decades. Maddox (The Times; 12th October, 2001) commented that, over time, formal aid to Saudi Arabia has been replaced by a series of major US-Saudi arms deals amounting to almost $94bn between 1950 and 1997 (about 25% of which were agreed after the Gulf War of 1991). In practice, then, US support has much to do with ensuring the security of its own oil supplies over and above any espoused democratic or humanitarian aims. The US military presence in Saudi Arabia - a nation which, ironically, some analysts see as both spawning the Al-Qaida terrorist group and helping to support it - serves to protect oil imports to the US which amounted, for example, to some 14% of oil requirements in 1999. Maddox notes a recent comment from former Secretary of State, Henry Kissinger, that the US cannot allow the region to be 'dominated by countries whose purposes are inimical to ours' presumably because of American strategic and economic interests which lie at the heart of the region.

At the same time, the US is viewed in the region as a global power that supports almost every action that Israel decides to take in its conflict with the Palestinians and other Arab states. Clearly, if the US means what it says about eradicating the terrorist threat in a campaign that may last for ten years, it may finally have to rethink its strategy regarding Israel. For, of the 369 terrorist organisations that the US estimates exist worldwide, 126 are in the Islamic world:

> and most are active mainly against their own governments. "Private" Saudi foundations, mostly royal, have for many years bankrolled a disturbingly high proportion of them (The Times: 12th October, 2001; p. 23).

The US will need the assistance of countries such as Saudi Arabia, Kuwait and Egypt (to whom it has provided over $50bn of military aid since 1991) if it is to effectively tackle terrorism and, to achieve this end, it may ultimately have to reduce its support for Israel, both financially ($18.8bn in military aid since 1991) and politically as the region evolves in the future.

However, as Maddox notes, the recent remarkable decline in wealth experienced by Saudi Arabia (per capita income falling from $28,000 in the 1980s to less than $10,000 in 2001) does give the US a new economic lever to employ to bolster Saudi support for its campaign whether it be through foreign direct investment to rebuild the Saudi economy or through political support for membership of the World Trade Organisation in due course.

As part of the moralising discourse of contemporary foreign policy, the terrorist attacks in the US in early September, 2001 were described by the British Prime Minister as attacks upon 'civilised values the world over' and it may be that they will be described by future historians as marking a turning point in world affairs. As the historian Michael Burleigh commented in the Sunday Times, 30th September, 2001:

> The world has been turned upside down. A decade of certainty in which America has enjoyed an unprecedented consumer boom, and during which the American defence budget was slashed from nearly 6% to about 3% of GDP, and the armed forces by one third, has abruptly given way to what future historians may call "an age of anxiety". World events cause children to have nightmares and the airports are almost deserted. The mood is palpable – and not just in America, for we are all terrorists' targets.

Burleigh makes the important point that, in this context at least, the apparent "victory" of the liberal democratic model over other alternatives, marked by the end of the Cold War and the collapse of communism, has yet to be fully realised. He notes that:

> Some even saw this as 'the end of history' in which event even the most broken-down wagons would eventually limp into the liberal-democratic capitalist encampment. If that scenario has failed to happen, we have now surely reached a palpable turning point of enormous importance...........the recent events in New York and Washington are, on several levels, an important turning point because the decisions the one remaining superpower makes as it deals with this crisis affect the whole world. Entire regions could be destabilised if those choices are wrong.

Indeed, of more direct relevance to our theme in this book, Burleigh comments that:

> Francis Fukuyama will rue the day he ever wrote about the triumph of western liberalism, embodied in the phrase 'the end of history'. It snakes and turns and surprises, but it has no ultimate ascertainable meaning.

> It is precisely because of the lack of any certainty about western liberalism that the west is putting so much effort into ensuring its dissemination and practice –either through conditions attaching to aid or the sale of arms. In the face of impending war with Iraq, the U.S and the UK have taken the process even further by strong-arming countries still equivocal about the war, (including Angola, Cameroon, Chile, Guinea, Mexico and Pakistan) by offering economic deals and aid in return for their support for military action ('The British do the diplomacy, and the Americans write the cheques', Guardian 28.2.02).

Implications at the corporate level

The close relationship between foreign, domestic, political and industrial strategy has even wider implications for peoples' lives. For example, the post-Cold War geo-political environment has had important consequences for those working in the defence and aerospace industries where the merger phenomenon, particularly in the US, has completely changed the structure, organisation and market behaviour of key players in recent years with major consequences for their employees.

In some ways representing a 'new industrial revolution', the US aerospace/defence merger process has been quite remarkable. With the end of the Cold War at the start of the 1990s and the huge defence budget cuts which followed, the US government became convinced that there were too many aerospace and defence companies operating in the now declining military market. They reasoned that massive rationalisation and industrial restructuring were essential to both restore and then preserve US economic and military competitive advantage in the global market through the elimination of excess capacity and the enhancement of the economies of scale and scope that would accompany such industrial reconstruction.

In 1992, the US government gave the go-ahead for the rationalisation process to begin, anticipating a wave of corporate mergers that would consolidate and downsize the US aerospace/defence industrial base. Crucially, it was made clear to the key corporate players that US anti-trust legislation would not be used to hamper the restructuring process. Over the next few years, a truly remarkable phase of intense merger activity ensued with over 30 aerospace/defence companies merging into 9, with 3 emerging as giant corporations on the global stage.

As part of this process, for example, Lockheed Martin was formed from the merger of Lockheed with Martin Marietta, incorporating divisions of Loral, General Electric and General Dynamics. This merger was justified as a strategy of vertical integration and brought together defence electronics business and information systems to target one of the few parts of the defence market where future expansion might be possible. Lockheed Martin emerged as one of the largest and most powerful aerospace/defence companies in the world with global sales of over $14bn. Since 1990, however, as a result of this corporate transformation, over 47,000 stakeholders in Lockheed Martin's labour force have lost their jobs.

Next, the decline in US defence spending in the 1990s and the consequent tightening of defence contracts brought two other vulnerable aerospace companies together, Northrop and Grumman into a partnership which was then augmented by the acquisition of Westinghouse's defence electronics business. This example of corporate transformation, while creating a powerful and defence-focused new business entity, also cost another 36,000 corporate stakeholders their jobs in the 1990s.

Finally, in 1996, the merger of Boeing, an aerospace giant with a remarkable commercial sector pedigree, and McDonnell Douglas, a leading, if somewhat vulnerable, aerospace contractor with strengths in the military sector, brought the prospect of greatly enhanced opportunities for military/civil synergies, technology transfers and significant cost savings within the new company. Having already acquired the defence and space business of Rockwell International, the merger represents an example of horizontal integration within the industry, giving the new corporate entity the widest possible range of military aircraft from fighters through helicopters to surveillance aircraft as well as a globally successful range of commercial aircraft (Boeing 747, 737, 757 etc). At the same time, however, employee stakeholders suffered the same fate as those mentioned previously with thousands of jobs disappearing as a result of the corporate transformation.

However, there are much broader but perhaps less obvious stakeholder issues involved in the US aerospace/defence revolution which are doubtless shared with that taking place in other important industrial sectors. Markusen (1997) makes the important point that, outside the United States, the US merger phenomenon has been viewed as essentially a Pentagon–led initiative to achieve massive economies of scale and scope in aerospace/defence production and further enhance US dominance and hegemony in the global arms market and geo-political power game. As a direct consequence of this perception, Markusen argues that European companies are now pursuing the same strategy of mergers and rationalisation in their aerospace and defence industries.

Markusen, however, challenges this view of US mergers, arguing that the merger phenomenon represents, in fact, a kind of neo-liberal market outcome, deriving its momentum from the interaction of two sets of markets, the defence supply market and the financial market. Far from initiating and leading the merger process, Markusen contends that, in practice, the Pentagon has:

> acquiesced in a strategy initiated by Wall Street investment bankers and a elect group of corporate CEOs. Although the mergers have been rationalized as cost-saving moves, driven by budgetary imperatives, they have been chiefly motivated by expectations of short term financial gain and long term enhanced market power and political clout (Markusen, 1997).

It is clear where gains occur in this example of corporate restructuring: industrial leaders and their key financiers stand to benefit significantly from the increased market power of the now intensely concentrated industry while their former employees, many with high skill profiles and long years of service to the industry, have seen their careers, income levels and future prospects sacrificed. It may well also be the case that the government (and therefore society and the economy more generally) becomes another loser in this far-reaching corporate restructuring process. Fewer more powerful companies in the industry clearly have the opportunity to lobby more effectively for a greater commitment of public funds to support the defence industry, especially support for the promotion of existing weapons system production. Markusen points out, for example, that in 1996, powerful lobbying in Congress added $11 billions to the Clinton defence budget, mainly for additional orders of existing weapons and for larger research and development contracts for ballistic missile defence. More recently, in 2002-3, the incoming US President – in response to the September 11th, 2001 terrorist outrage in the US – has driven through Congress one of the largest increases in US defence spending for a generation.

More remarkable still, from the viewpoint of tax-payers, there is evidence that the US government, perhaps unwittingly, has acted directly to support the merger movement with public funds, thereby diverting otherwise socially beneficial taxpayer contributions away from the majority of 'stakeholders' and into the hands of a few powerful industrial and financial market players. The introduction of the Morris tax scheme effectively meant that US defence companies could be reimbursed for significant costs associated with the merger process. As a result of this scheme – and against expectations – large US defence contractors remained generally profitable during the defence cuts of the 1990s, a remarkable and unprecedented development given the decline in profitability suffered by defence contractors during earlier experiences of large defence expenditure cuts such as those after World War I and II, Korea and Vietnam. Analysts suggest that, as a result of the merger subsidy, companies such as Lockheed Martin, as an example, saved some $6 billion in 1999 and about $2.6

billions each year thereafter. This kind of merger subsidy effectively constitutes an indirect grant from the US government, enabling recipient companies concerned to re-deploy such funds into alternative areas such as research and development, marketing and/or cost reduction strategies.

The controversial nature of such a merger subsidy surrounds the way in which cost-savings have been used against the majority of employees, key stakeholders, in theory only. As Markusen (1997) notes cost reimbursement was possible for:

> court costs for opposing worker severance suits or for attempting to lower local property tax assessments, costs involved in destroying productive capacity that might otherwise have been sold to competitors, and costs incurred in moving people and equipment to lower cost and union-free regions, any of which would spark social protest if widely understood. Socially benign purposes, such as severance pay and worker adjustment assistance (but not conversion or civilian job creation) can also be covered (Markusen, 1997).

US hegemonic power and the stakeholder dimension

One of the key problems in developing a more democratic, equitable and accountable global security architecture is the fact that only one nation now has genuine 'global reach', the combination of economic and military strength that allows it to extend its influence across the globe. The power of the United States in this respect is unmatched, which creates a somewhat unbalanced global security system, both in terms of influence and financing, when it comes to a NATO or UN response to an evolving crisis. The US, time and again, is seen to take the lead role in UN or NATO allied actions (military and/or political) and, at the same time, tends to bear a disproportionate share of the burden of military expenditure.

Strategically - and technologically - the US remains at the leading edge of global military power. As noted above, significant defence expenditure cuts were implemented in the US during the last decade with substantial regional economic impact but it is important to remember that the US defence budget still exceeds by a considerable margin the combined defence budgets of the next eight highest defence spending countries (Russia, Japan, France, UK, Germany, China, Italy and Saudi Arabia).

Such an immense defence provision ensures that the US is the only country in the world with the military strength, mobility, logistical support and access to leading-edge communications and intelligence systems that allow it to undertake large-scale military operations with maximum global reach. Nor can there be any question that the US intends to maintain its unique global military power in the future and the hegemonic influence that goes with it. For example, the Clinton administration's 1997 Quadrennial Defence Review set out clearly the future approach of the US to its global military role. Recognising that technology is altering fundamentally the entire nature and conduct of military strategy, the Review identified a new conceptual framework "Vision 2010" which has been adopted to ensure that the

US secures and maintains 'full spectrum dominance', particularly in the collecting, processing and dissemination of critical information, essential to battlefield victory. In 1998, the Clinton defence budget request was formulated to ensure that the US could operate successfully in regional conflicts across the world, as and when they arose.

Since 1999, the US defence budget has continued support for this strategy with emphasis being given to financing the new technologies required to deliver the required 'full spectrum dominance'. This evolving strategy clearly has implications for industrial stakeholders, especially for those companies and their labour forces developing, manufacturing and servicing products relevant for the military's new technological requirements in respect of seven key areas: command, control, communication, computers, intelligence, surveillance and reconnaissance (C4ISR).

Attempting to restore the balance: the European Dimension

Given the technological supremacy of the US in the military sphere and its unmatched 'global reach', it is difficult to envisage any countervailing power to the US and its undoubted capabilities in terms of 'full spectrum dominance'. On their own, the individual European military powers can only expect to play a minor, subordinate role within NATO with their 'voices' somewhat muted as a result. While they will be consulted by the US and incorporated in agreed Nato action plans, the US remains individually the single most powerful member and commits a significantly higher proportion of its resources to the Nato budget. The only really viable challenge to US supremacy in this respect would appear if the members of Nato Europe (or a similar grouping) were able to co-ordinate their approach to foreign policy and associated military action (and perhaps, ultimately, arms procurement) and speak with a single voice on global affairs. Recent discussion within Europe concerning the potential for a European defence force has already encountered much dissension at the political level and some critics have perceived such a force as potentially weakening Nato rather than addressing the burden-sharing problem.

Despite its inclusion as a stated objective of the Maastricht Treaty (Title V, Article J.4), the slow and cumbersome process of negotiating and implementing European Union foreign and defence policy reveals only too clearly the degree to which vested European economic interests, as they are reflected in global security strategy, differ in their positions and expectations. Nevertheless, limited progress towards a European viewpoint on matters of foreign policy and security architecture is being made. For example, the formation of the Western European Armaments Group (WEAG) in 1993 represented one such step. This initiative involved initially a bilateral agreement on military matters between France and Germany, with increasing interest and involvement by Britain and Italy as the more ambitious elements of its perceived role were scaled down. The establishment of OCCAR, too, carries the process a little further, although the emphasis here is more on steps towards unifying European *arms purchase* rather than developing or modifying military strategy and foreign policy.

This focus on the eventual unification of military procurement across Europe might be seen as a first step along the road towards the attainment of a more wide-ranging consensus within Europe on the deeper issues of global security and foreign affairs. Even here, however, the route to the desired goal is far from easy. The efficacy of EU policy on arms purchase co-ordination has been hampered by Article 223 of the Treaty of Rome which exempts the defence industries in Europe from regulations concerning competition and monopoly, which so constrain the behaviour of other industries. Furthermore, at the heart of the European arms procurement debate is a fundamental and complex question about its precise purpose and the degree to which individual national viewpoints and interests can actually be represented adequately within an organisation where unity of vision and purpose must be the crucial objective.

A stakeholder-based security system would surely encompass, within its decision-making structures, the views and objectives of all relevant players. Apologists would argue that the first signs of such a system are gradually emerging in the form of security partnerships which, taken together, appear to offer an enhanced prospect of global stability. From such a naïve perspective, four developments in particular stand out as significant:

- the Partnership for Peace initiative signed in 1994 between NATO and its 'co-operation partners' from the former USSR and from Eastern Europe;

- the establishment of the Euro-Atlantic Council in May 1997 to expand the political aspects of the Partnership for Peace structure and increase the potential for practical military co-operation across Europe; and

- the agreements in May-June 1997 to sign the NATO-Russia Founding Act and the NATO-Ukraine Charter;

- the invitation to the Czech Republic, Hungary and Poland in 1998 to begin the process of joining NATO, finally accomplished in early 1999.

In each case, clear attempts are being made to involve a wider group of countries in security partnerships but whether these initiatives will result in wider stakeholder participation in actual decision-making and policy implementation in the future is less certain.

The peace dividend - lost opportunity for a 'stakeholders' reward?

The sudden cessation of the Cold War at the end of the 1980s, the collapse of Communism that followed and the subsequent wave of economic and political liberalisation unleashed across the former Soviet Union, Eastern and Central Europe, gave the world the opportunity to secure a 'peace dividend' as a result of deep and apparently permanent defence cuts. Here, at last, was a real opportunity for politicians to address broader social and political stakeholder interests, not simply narrow economic ones - and ensure that a significant proportion of the massive sums devoted to military production during the Cold War would now be redeployed to enhance welfare and other social provision. Alternatively, such expenditure could now be diverted to new, more productive civil investment, stimulating economic growth and the attainment of high wage, high productivity economies with attendant benefits for all.

The scale of resources absorbed by the global military system has been unquestionably immense. In 1990, world military expenditure amounted to almost $1,000 billion per annum of which some 60% was attributable to military provision associated with the Cold War. (Hartley et al, 1993). By 1996, this had decreased to about $800bn, the lowest level since 1966 and about 40% below its 1987 peak (for an excellent discussion of world military expenditure, see Brzoska, 1995). In the US, defence expenditure has declined by about one-third since 1987 and US weapons procurement by about two-thirds. In addition, recent estimates for future US defence budgets suggest a further reduction in expenditure of 10% up to 2002. While not unprecedented in scale, most analysts viewed these defence cuts as being irreversible in the light of the end of the Cold War and the superpower arms race that was its central feature.

The opportunities for real stakeholder rewards from 1990 onwards were considerable. Since 1945, between $30 and $35 trillion has been devoted to world military expenditure (Felice, 1998, p.36) and, currently, annual global military expenditure equals approximately the income of half of the world's population. Taking the military expenditure total for the developing countries of the world alone, just one-eighth of that total could be sufficient to provide primary health care for everyone. A further 8% of the total would ensure access to family planning for everyone with, crucially, the world's exploding population stabilising by 2015. Finally, it has been estimated that it would take only 4% of developing countries annual military budgets to extend primary education on a universal basis, cutting adult illiteracy by half (Felice, 1998, p. 32).

In the immediate aftermath of the end of the Cold War, public expectations were high concerning the stakeholder gains to be derived from improved public services (education, health, welfare) and rural amenities (see, for example, Dowdall and Braddon, 1995) and for improved civil sector development, especially for civil research and development which, some analysts argued, had previously been 'crowded out' by high levels of defence expenditure. Significant improvements in the global human condition were thought to be possible even with a relatively modest peace dividend. Arias noted that, for example:

> If we redirected just $40 billion of those resources over the next 10 years to fighting poverty, all of the world's population would enjoy basic social services, such as education, health care and nutrition, reproductive health, clean water and sanitation. Another $40 billion would provide all people on the planet with an income above the poverty line for their country (Arias, 1997).

Such immense stakeholder rewards could not be expected instantly. It was anticipated that the acquisition of a genuine and lasting peace dividend would require time for the adjustment process to work and considerable flexibility in the factors of production, so that the switch from military to civil production (and its associated income and employment effects) could take place smoothly and with minimal economic dislocation. The stakeholder benefits from 'global peace' were given great stress by politicians who were only too pleased to welcome the end of the Cold War and to highlight the unprecedented opportunities it offered.

Reluctant to allow government intervention to assist in the peace dividend acquisition process, their largely neo-liberal persuasion led them to prefer a market solution. Not only did they tend to downplay the short-run economic dislocation that would emanate from defence cutbacks and the unavoidable costs associated with the disarmament process (for an interesting analysis of these costs, see Renner M., 1996) but also seemed to believe that market forces, left to their own devices, would stimulate resource-switching from the military sector into civil production and welfare provision and generate new prosperity. Market adjustment would, it seemed, bring stakeholders the rewards they had long awaited, without formal government intervention.

The peace dividend was perceived as desirable in terms of its potential for generating both faster economic growth and higher government expenditure on social provision. In terms of measurable benefit, between 1990 and 1995, Bischak (1997) suggests that modest increases in public spending of some $9.4 billion on areas such as infrastructure, construction, transportation, community, regional development, environment, community health and education and training were facilitated by military expenditure cuts. Yet, as Chan (1996) noted, there is little real evidence to support the proposition that most stakeholders will gain from such a dividend since faster economic growth often tends to exacerbate rather than resolve income inequity and high levels of government expenditure, through large public sector deficits and high inflation, and can be particularly detrimental to the poor.

Brommelhorster and Dedek suggest that the process of acquiring a peace dividend (and therefore the stakeholder rewards to be derived from it) should be considered in three stages: a resource dividend, a product dividend and a welfare dividend. The resource dividend amounts to the direct savings resulting from the defence cuts (although this is unlikely to equal the actual reduction in military expenditure since eliminating weapon systems and military installations, particularly nuclear, is a high cost process and one likely to absorb a significant part of any peace dividend for many years). Perhaps here the stakeholder reward is to be measured more in terms of a scaling down of the nuclear threat than in terms of financial resources. The product dividend then should appear as the resources freed from the military sector are redirected to the civil sector and stimulate enhanced production efficiency and new wealth generation. Finally, and most importantly, the welfare dividend would be captured by society as social welfare provision (health, education etc).

Earlier in the chapter, we noted the attempts to construct a more widely-based partnership approach to global security decision-making (particularly within Europe). While the partnership approach may allow the voices of those previously excluded from the decision-making process to be heard, the expectation would naturally follow that these new participants would bear a more realistic share of the burden of financing military expenditure. Clearly for poorer countries this is less of an option.

For example, at the more extreme end of potential peace dividend estimates, Forsberg (1992) estimated that a genuine global 'co-operative security' strategy would enable the US to reduce its defence budget by some 80%, amounting to savings of some $180 billions per year. Kaufmann and Steinbruner (1991) have suggested that such a cooperative strategy, together with a switch in focus from offensive to defensive-only military provision, would save the US at least some $420 billion in a decade. Other countries would gain an enhanced strategic role in security decision-making as a result but would have to contribute a greater proportion of their national wealth to fund the new strategy. We then have to ask – to what end and for what purpose? The higher military spending of the US reflects, surely its own overwhelming strategic and economic interests in different parts of the world.

Finally, the notion that stakeholders globally can expect to benefit from the end of the Cold War is questionable in the face of geo-political instability and vast economic inequalities. To illustrate the point, Allison et al (1996) point out that the collapse of the former Soviet empire in the early 1990s left vast quantities of highly dangerous weapons-grade nuclear material in vulnerable stockpiles across the former Soviet Union, providing international terrorists and/or 'rogue' states with a potential source of sophisticated weaponry. For example, on at least six occasions since 1991, unsuccessful attempts have been made to sell stolen Russian nuclear materials. There is enough Russian nuclear material to enable the manufacture of over 100,000 nuclear weapons. It is currently held in stockpiles with security conditions described by the authors as: "questionable at best, non-existent at worst".

The conclusion must be drawn after a decade of defence cuts that, for the most part, 'stakeholders', (if we are to take the concept at face value) around the globe have yet to see the rewards of a genuine and sustained peace dividend through unfettered market adjustment. For neo-liberal economists and politicians persuaded of the supreme efficacy of the market in resolving the economic damage attributable to such a massive exogenous shock as the end of the Cold War, the experience of the last decade in failing to deliver a genuine and long-lasting peace dividend must have been surprising. Instead of economic adjustment to military expenditure contraction culminating in significant stakeholder rewards through the acquisition of a peace dividend, the process of market adjustment has actually been characterised by an array of obstacles, delays and dis-equilibria which have both eroded that dividend and denied stakeholders in the global security arena (Braddon, 2000).

Chapter 7

Communitarian orthodoxy and the Third Way

It has become fashionable for social commentators, politicians and business leaders alike to focus their attention on the moral and ethical behaviour of individuals as a means of regenerating a sense of social cohesion and responsibility towards local communities. The significance of cultural attitudes and value systems for a revised social democratic platform is given particular priority in welfare restructuring programmes designed to encourage individual responsibility for a range of duties hitherto performed by the state. Attempts to redraw the boundaries between state and civil society and, in the process, notions of citizenship, have tended to draw piecemeal on communitarian philosophy.

While communitarian philosophers point to the inextricable relationship between individual/group identity and society and refer to the necessity of a more receptive and *grounded* approach to democracy, the prevailing tendency in the welfare restructuring programmes of Britain, America and New Zealand, for example, is a top-down approach to the reconstruction of communities. This chapter, attempts to distinguish a truly communitarian approach to politics, as opposed to the modified communitarianism of Anglo Saxon social policy. The tenets of communitarianism must be distinguished from stakeholding and the Third Way, since they are often confused in political rhetoric. It is also important to identify the central elements of communitarian philosophy and to highlight the insights it offers to a revised, enlightened, democratic project. This is, as we shall argue, of greater democratic potential than the highly diluted elements of communitarianism that now prevail in the language of community.

Fundamental to Communitarian thought is the idea that political identity and ideas surrounding the common 'good' derive from specific experiences and linguistic frameworks. In other words rational decision-making relies upon sociologically contextualised interpretative frameworks where the meaning of ideas and policies will depend upon one's personal social, economic and political history. Practical, substantive, reasoning (Taylor, 1990) which evolves from personal history and experiences is favoured over what has been described as the antecedent a-historical individual assumed in ideas of liberal democracy.

Classical liberal theory rests upon the assumption that, as essentially rational decision-makers, individuals are capable of making choices between abstract alternatives, *regardless* of their daily experiences and the socially embedded matrices of meaning in which they occur. As Mulhall and Swift (1992) point out *procedural* issues which stipulated criteria for the logical formulation of arguments leading to conclusions about 'universal right' were favoured over and above *substantive* or *practical reasoning*. The latter focuses upon the *ways* in which ethical issues emerge out of daily routines, interactions and social structures. It looks to the socially incumbent nature of individual, social or political identity, this having fairly substantial ramifications for ethical or moral issues which are of such interest to politicians.

Without recognising the particular histories and cultures that inform ethical decision-making, choices become reduced to a series of arbitrary judgements and values which may be freely chosen at will. Any reference to the history of political struggles will demonstrate that this is clearly not the case. We might cite a number of contemporary examples - the difficulties currently surrounding maintaining the 'peace treaty' in Northern Ireland: the struggle of the Kurds, Palestinians or those struggling to survive in Afghanistan. To point to the simple 'truth' of the 'good' outside of any socio-historical context is politically unsophisticated and obliterates genuine debate.

As we witnessed in the allies stance on Serbia, decisions surrounding air-strikes were at times made almost unilaterally. It is unilateral decision-making that is also behind a number of mainstream policies from welfare to the treatment of refugees. Disguising its value-laden character with the language of 'objectivity' and value freedom in judgement, liberalism is actually ideologically loaded. It represents sectional interests in universal terms without acknowledging the possibility of dissent.

Feminist political philosophers have been particularly critical of the disembodied, abstract reasoning on which liberalism relied, precisely because it rested upon and was blind to differential and often highly inequitable experiences of 'citizens' who may have vastly divergent experiences of the nation state on which conceptualisations of citizenship relied. Such blindness to the specific historical and social experiences of whole collectivities is seen to mark a more general alienation of ideas from 'practice'. As we shall see, similar tendencies in social policies which abstract 'community' or 'stakeholders', from embodied or material interests– may also result – for all their reference to the language of civil rights, and political inclusion – to social exclusion and inequality.

Communitarian philosophy

Marxist philosophy pointed to the inherently ideological character of notions of 'universal rights' (see Marx, 'On the Jewish Question') since this denied the existence of sectional (class) interests and conflictual historical dynamics that determined them. The communitarian critique, that people are actually constituted by the kinds of conditions in which they live and the communities that frame them, (Sandel, 1982) obviously has a different political inflection. Yet parallels may be drawn between the Marxist conceptualisation of 'praxis' (the unity of political thought and practice) and the 'practical reasoning' favoured by some communitarian philosophers. This is the idea that liberalism must accommodate specific socio-historical experiences of social groups and individuals.

Differentiating the two traditions are their respective positions on the character of the nation state. While one highlights the inherently undemocratic nature of the capitalist state because of its immersion in bourgeois interests, the other prefers to critique a series of political ideas and assumptions about the human condition, that have become embodied in institutional practices, bureaucracies and government policies. It is argued that serious modification of these implicit assumptions would entail the accommodation of histories and experiences lying outside the objectivist gaze and experiences of the relatively narrow social groupings who make decisions on everybody else's behalf. But it is not a question of tinkering with existing institutional structures to make them more 'user-friendly' for hitherto underrepresented groups. The more substantive political tasks of goal setting and prioritisation would need to be completely re-conceptualised.

MacKintyre (1990) refers to this way of looking at the relationship between individual and broader social and political processes which have influenced them, in terms of the 'encumbered self', the idea that we cannot divorce questions of who we are; where we are going, or how we think and respond to political and ethical issues, without reference to our personal and collective histories and the political, economic and cultural contexts in which those histories have unfolded. As MacKintyre emphasises, individuals are not antecedent to political processes but, in their socio-economic and historical entirety, should be regarded *as intrinsically a part of them*. Individuals are constituted by political frameworks and therefore have a prior interest in contributing to those frameworks. As such, there would need to be a wide debate about the usefulness of existing frameworks not only for the modern world, but also in terms of their representation of diverse histories.

Any government interested in the moral and political direction of their country should take note. Recognition of the situated self would encourage citizens to adopt a deeper, more engaged relationship with the moral and political issues of the day. Our development as *situated* selves is inextricably bound-up with our development as moral and political beings. A top down approach to the re-moralisation of society is unlikely to bear fruit. To be a good person, to possess moral virtue is to be the best a person can be in the given circumstances and roles which are a part of them and of the society in which they live.

The divorce of ethics from concrete social contexts leads to 'emotivism', the idea that moral behaviour of different (abstract, disembodied) individuals could be cohered through reasoned argument alone. Broader principles governing ideas of the social 'good' cannot be established simply through abstract argument since arguments can only be rationalised and justified internally, according to their own set of premises. This can lead, according to McIntyre, a clashing of arbitrary personal wills which are somehow displaced onto arguments that appear outside of the needs and embodied interests of individuals.   The major problem with emotivism is that there is no conception of the *persons possessing reason* to judge between alternative perspectives. McIntyre also highlights the implications of emotivist *sociology* that may ultimately lead to a situation in which there can be no judgement about the virtue of particular roles or occupations, except that individuals have chosen to engage in them. As we shall see later, such criticisms may be directed at notable developments within mainstream sociology whose conclusions about modern society (and the policy recommendations which arise from these conclusions) have become over-reliant on abstracted notions of individual choice in the pursuit of free-floating and therefore quite arbitrary 'lifestyle practices'. Again, as Mulhall and Swift summarise:

> In effect, then, the modern self that hangs together with and is secreted from the social context of emotivism is fixed or bounded independently of any of its social embodiments or characteristics, and lacks a rational history. Neither its identity at any given time nor its identity over time are fixed by or dependent upon its attitudes, characteristics or life story; neither its personality not its history are part of its substance; indeed, that substance assumes an abstract and ghostly character (Mulhall and Swift, 1992, p.77).

Judgements about what constitutes the social 'good' cannot be drawn outside the practices in which virtues manifest themselves. A failure to locate ethical priorities within specific socio-historical contexts ultimately leads to a reading of particular or current ethical values as objective universal ones.

Significantly for our discussion of stakeholding, polity should work in tandem with civil society as this is constantly evolving, at once embracing universal ideals, while actively incorporating differential experiences. However, in order for this to occur, the condition of informed public debate would need to be met through the principles of freedom of speech, appropriate vehicles for the expression of diverse debates and ideas. The relative balance of particular and universal interests needs to be carefully maintained and any tendencies towards centralisation of political and corporate power checked. The re-vitalisation of local and regional political structures would represent a crucial and important counter to increasing centralisation of political decision-making throughout Europe for example. The Enlightenment project became corrupted by a failure on the part of nineteenth century philosophers to distinguish between, or for that matter attempt to relate, '*being*' and '*potential*'. This was achievable under the more ancient Aristotelian approach to ethics but lost later on when ethics was presented in terms of oppositional abstract debates. As Mulhall and Swift comment:

> Those rules had been developed within a wider moral scheme which had dominated the medieval period and had originated with Aristotle. Within that framework, there is a sharp distinction between 'man as he happens to be' and 'man as he could be if he realised his essential nature'. Ethics is seen as the science that enabled human beings to understand how to make the transition from the former to the latter state. What this presupposed is a distinction between potentiality and its fulfilment in reality and an account of what the true end or fulfilment of human nature might be. It viewed human nature as initially discrepant with the precepts of ethics and so in need of transformation through experience and the tutelage of practical reason until it fulfilled its potential (reached its telos) (Mulhall and Swift, 1996, p.78).

The idea that we should retain some of the principal aims of the Enlightenment is what differentiates Communitarian thinkers like MacIntyre from sociologists like Anthony Giddens. Both may point to the limitation of assumptions underpinning current traditions but, while one focuses upon individual decision-making and individual consciousness of ethical behaviour, the other stresses the crucial role of the collective in determining and shaping the roles and responsibilities of society. For one, the community is a collection of localised practices and customs which may be drawn upon in individual decision-making to help formulate identity, which may then influence political behaviour; while, for the other, it is intricately a *part of* identity which cannot exist outside of it and is in turn, an intricate component of political behaviour.

A revised, humanistic, Enlightenment project has the potential to give more accurate voice to oppressed groups who often encounter the dilemma between making political claims along the lines of universal principles, (for example, basic human rights) while retaining the integrity of their particular historical and cultural experiences. Obviously, such a project would have to acknowledge different forms of oppression to begin with - it would also have to assume the existence of ultimate human goals and potential. It is to this which McIntyre is referring in his argument for the importance of a human telos, this involving the matching of ethical ideals with human potential. The latter is of course shaped fundamentally by specific socio-economic and historical contexts that are often unhelpfully ignored in social policy.

Implications for globalisation

Some contemporary theorists have talked about the potential for the state to deal with what has become a legitimation crisis in the face of its inability to appear neutral or to resolve tensions between competing interests in the face of globalisation. The closer forging of civil society (which is itself dominated by business interests), and polity may be one contributing factor to such a crisis. Potentially radical in its implications, the importance of localities in political and moral behaviour was regarded as direct means of widening the social basis of policy at a grass-roots level. Born, as noted earlier, out of the feminist and civil rights movements of the 1960s, much has been written of the ways in which grassroots ideas about the nature of the relationship between local and central political decision-making were diluted and adapted for a 'New Right' populist political programme. With a 'New Labour' Government now in its second term of office in the UK, these ideas (subject as they were to modification of New Right styled neo-liberal economic policy) have been re-inserted into a weakened social democratic programme. The result is the worst of all worlds; powerful sectional interests are represented in both pluralistic and universal terms. Appeals to electorates tend to pivot upon notions of diversity and difference on the one hand, and the imposition of centralised concepts of national identity, on the other. This is particularly significant in the UK where training of immigrants and refugees in the culture of 'Britishness', is contrasted with the rhetoric of social diversity and inclusion, for example, which New Labour often deploy as part of their third way approach. A reactive and ad-hoc approach to social issues amounts to a failure to genuinely engage with citizens or for that matter stakeholders who to be truly represented, would need to be recognized as historical subjects, faced with concrete material constraints as well as limited opportunities for change and self-fulfilment and political expression. Such constraints and opportunities need genuine acknowledgement and policies need to be tailor-made to accommodate and modify such experiences before individuals can really in-put into broader social or political projects.

Communitarian social policy

There are clear differences between a critical communitarian perspective and communitarian social policy. The former does not necessarily reject liberalism or the Enlightement project from which it was born; the latter caricatures some of the main tenets of philosophical communitarianism in the pursuit of policies which are far from democratic. A popular characterisation of communitarianism is one derived from predominant trends in social policy. However, in relation to the current phase of global economic restructuring in accordance with the principles of neo-liberalism, communitarianism has a variety of theoretical and practical inflections. Indeed, this ambiguity makes it so popular in the current restructuring of the welfare state (Clarke and Newman, 1998). As Clarke and Newman argue:

> communitarianism has a multi-faceted appeal, drawing on diverse sets of images. The first is a nostalgic sense of sturdy and self-reliant communities...the community denotes networks of relationships and sustain established ways of being and behaving: community as a moral order. The second address of communitarianism is to the field of community activism. Community here is identified as a mobilising focus for collective action - in defence of local interests and institutions...and, more expansively, in the creation of new collective resources through self-provisioning...Such conceptions draw on the increasing vitality of the voluntary sector in shaping a welfare pluralism alongside state and market forms, assisting in welfare provision, sustaining a diversity of needs and playing a role in community regeneration...The final form of address in communitarianism is to a conception of communities of common identities or interests. Here, communities are affective or identity based rather than bounded spatial entities, though they may overlap in places (Clarke and Newman, 1998, p.132)

Communitarian philosophy emphasises the democratic importance of the entwining of political identity and *'community'*, read in terms of a host of historically complex lived experiences. Rather than, focusing upon the lessons such insights might offer for a revised and enlightened democratic project, sensitive and responsive to the ways in which ideas of justice, truth, freedom and ethics are shaped by a history which is in many ways socially flawed, mainstream social policy, influenced by the pragmatic turn of politicians grappling with the dilemmas of societal fragmentation, became preoccupied, with *re-creating* communities.   Ironically, what started out as a critique of the abstracted universalist claims associated with the key principles of the Enlightenment, has now become itself an abstraction, divorced from the networks, relationships and histories which continue to be decimated by policies focused upon 'the market', over and above broader human needs.   To justify wars, revolutions and vast economic and social upheaval, histories, identities and narratives of society or community get officially re-written. The re-writing of identity, culture and history is central to shaping political and social behaviour so that it can be adapted to prevailing government/state policies and strategies. The ultimate aim is to influence the underpinning belief systems of societal members.

There is often an uncomfortable disjunction, however, between the espousal of particular beliefs in political rhetoric and more influential systemic factors these having a greater bearing on human perceptions and behaviour. Communities of belief cannot easily emanate from official or bureaucratic tampering, even though this is the order of the day, not just for the UK, but also for America. As argued by Lasch, belief cannot simply be reinvented because it might serve a helpful social and moral purpose. The task is more complicated.

> *It is to reinvent a value system in which obligations are stressed along with rights -* and so underpin democracy and wider society. The way forward must be to transform the institutions of market capitalism so that, instead of embodying networks of unravellable spot-market relations, there are new legal obligations to acknowledge a reciprocity of obligation. *Moreover, the work must begin at the top* (Lasch, 1996, p. 95) (our italics).

A far cry from Lasch's appeal to a root and branch overhaul of the senior players in the institutions of market capitalism, it is the broader social base and the lower echelons of society who are targeted for cultural re-engineering. As argued in previous chapters, the re-forging of the relationship between *business* and civil society, (as an aspect of public sector spending reductions, restructuring and the growing reliance on private finance to re-build welfare states) coincides with the shifting of political and social responsibility onto poorer members of society who have the task of community responsibility for socially and economically decimated wastelands of foot-loose capitalism.

Disregarding the broader economic and political culture that has given rise to self-interested elites and a culture of narcissm, 'values' have become isolated from broader political economy and re-packaged as narrowly cultural phenomena.

Plant (2001) has argued that the preoccupation with *values* is typical of Labour parties jettisoning socialist objectives as these were bound up with some notion of redistribution of wealth or common ownership of the means of production (in Britain witnessed in the abandonment of clause 4). Values, rather than interests, are designed to appeal to an apparently broad based middle class electorate. The reinvention of values systems has acquired a high profile in New Labour's policies which have now taken on the responsibility for advising a whole range of social groups on how they should behave if they are to be 'socially included'. Tensions proliferate between this kind of increasing cultural and moral interventionism and rhetoric celebrating individuality and diversity in 'multi-cultural' Britain. At the same time, to deny the relationship between culture and economy and the latter's impact upon the lives of whole groups of people is to fuel a relativistic approach to identities and rights, this only serving to exacerbate the self-referential 'moral crisis' modern social policy is meant to address.

Paradoxically, centralisation of government decision-making as a reaction to the contradictory and multifarious pressures of globalisation actually relies upon the 'dis-aggregation of the social' (Rose, 1996). The aggressive spread of neo-liberal flexible accumulation policies have rested upon the reconstitution of citizens as 'consumers' and globally flexible workers disconnected from place or history (Casey, 1998; Hoogevelt, 1998; Sennett, 1998).The implications for democracy are such that moral relativism replaces any broader social vision and, consequently, allows democracy to be hijacked by objectively more powerful interest groups (Bauman, 1996, Lasch, 1992).

Government support for such sectional interests is now a common news item. While business elites take on greater significance in pushing through policies that favour global corporations, at the grassroots political level there is a degeneration of aspirations to personal self-interest. Current social policy continues to encourage an almost tribal orientation to politics, by referencing the particularities of group experience while ensuring government holds a tight rein over the activities of local government (see Bauman, 1993).

Political apathy is borne out of a suspicion of unrepresentative politicians and a prevailing sense of powerlessness. We have already noted such feelings of alienation to impact upon the breakdown of social solidarity. We are already witnessing this with poorer sections of society living in impoverished circumstances and in under-resourced tower blocks, fighting similarly impoverished asylum seekers, sometimes with hugely tragic consequences. We see it also in the venting of frustration between Afro-Caribbean and Somali communities and we see it in the more generalized crimes against persons that hit the headlines everyday.

This does not occur in all countries. Those with a federal framework (e.g. Germany) have quite different dilemmas to face; for example, the tension between the more conservative principalities who take a relatively harsh approach to the treatment of asylum seekers and a central government which may wish to take a more enlightened and universal perspective. Simultaneously, international bodies are attempting to 'harmonise' policies that are divorced from local interests while playing on notions of cultural diversity.

In the current political climate, Liberal ideas foregrounding universalism and the automatic conferring of rights on affiliation to some abstract notion of 'nation'- are also problematic due to their reliance on the 'lowest common denominator' of collective experience. This encourages a kind of passive herd-like instinct reaction to critical social and political issues, rather than reflective engagement. Manipulative political leaders, who play alternately or simultaneously on such universalism and crude notions of cultural identity and diversity, may unwittingly become embroiled in a proliferation of problems associated with passivity and self-interested relativism. This is a consequence of a failure to suitably empower people politically or economically. A thriving public and political space would allow appropriate levels of individual moral and ethical autonomy from government, this being favourable to healthy critical debate and a safeguard against political or social tyranny. The prevailing moralizing political rhetoric surrounding the interventionist foreign policies of the UK and the US are potentially sobering examples. Freedom of speech requires the healthy maintenance of the private sphere, where moral behaviour is a matter of individual conscience, rather than circumscribed by politicians who are often out of touch with their electorates.

Communitarianism has been bastardised in key areas of life to create, rather than respond to, flexible workforces by emphasising self-interested policy communities with different needs and interests (for example, aids victims versus the disabled, elderly, women, blacks, etc.). Ralston-Saul (1997) argues that such practices are encouraged by the encroachment of corporatism that renders political government near redundant in the face of the growing influence of managers and bureaucrats on social policy. Interest groups are dominated by business lobbyists which, some argue, now possess greater power than democratically elected government (Monbiot 2001); indeed, some see these becoming **the** fundamental political units. The degree to which corporatism may be rendering all of us politically passive or impotent is bad enough. There may be, however, more sinister political ramifications that are borne out of a narrowing of political vision to self-interested local affiliations, this allowing the continuing colonisation of political space by business lobbyists.

Comparisons may be made between contemporary corporatism and the corporatist movement in Germany, Italy and France that later developed into Fascism. It is true that the similarities appear to be quite stark as Ralston-Saul outlines, the corporatism of the 1920s entailed:

> devolving power to economic and social interest groups; pursuing entrepreneurial initiative in areas normally reserved for public bodies, obliterating the boundaries between public and private interest and.....challenging, in turn, the idea of public interest (Ralston-Saul, 1997, p. 91-92).

It is a salutary reminder in relation to the concept of the Third Way that corporatism is beyond left and right:

> ...corporatism cuts across political lines. The official voices of reform are as much a part of the structure as are the voices of the Right (Ralston-Saul, 1997, p.97).

Loyalty to the corporation is, itself, a corporation-led movement; sentiments echoed by Eldman (1999) who in remarking in particular on the concept of the 'Third Way' states:

The Third Way turns out to mean not a genuine three-way partnership and division of responsibility, but abdication of governmental responsibility to an amorphous group of people and institutions in the private sector. The social justice envisaged by Third Way proponents turns out to be a matter of the largesse of private actors. The personal responsibility that the Third Way calls for turns out to be the responsibility of the poor to behave themselves better, not a responsibility that extends across all the institutions of society. Corporations and wealthy individuals are still entitled to lobby the government for subsidies that seem startlingly like something for nothing, and nobody appears to have responsibility to help the poor except themselves (Eldman, 1999, p.14).

To recapitulate, we are faced with several inter-related developments that are critical for a revised social democratic programme. Firstly, there is the growing capacity of powerful lobbying groups, already better equipped and positioned to manipulate and influence government for their own purposes, to curry favour with governments whose prime aim is to shore-up big business. This is encouraged by neo-liberal economic policy that has favoured the unrestricted movement of financial capital through the vehicles of multinational corporations, this development, in turn, impacting upon the ability of nation states to effectively 'manage' their own economies in line with broader social or political priorities. Finally the increasing reliance of welfare states (in those countries most influenced by the Thatcherite legacy) on the promotion of individualistic orientations to community, health, policing, housing and education, is part and parcel of the retreat of government from the responsibilities of government and the further erosion of a culture of genuine social or community responsibility.

The decline of public space in favour of narrow corporate interests leads to an 'unconscious civilisation' (Ralston-Saul, 1997). This relates to the processes of 'forgetting' human roles and purposes in favour of the market (Sennett, 1998). 'Forgetting' human roles is what sociologists have classically related to the experience of *anomie* or a feeling of normlessness (Durkheim 1933) while psychoanalysts have highlighted the significance of forgetting for the repression of problematic feelings or issues which cannot be consciously faced. Significantly such processes of repression are often bound up with depression, the fastest growing illness in the modern world (see the World Health Report, 2001). It is often associated with a morbid self-preoccupation and a feeling of physical, psychological and social impotence due to limited outlets for the expression of legitimate grievances or needs (which are themselves growing in the face of increasing work pressures, stress and insecurity of employment or lifestyles). It is perhaps not surprising that the decline of alternative constructive channels of political communication and representation coincides with the growing popularity of chat shows urging the poorest members of society to bear their raw and unprocessed emotions. Social, political and economic issues are telescoped into crudely psychological experiences with little attention to the relationship between the individual psyche and broader social and institutional processes of which we are all a part.

No vision

Stuart Hall (1998) has referred to the Third Way, for example, in terms of a kind of political parade, the 'Great Moving Nowhere Show'. The Third Way is seen as an apologia for the limited vision of prevailing neoliberal policies. The anti-progressive nature of the Third Way was prefigured by Fukuyama's 'The End of History' (Fukuyama, 1993) a popular book in business and political circles as well as a convenient phrase to represent 'business as usual' with very little possibility of serious modification to (free) markets.

The inherent anti-progressivism of such opinions encourages the self-absorbed and exploitative social relationships which policy is meant to be solving. Instead, as Rustin (1995) notes, tensions and problems which are endemic to modern capitalism are simply displaced onto policies and strategies which amount to little more than tinkering, but which give the impression of good things happening:

> To displace the agenda on to some other topic, where political progress may be made, and some solutions may be found, gives an impression of optimism, even if it also tacitly colludes with a lasting political defeat...so pragmatic and present oriented has modern politics become that it seems to be impossible to tolerate a disjunction between the truthful statement of a problem and absence of an immediate solution to it. The very idea of long-term aims, not capable of immediate fulfilment, has been abandoned... (Rustin 1995:23).

The abandonment of longer-term social or economic aims is accompanied by reluctance on the part of government to prioritise public resources. Instead matters of expediency dominate, while in the British case in particular, government can deflect attention from a general lack of political direction by insisting that members of civil society engage with government imposed rules. Of course this is associated with a continued emphasis upon privatisation as pointed out by Nuti:

> Commitment to continued privatisation of state assets and to competition, with state regulation taking the form of setting the rules of the game instead of direct interference in resource allocation (Nuti, 1999, p. 62).

Unfortunately, the hallmarks of the more progressive principles of the Enlightenment, claims to universalism, the importance of rights surrounding the abstract political individual and a stress upon rationality - are being telescoped by what is becoming a kind of communitarian orthodoxy as governments intervene in issues once thought of as belonging to the private sphere to encourage appropriate cultures, attitudes and behaviour within their 'communities'.

The new governance

The ideological vacuum left by the fall of the Berlin Wall in 1989 has for some time become filled with concerns about social and political order. Outside of the constraining influence of clearly demarcated international relations, problems are perceived to spring up Medusa-like anywhere and at any time. Attempts to generate a new type of social order require organs of government to keep a closer ear on what is happening on the ground, below the level of the nation state, while supranational organs of governance have been created in recent years, as a means of harmonising a range of national and international policies directed at issues of terrorism, international crime, Asylum and refugee movements etc – all with the aim of maintaining optimum conditions for the unobstructed activities of modern capital. Both levels of governance mean that governments and their official bodies are in a stronger position to respond and intervene in activities regarded to be at cross purposes with the Shumpetarian ideals of neoliberalism and free-trade. Indeed, the Schumpetarian 'workfare' state (Jessop, 1994; 2001) is designed to encourage appropriate attitudes towards flexible labour markets.   Harris uses the phrase advanced Liberal governance to describe the innovative ways in which governments must appeal to and re-position citizens to meet with requirements of an international neoliberal and post-Fordist agenda. (Open University Study Guide, p.22). As Harris states:

> ...advanced liberalism progressively deploys the language of economic theory to manage social and political affairs. If the economy was a self-governing entity under classical political economy and an interdependent domain under Keynesian economics, it is now an inclusive mode of operation that *subsumes the social...* (our emphasis) (M Harris, 1999).

The new governance attempts to reconcile a number of conflicting political, social and economic pressures. Such contradictory pressures result in ambiguous political strategies and rhetoric. On the one hand, the role of and regeneration of civil society and 'civic' institutions to meet 'moral' and political agendas is emphasised by politicians (see, for example, 'Defeat of Milosevic a 'Moral Imperative'; Tony Blair's address to Nato, *The Times*, 21.4.99) at the levels of domestic and foreign policy, whether they are designing the architecture of aid and financial investment (see F.T Index 2002) in poorer countries, or restructuring welfare states at home. At home and abroad emphasis upon individual responsibility within decentralised political structures is regarded not simply as desirable but *imperative*. This is witnessed, as we have already discussed in a range of international publications from those of the World Bank, the IMF, and World Health reports – to those, within a range of national contexts where welfare state restructuring continues to reflect the demands of global business. In Britian, the current 'Best Value' regime is a typical example (see Maile and Hoggett 2001). Widened participation in decision-making, in the form of the expression of *consumer* rather than *citizen* views is a condition attaching to central government funding and cooperation and is a fundamental requirement of Auditors.

Moralising discourses are deployed to cohere support nationally, for the targeting of welfare 'scroungers', (single parents or asylum seekers) and for the imposition of western-style democractic political processes on countries already disadvantaged by unequal trading relations through, for example, trade embargos. This has been the character of western foreign policy since September 11th, particularly in relation to Iraq. When this strategy fails military might is preferred, a fact illustrated by the current insistence by America and its main supporter, Britain, that Iraq should be bombed into conformity with Western versions of democracy in spite of the controversy this has generated among political analysts, journalists and citizens more generally (see The Guardian 25.9.02).

The third way

As already argued, broader social and political visions, stressing an entirely alternative society, are giving way to the promulgation of a sobering pragmatism. Pragmatism is itself ideological in the prevailing celebration and rhetoric surrounding the pursuit of *practical* solutions to problems as they arise in the *here and now* (as if history and relative power differentials between institutions and countries, which all contribute to shaping the 'practical', did not exist). Yet, in spite of the ideologically loaded nature of the term, the Blair approach in the UK is keen to convey to us that pragmatism stands in opposition to 'dogma' or ideology.

Moreover, intellectual debate is frowned upon in Blair's 'knowledge-driven' society. *Pragmatism* is represented as more in touch with the practical needs of business and 'the people' – as opposed to *philosophy* which is regarded as abstract and overly intellectualist. It is often counterposed to intellectualism and ideology. Of course this counterposition is ideological in itself both in its failure to register pragmatism as a well known philosophical perspective and in terms of the ways in which 'pragmatism' is presented as autonomous from any particular political perspective, when of course, this is patently untrue.

It is not just the arcane thought of armchair socialists who have come under attack for their lack of realism. The more prosaic insights of stakeholding have also been represented as utopian. Curiously, while other countries are expected to conform (and we are not arguing in any simplistic way that this is actually occurring) to Anglo-Saxon economic models led by the US and the UK, it has been argued that attempts to map Rhineland welfare models to Anglo-Saxon countries amounts to lack of sensitivity towards the different cultural and historical traditions of countries like Britain and America.

'Vive la difference' was the strong message in Giddens' Third Way approach. It was a plea to let us acknowledge the nationally-specific needs of more flexible-oriented, market-styled solutions of Anglo-Saxon capitalism. Apparently, this requires a more 'fleet-footed' responsive approach to the turbulent world in which we find ourselves (Giddens, 2000, p. 153). Described by David Starkey as Blair's 'intellectual guru', Giddens' Third Way is regarded, in Starkey's terms, 'like the holy grail...elusive' (Sunday Times, 21st March, 1999). He goes on to comment that 'at the moment the Third Way appears like mere expediency; 'what matters is what works', in Blair's own revealing phrase'.

Yet Giddens depicts the Third Way in more radical terms associating it with a 'new' political - post-Cold War order. He argues that the old left/right divide belonged to a politically and economically polarised world, rooted in questions about the nature and role of the state. Communism and socialism stressed, to varying degrees, state intervention in or planning of the economy to reduce the worst aspects of capitalism. Neo-liberalism and conservatism respectively highlighted the freedom of markets and individuals and the state's role in upholding traditions of church, family and morality.

Both broad political programmes, according to Giddens, rested upon these two fundamental positions which are no longer relevant due to the fact that:

> with the demise of socialism as a theory of economic management, one of the major division lines between left and right has disappeared, at least for the foreseeable future (Giddens, 1998, p.43).

However, each perspective will accommodate the opposing views to retain or gain power. The left, for Giddens, continues but it is a 'left of the radical centre'. So what does this Third Way or 'radical centre' actually amount to?

The evolution of ideas surrounding the Third Way can be traced back to the early 1980s when the German Social Democratic parties and those of the Netherlands retrenched in response to perceptions about the internationalisation of the economy. Left wing and social democratic parties throughout Europe began to argue that the market should no longer be regarded as a bogeyman, preying upon the poor and helpless, but needed to be seen as a resource for distributing social and economic goods. While other European parties are cautious in their pragmatic orientation to markets and are concerned to ensure safeguards are in place for employees and single parents etc, the UK has embraced many of the key principles of what may be called the 'Americanised' workfare system.

In keeping with the prevailing political sentiments of the day, Giddens argues that we should continue to use the phrase, Third Way, as much for its increasing *popularity* as for its inherent appeal to *pragmatic* solutions for the various problems thrown up by globalisation. This is in spite of the sustained criticisms of the concept. Nevertheless, the Third Way, is particularly useful for promoting the ideas of social inclusion – these already pointing to the possibility of a variety of identity groups who may to date be losing out economically, socially and politically and whose social *exclusion* cannot simply be traced to economic factors. The pluralistic and socially integrative appeal of the Third Way indicates the redundancy of traditional left or right political orientations (Giddens 2000:41). A focus upon *lifestyles* has a *cultural* rather than economic bias. Inequalities reflect processes of group dynamics and unequal opportunity over and above the distribution of societal, political and economic resources (Giddens, 2000, p.2).

Wealth creation, rather than *wealth distribution,* through individual effort and improvement is a central plank of the Third Way. It relies upon supply side economics. Individual effort and training becomes the driving forces of successful economies, rather than a Keynesian focus upon creating high employment levels and hence maintaining markets through spending. This shift in emphasis means that *cultural* processes and social processes surrounding skills learning, motivation and enterprise become the driving forces of economic success. This sociological promotion of the cultural is a component of supply side or 'generative' bottom-up politics, born out of dialogue and listening, to deal with some of the pressures experienced by nation states.

As an example of Giddens' bias towards the new culturally influenced governance, he states:

> Economic globalization has, by and large, been a success. The problem is how to maximise its positive consequences while limiting its less fortunate effects and to encourage more and more poor countries to enter into the dynamic global economy (Giddens, 2000, p.125).

His depiction of globalisation as a complex dynamic between economies, technological systems and changing institutional and personal relationships, (see Runaway World, 1999, pp.12 and 13) loses salience as attention comes instead to be focused upon a policy agenda which highlights the inherently cultural and technological character of globalisation and underplays the economic.

Technological change is singled out as having played an important part in creating a better informed public and is therefore linked with the democratising process, one that can seemingly brook no obstacles to its continuing spread and impact. In addition, the rise of information technology for changing the class base of social democracy (the growth of 'wired workers' for example) feeds the decline of party political issues to ones which cross party lines in a middle class, individualistic culture favouring lifestyle politics. Productivity through appropriate use of human resources and processing of information in the service economy, rather than productivism which has been associated with a culture geared towards the manufacturing of physical objects, are respectively associated with civic democratisation and undemocratic, top-down, state planning.

For Giddens, democratisation and education are regarded as key to economic success, something only likely to be obstructed by corrupt governments, hierarchical institutions and unequal gender relationships.   We need therefore to:

> experiment with alternative democratic procedures, especially when these might help bring political decision making close to the everyday concerns of citizen (Giddens, 1999, p.77).

This is a laudable aim but unless broader economic influences are acknowledged such experiments may fall far short of enhanced democracy. There is much evidence that the 'participation' programmes which have become the common currency of international agencies and governments serve only to reflect their biased political and economic agendas (Balanya, Doherty, Hoedeman, Ma'anit and Wesselius, 2000). Again, an emphasis upon 'democratisation' is directly linked with policies throughout the West which are bound up with the restructuring of international and military relationships these relying on unilateral military intervention in 'immoral' or culturally 'backward' countries. As already argued, there is a large disjunction between rhetoric and reality here.

An *overemphasis* upon culture and technology serves to replace one type of determinism (economic) with another. The debate between Giddens and Hutton (2000) illustrates the point very well. Hutton can hardly be called a radical but he does have a realistic insight into the ways in which *economic processes* influence social life. Hutton's rather scathing rejoinder to Giddens' positive interpretation of the creative potential of markets and the social impact of the 'knowledge economy' is revealing of an inherent ambivalence in Giddens' account:

> Well, which is it to be - regulation because capitalism can be destructive now that communism has left a gap or starry-eyed faith in capitalism's boundless creativity? Don't traduce Schumpeter. Your argument and his are essentially the same: capitalism may be ruthlessly destructive but it is also creative. At one moment you want to celebrate capitalism, at another you're wary of it, but without - unlike Schumpeter - offering an integrated view of how both positions could be true (Giddens and Hutton, 2000)

Hutton argues that it is wrong to prioritise the political import of technologically driven innovations and to associate knowledge with the service sector. An emphasis upon knowledge as a driver of globalisation:

> can lead to dubious analysis and even more dubious policy prescriptions (Giddens and Hutton, 2000, p.5).

As we stressed elsewhere in this book, whatever the benefits may be, there are untold levels of poverty and extreme forms of exploitation associated with economic globalisation. Technology is a facet of this process but as Corfe (2000) argues, it tends to be used as a means of intensifying work processes in some parts of the world:

> In such instances the benefits of scientific progress - not to mention the advance of employees' rights and conditions - are put into reverse gear. Everywhere there is insecurity, and always the needs of long-term planning in maximising market share for the benefit of the community is sacrificed for the short-term demands of shareholders (Corfe, 2000, p.6).

Such observations lend an ironic inflection to Giddens' 'Runaway World', a title which, some might suggest serves as an apologia for the status quo. Hutton and Giddens book 'On the Edge' is equally ambiguous title which may read in terms of the potential of a yet unknown new millennium, full of exciting possibilities; or to the extreme anxiety and stress of modern capitalism where suicide rates are increasing. It is a title that captures the different perspectives of its joint editors. While Hutton is well known for championing new forms of regulation to redress the malpractices of global financial institutions and economic inequalities within richer as well as poorer countries (see also Corfe, 2000), Giddens argues that there are political and economic pressures which make any possibility of planning redundant in a 'post-scarcity' society The economic is presented in terms of the evolution of complex inter and intra-organisational structures which, facilitated by technological innovations and developments in transport – stretch like a network across the globe. Attention is therefore turned away from the economic, whose progression cannot – it would appear – be curtailed, to the cultural sphere that must be shaped and modified.

A failure to adduce any cultural or social determinacy to the economy is problematic given the current economic inequalities of the global order. Even a traditionally 'conservative' paper like The Times is cognizant of the fundamental power of the economy in a global capitalist society (Power List, 1999, p.4) while David Smith, Economics Editor for the Sunday Times, adopts an ironic tone in his observation about the role of monetary authorities:

> Within this decade we have witnessed the powerlessness of governments in the face of the financial markets - for example, sterling's embarrassing exit from the European Exchange Rate Mechanism in September 1992 - although we have also seen, more recently, the monetary authorities successfully steering a course through financial hurricanes.

Yet, as Nuti (1999, p.60) argues, it is recognised even by the former proponents of neo-liberalism that things have been allowed to go too far:

> at a time when the need for international surveillance, regulation and intervention was being recognised even by the staunchest defenders of neo-liberalism' (see also Hobsbawm, 1998).

Given Giddens' failure to properly acknowledge the economic, it is easy to see why the Third Way is considered to lend support for much of the free market thinking and mechanisms put in place by the Reagan and Thatcher governments. It is the impact of societal fragmentation on effective economic growth which is prioritised over and above the impact of the economy on social systems. Social systems must adapt to the needs of the economy, the two levels becoming analytically fused in the all-encompassing Third Way.

Contrary to the argument that the Third Way has universal meaning it became associated with the Clinton-Blair-Schroeder 'modernising' project (see Janet Newman, 2000, Clark and Newman, 1999) with an emphasis upon a supply-side approach to the economic needs of entrepreneurialism, market and labour flexibility, reduced public expenditure, the decline of collective bargaining and the greater involvement of community forms of organisation in the delivery of welfare and in the integration of morally responsible citizens.

There are a number of related issues which are being highlighted by a range of policy advisers and business leaders which may fit with what Giddens argues are the 'five dilemmas' of the modern world, namely:

- The implications of globalisation;
- individualism;
- the meaning of left and right;
- political agency and the movement away from orthodox mechanisms of democracy;
- issues about the potential integration of ecological problems into social democratic politics.

Generally, conceptualisations of welfare have traditionally pivoted upon the now outmoded economic and political structures of *modernity*. Modernity is characterised by mass production methods, full-time male employment, clear family roles and values, a highly gendered division of paid and domestic labour and the concerns about redistributing scarce resources.

The challenge presented by globalisation, neo-liberal economic policy, and flexible working and accumulation practices have seriously impacted upon traditional ways of life, necessitating re-conceptualisations of welfare and the national state on which it was based. In terms of changing value systems, employment, the increasing integration of global cultures and economies, political programmes must now appeal to the diverse and often fragmented beliefs and experiences of a more politically heterogeneous social body. This is encapsulated by the phrase 'post-productivist' or 'post-scarcity' society. Such thinking is targeted at middle class voters whose cultural value systems and voting patterns can no longer be associated with the left-right agenda of class politics.

At the core of this 'radical centre' is an individualisation of political and social issues, particularly in relation to conceptualisations of 'risk'. Risks of unemployment, risks of industrial injury, risks of sickness and old age remain, but they are being replaced by risks that cut across class lines. In sum, there is a reassessment of risk away from that produced by modernity, (industrialism, war, as something external to us) to 'manufactured risk', risk which has become internalised and which is endemic to late or postmodernity (Beck, 1993).

Manufactured risks are those produced by the very activities of modernity: the impact of technology and the self-limiting impulses of profit-orientated attitudes to the environment. The idea that resources can be plundered indefinitely has resulted in all kinds of ecological and social crises that permeate our lives on a global scale. In addition, risk is no longer external; technological and scientific developments mean that risk is something we may embody, literally, as science infiltrates our physical selves.

It is *not what we have* as social collectivists, or classes, but *how we live* as individuals that, along with the end of the Cold War and the polarised world that gave birth to left-right thinking in the first place, influences the need for a Third Way. The 'radical centre' that Giddens refers to is radical in its potential to seriously impact upon a truly democratic politics that is practical, individualised, local, cosmopolitan and 'life centred':

> I shall take it 'third way' refers to a framework of thinking and policy-making that seeks to adapt social democracy to a world which has changed fundamentally over the past two or three decades. It is a third way in the sense that it is an attempt to transcend both old style social democracy and neoliberalism (Giddens, 1998, p.26).

Having an agenda that is different to the concerns of communism, socialism or conservatism, the Third Way is indeed, pragmatic. Idealism must be fully grounded in experiences and practical need. In particular, it must be designed in recognition of the need for self-actualisation through work, individual self-expression and fulfilment. The renewal of civil society to foster a spirit of community is thought to involve public/private sector partnerships and partnerships between government, industry and the voluntary sector. A pivotal concern is with the active renewal of authority, since it is this that appears to be posing the greatest potential problems for government and industry. Civil society is usually conflated with an enhanced role for 'civic' institutions, something that falls far short of the vision of communitarian philosophy.

It is not surprising, therefore, that the various terms and phrases which are associated with the Third Way are evocative of management discourses, as these reflect the recasting of social and political life along business lines. Perhaps the most obvious, although contentious, example is the phrase 'social inclusion'. It would appear, as many authors (Levitas, 1999; Lister, 1998) have suggested, that this phrase may be substituted for equality of opportunity within a workplace framework.

Yet, ideologically, it is a rather clever phrase, subject to appeal to a variety of causes, individual and collective experiences. It draws upon and appears to empathise with images of the socially, politically and economically disenfranchised. In this sense it is sociological, recognising the oppressed. Yet it is also a highly individualistic conception. It is a dis-enfranchisement that may affect any number of social groups and individuals. Thus, it is not solely dictated by social class, gender, ethnicity, sexual orientation or any other collective experience. Indeed it is both individual *and* social, a reference to both 1960s radicalism (the civil rights and feminist movements) which twinned the 'personal and political', while simultaneously evoking the individualism and social responsibility of late conservatism.

The idea that the neo-liberal economy should be serviced by governments and citizens (national and international, paid and unpaid) is an assumption that lies deep within the core of the Third Way (see Hall, 1998). Its focus upon the re-evaluation of individual and societal values detracts from the pursuit of a radically alternative economic policy or for that matter any radical centre (see Held, 1995; Etzioni, 1997). The fact that corporations are being urged to intervene in the management of civil societies everywhere seems to be ignored. Different rates of economic, social and technological change are perceived to be evidence of the need for even greater 'global' harmonisation and intervention through, for example, the setting out of supra-national legal frameworks for governance, welfare, banking and finance.

In relation to this, it has been argued that the Third Way entails opportunistic responses to the here and now, rather than a coherent future plan of action. This pragmatic turn in political discourse has led a number of commentators and writers to dismiss the Third Way as little more than a post-hoc justification for anything and everything (see, for example, Faux, 1999 and Hall, 1998.) It has also been associated with the increasing commercialisation of politics which is being packaged to appeal to shifting moods of the voting population, rather than to encourage genuine critical debate (see Corfe, 2000). Giddens summarises critiques of the Third Way as including accusations that it is:

> amorphous and lacking in direction; conservative, uncritically accepting of neo-liberalism and the global market place and biased towards Anglo-Saxon contexts; economically vague and poor on ecological issues (Giddens, 2000, p.25).

As we have already indicated there is a growing recognition on the part of the general public as well as academics that political institutions are becoming more and more centralised. Giddens is optimistic about the capacity for a scaled-down government, for democracy, while hinting at 'New Labour's ready embrace of his ideas which have taken note of the fact that central government can be more influential through the devolution of some of its functions (Giddens, 2000, p.57).

Equating democracy with decentralisation of decision-making is deeply problematic given the extensive and wide ranging research spanning sociological, political and organisational theory that suggests that the relationship between the two is not so clear-cut (see Nuti, 1999). Although, as Giddens, (following the insights of the management gurus of the 1980s), argues bureaucracies are stifling of creativity and independence of thought; for the moment forgetting the more complex analysis offered by the highly influential German sociologist, Max Weber, that what determines levels of democracy are fundamental aims and commitments (substantive values and substantive rationality) rather than specific organisational structures per se, these reflecting a rather more superficial and potentially undemocratic technical rationality. Hence it is quite possible for substantive values to take a variety of technical or instrumental forms, whether it is the classic hierarchical bureaucracy, or the streamlined management structures so popular with those wishing to create an 'enterprise culture'. Moreover, the commitments of multinationals to profit-seeking has meant that decentralisation has been part and parcel of the centralisation of decision-making at corporate and government levels and labour intensification, bringing with it longer working hours, the reduction of employment, health and safety conditions, the capacity for employers to hire and fire at speed and pay lower wages, all helping to enhance shareholder returns. Yet an overemphasis upon the needs of consumers over and above producers or citizens leads Giddens to take these private sector models as examples of good government:

> As private companies downsized, adopted flatter hierarchies and sought to become more responsive to customer needs, the limitations of bureaucratic state institutions stood out in relief... 'Third Way' politics looks to transform government and the state -

to make them as effective and quick on their feet as many sectors of business have now become (Giddens, 2000, pp. 57-58).

Newman (2000) has argued that 'participative democracy' (as opposed to representative democracy) may be equated with the increasing use of questionnaires and focus groups borrowed from the discipline of marketing and public relations where the views of citizens are reduced to box ticking. The UK government's modernisation project reflects these views, modernisation being associated with an emphasis upon public/private sector partnerships, for example the Private Finance Initiative, and a regime of Best Value (see Policy and Politics, volume 29, no. 4 for a more detailed discussion), based upon notions of 'quality services' borrowed from the private sector.

References to social inclusion within these public-private partnerships proliferate in government publications that stipulate rules and conditions attaching to funding at local authority levels (the White Paper 'Modernising Government'). Risk is regarded as a healthy adjunct to innovation and prosperity: entrepreneurs are held in awe for their creativity (only within the context of responding to the global economy) while human capital, economic efficiency and civic cohesion are viewed as the bedrock of a healthy and fair society. Yet local councillors, professionals and other welfare workers suffer the reduced vision of unrealistic target setting by government (note in particular the refugee crisis), funding restrictions and the ever ready gaze of the Audit Commission, endorsed by the extra powers given to the Secretary of State to intervene if local authorities are seen to be acting too 'creatively'.

As we have seen, it is much easier now for companies to re-locate their production sites to areas of the world that offer the cheapest labour and resources. Associated with these developments are a proliferation of aggressive corporate take-overs and asset stripping. With all their implications for company closures and unemployment, such activities are fuelled by pressure upon managers to satisfy the aim of realising quick shareholder returns and to gain higher bonuses and salaries for their efforts. It is this highly prized skill for which managers are paid such high salaries according to Plender (1997). Strategies to increase firm size (of which take-overs and mergers have become a modern day motif) will be in the financial interests of executives, regardless of the long-term benefit to the company (see, for example, TUC, 1996, p.45).

The 'personal is political' refrain

Giddens emphasises the potential of individual human agency, a laudable stress and an important redress to the overarching principles and assumptions generalised into social policy from often fairly narrow, sectional interests. It is an approach which, taken at face value, serves to treat individuals with respect rather than patronage; it is essentially an optimistic view of human potential which should be applauded. It is refreshing to note the importance Giddens gives to the part our own capacities play in shaping the world in which we live; that we are not simply victims of circumstance; that there are differences in our orientation to poverty, unemployment and opportunity. It is uplifting to see these differences between us so acknowledged. To recognise these differences is not to adopt a callous individualistic political perspective. Such acknowledgement can take into consideration the histories and structural or institutional practices which may give birth to poverty and inequality. If anything Giddens' changed emphasis may lead to welcome but limited fine-tuning of policies to meet individual needs as they have been shaped by previous societal processes and individual effort or orientation wherever this may occur in, to use Giddens' phrase, 'the lifecycle'.

However, to argue that the 'pure' relationship based upon trust, reciprocity, understanding and above all communication offers qualities that can be generalised to other spheres of life is naïve in the prevailing political climate. This is not to argue that personal relationships should not be worked on and that we should forgo advancing our self-understanding and understanding of others, but that there is a danger in the context of the increasing incursion of the public sphere into private life and relationships that a preoccupation with establishing 'pure relationships' could become part of a psycho-social and political cul-de-sac.

Another brand name goes to the wall

We argued earlier that the ideals and policy agenda associated with stakeholding have been driven from the political arena by the neo-liberalist revival: some commentators now argue that the Third Way has met the same fate. Tom Baldwin (The Times, 15/12/2000, p.4), for example, citing President Clinton's final speech on his last UK visit as President in December 2000, commented that:

> Bill Clinton's passing reference to the 'Third Way' yesterday could not disguise the fact that the political project he and Tony Blair embarked on is now effectively sidelined. The two leaders had tried to build a worldwide alliance of centrist politicians who were prepared to combine the best of market economics with a concern for social justice.... Mr Clinton said yesterday that the term has been viewed 'as more of a political term than one that has actual policy substance'. The arrival of George W. Bush in the White House only confirms that it was a fad that has gone out of fashion.

With reference to the series of Third Way international conferences organised by Blair and his chief policy adviser, David Milliband, Baldwin quotes a senior colleague of Blair as stating:

> The effort that went into these self-congratulatory festivals would have been better spent on coming up with some real policies for our manifesto. I'm fed up hearing about how they've clocked up the air miles doing the Third Way by first class (The Times, 15/12/2000).

As Baldwin notes, interestingly, one of those principally involved in the Third Way initiative, the German Chancellor, Herr Schroeder, decided to rename the Berlin Third Way conference 'Progressive Governance' instead. After noting that the Third Way approach was regarded by Al Gore's Presidential campaign team as a 'tarnished brand' and that 'compassionate conservatism' had emerged as the victor in the US elections, Baldwin concludes by commenting that:

> Others say that the search for signs of life in the Third Way need go no further than the launch this week in London of a new organisation called Policy Network, which aims to bring together progressive thinking on the Internet. But most, watching the last jet vapours of AirForce One fading as Mr Clinton headed back to America, would say the Third Way has had its day (Martin Fletcher and Philip Webster, The Times, 15/12/2000, p.4).

Conclusion

Throughout this book we have examined the conditions under which the potentially more critical dimensions of stakeholding have become much diluted in the face of the neoliberal policies pursued by financial institutions like the IMF and World Bank. Countries formerly identified with alternative types of capitalism and held up as good examples to follow, in the stakeholding debates of the 1990s, have themselves come under considerable pressure to change their welfare and economic policies in conformity with the establishment of optimal conditions for free-flowing investment practices. The Anglo-Saxon models of capitalism, with their focus upon non or under-unionised workplace relations, rather than the more socially progressive institutional economic and political relations which characterised Rhenish or Rhineland approaches are proving more conducive to neoliberalism. As indicated in chapters 4 and 5, the Anglo-Saxon model highlights the respective role of individual employees, customers, suppliers and shareholders in *company* decision-making, an approach which is redolent of human resource management strategies. The localised and individualised approach to employee relations has carried with it, not the greater expression of diverse interests but the erosion of trade union power, the decline of collective bargaining and growing pay differentials.

The achievement of a more egalitarian and inclusive society would entail a radical re-conceptualisation of company ownership (Kay, 1996; Perkin, 1996) at both national and international levels, especially in the context of various economic and business dynamics identified in chapter one (see Thompson, 1997; Plender, 1997, p.17). The balancing of different and sometimes conflicting interests could not occur without some attention paid to the prioritisation of interests. This in turn would require consideration of the relative impact of policies on particular stakeholder groups at any one time. The relative weight given to different stakeholder interests, and the specific rights that would give each group authority in the expression of these interests, needs to be defined (Gamble and Kelly 1997). Associated with this is a need to re-evaluate institutional structures and entrenched traditions that may obstruct open debate and participation. There is a pressing need to explore alternative approaches to new social, political and economic problems wrought by neo-liberalism and the cessation of the cold war. In relation to processes of *political* prioritisation the concept of stakeholding, could serve to draw attention to unjust vested institutional interests and practices. For positive and more democratic developments to occur there would need to be a more critical analysis of the cultural and political symbols associated with citizenship in general. What it means to be 'British', 'European', 'international', 'global' or a 'stakeholder' is as much a *cultural* as an economic, social or political project. It is one which urgently needs to *engage with* citizens' interests as these interests evolve from particular as well as general histories, experiences, aspirations and needs. Such an approach would be a far cry from the false interests forged from policy networks and categories informing the mechanisms and procedures of the new governance referred to in chapters 6 and 7. The regeneration of local political and organisational structures, independent of central governments or international directives would be critical to establishing a more democratic approach to critical issues of our day than we have witnessed recently. In exploring alternative approaches, the global economy should not be used as an excuse for blocking change, since governments themselves still have a significant degree of autonomy.

Stakeholding might be too limited when it comes to exploring more egalitarian and democratic approaches to modern dilemma. The term, when loosely applied, implies *categories* of people (those in work, those out of work, the poor, refugees, asylum seekers etc.) rather than a society that is constantly changing according to the relative strengths and power of its *citizens*. Automatically, as soon as the question of citizenship is raised, there is more of a focus 'on process', which in turn, relies upon the expression of voice and agency (Lister, 1997, p.99). Although it is important to note the dynamic character of economic and social processes and their effects, we still need to address questions of 'interests' while acknowledging that these may change. However, such interests need to evolve from the histories, practical experiences and needs of localities.

At a more formal level, Barnett (1997) argues that there needs to be a practical commitment to providing a framework of 'reciprocal rights and interests' and in turn, a 'positive approach to change and to openness...at the heart of government itself where it is now needed most of all' (Barnett, 1997, p.87). Some would argue that there should also be a fundamental reform of issues of 'sovereignty', not only at governmental level but also, say, at the level of the workplace. Talking with employees, every now and again when issues are becoming critical does not really constitute 'involvement' (Held, 1997, p.253). New methods of negotiation and new frameworks within which the diverse members of any organisation are able to make decisions are crucial for the kinds of dilemmas and problems thrown up by 'globalisation'. Above all, perhaps, there is the need for clearly defined frameworks that can only enhance genuine open debate.

At the moment we are living in a society led overwhelmingly by bureaucratic officials and auditors. Sometimes it is possible for different interests to be co-opted into the official vehicles of public expression created by them. As already stated, the more radical dimensions of stakeholding as these were associated with

debates about the relationship between banking, finance and business appeared far
more controversial than the vocabulary of 'stakeholder' or for that matter
'community' so easily bandied about in the apparently all-inclusive and anodyne
'Third Way'. In keeping with the emergence of new governance structures and
rationales, Communitarianism would seem to have gone the way of stakeholding. A
potentially highly progressive political philosophy which offered a critique of the
tendency for classical liberal thought to abstract citizens from their concrete histories
or experiences, has been emptied of original content; reduced instead to another empty
category in falsely created interest groups or 'communities'.

Stakeholding seemed, for many, to offer such promise for a newly
formulated social democratic framework during the middle of the 1990s.
Unfortunately, the main drivers of the much vaunted 'global economy', major
financial institutions, gigantic corporate entities and the various governance
structures and political institutions which support them – in addition to levels of
integration and networks of significant global economic players limits the scope
for more radical alternatives. Without a serious commitment to challenging
neoliberal orthodoxy, stakeholding really is meaningless and will not deliver the
more socially inclusive agenda it once promised. Stakeholding has become one of
a series of much-diluted political vocabularies and phrases that have little political
bite beyond their usefulness in the construction of yet more, potentially
authoritarian governance structures.

Issues of international and national security are prominent in the re-forging
of state and civil society. Increasingly it is the organs of civil society that are being
co-opted into broader political and economic agendas. The short-lived 'peace-
dividend' was a part of this approach to the management and containment of the
unruly market, political and social forces of a post-cold war order. When such
strategies do not work, as we are witnessing at the time of finalising this book, leading
international players, dominated by US foreign policy and economic interests and
networks - resort to threats of war and military intervention once again. We have
argued that there is an intimate relationship between defence economics and military
strategy, this further being related to inequalities in defence and military capabilities.
It would appear, that the hegemonic power of the US and its allies remains particularly
relevant for the terms and rules of engagement operating at the international level –
Iraq being a salient case in point.

On a more positive note, political developments since September 11th 2001
have shown just how informed the general public are in relation to critical
international issues. Leading politicians may be cynical in their pursuit of 'pragmatic'
solutions at whatever cost, but the majority of their citizens are not. Governments will
have to show in future that they are more than prepared to respond to public pressure
and debate. The predominant Anglo-Saxon stakeholding model does little more than
pay lip service to the opinions of those who have lost much in terms of real political
and economic bargaining power in recent years. They include a large proportion of
those employed on relatively low wages and those who through no fault of their own
find themselves dependent on welfare states, or governments, as they flee

economically disrupted and conflict ridden countries - often created by the foreign policies and economic activities of the richer part of the world.

'Stakeholding', the 'Third Way' and 'Communitarianism' have all been marshalled to deal directly with the vagaries of neo-liberalism. Once we contrast the theoretical underpinnings of these ideas with their harnessing to prevailing international and economic policies, we can see that in practice at least, they are far too limited in their scope to seriously redress the spectre of war and autocratic power that the Allied leaders, in spite of their increasingly centralised approaches to political authority, claim to oppose.

As we have indicated in this book, economic, political and social inequalities are clearly evident throughout the world, within as well as between nation-states. They would appear to be getting worse. Governments are still reeling from the hatred and frustration borne out of perceived injustices domestically and abroad. Now, some might say thankfully, they must deal with new types of street and grass-roots protest. Such protests cannot be silenced by the mechanisms of governance so designed to co-opt and incorporate them. Democracy is in crisis. Local people all over the world need to be heard, respected and represented according to the circumstances they face and the histories they have shared. Catch-all easy phrases which continue to deny such histories and interests are bound to fail in delivering policies which are progressive, enlightened, sophisticated, realistic and just. Finally, unless there are serious attempts to address these issues through the appropriate balancing of local, regional, national and international interests, governments already plagued by reduced electoral turnout and public suspicion of politicians, will continue to face a crisis of legitimation in the face of growing awareness of inequalities both at home and abroad.

Bibliography

Ackerman B, and Alstott A, (1999), *The Stakeholder Society*, Yale University Press, London

Ackerman B, and Allstott A, (2000), *The Individualist's Case for Stakeholding*

Aglietta M, (1979), 'A Theory of Capitalist Regulation: The US Experience', *NLB*, London

Albert M, and Gonenc R, (1996), 'The Future of Rhenish Capitalism', *The Political Quarterly*, 67, 2, 184-193

Albrow M, (1996), *The Global Age: State and Society beyond Modernity*, Polity Press, Cambridge

Alcock P, (1996), *Social Policy In Britain: Themes and Issues*, MacMillan Press Ltd, London

Allison G, Cote O, Falkenrath R, and Miller S, (1996), *Avoiding Nuclear Anarchy: Containing the Threat of Loose Russian Nuclear Weapons and Fissile Material*, MIT Press

Amin A, (1983), 'Restructuring in Fiat and the decentralization of production in southern Italy', in Hudson R and Lewis J, *Dependent Development in Southern Europe*, Methuen, London

Arias O, (1997), The Price of Peace, *B ICC Bulletin*, No. 5, 1 October

Atkinson J, (1984), 'Manpower Strategies for Flexible Organisations', *Personnel Management*, August

Avineri S, (1969), *The Social and Political Thought of Karl Marx*, Cambridge University Press, Cambridge

Balanya B, Doherty A, Hoedeman O, Ma'anit A, and Wesselius E, (2000), *Europe Inc: Regional & Global Restructuring and the Rise of Corporate Power*, Pluto Press, London

Barnett A, (1997), *Towards a Stakeholder Democracy*, in Kelly, Kelly and Gamble, ibid

Bassett P, (1994), 'Britain adopting 'Victorian' employee relations methods', *The Times*, February 15th

Baudrillard J, in Poster M, (ed), (2001), *Jean Baudrillard: Selected Writings*, Polity Press, Cambridge

Bauman Z, (1992), *Intimations of Postmodernity*, Routledge, London

Bauman Z, (1993), *Postmodern Ethics*, Blackwell, Oxford

Bauman Z, (1997), *Postmodernity and its Discontents*, Polity Press, Cambridge

Bauman Z, (1998), *Globalization: The Human Consequences*, Polity Press, Cambridge

Beck U, (1992), *Risk Society: Towards a New Modernity*, Sage, London

Beck U, (2000), *The Brave New World of Work*, Polity Press, Cambridge

Bendix R, (1963), *Work and Authority in Industry*, Harper and Row, New York

Bischak G, (1997), *What happened to the Peace Dividend?* See http:llwww.webcom.com/ncecd/div.html

Bobbio N, (1990*), Liberalism and Democracy*, Verso, London

Bovaird T, and Halachmi A, (2001), 'Learning from International Approaches to Best Value', *Policy and Politics*, volume 29, October, The Policy Press, Bristol

Braddon DL, and Dowdall P G, (1996), 'Flexible Networks and the Restructuring of the Regional Defence Industrial Base: The Case of Southwest England', *Defence and Peace Economics*, Vol. 7

Braddon DL, *Exploding the Myth? The Peace Dividend, Regions and Market Adjustment*, Routledge, 2000

Bradshaw P, (2000), The Financial Mail on Sunday, 30th July

Brommelhorster and Dedek, (1998), *Changing Priorities of Military Expenditures and the Results of the Peace Dividend*, BICC Peace Dividend Project, September

Brzoska M, (1995) World Military Expenditures, in Hartley K. and Sandler 1, (eds) *Handbook of Defence Economics*, Elsevier Science B.V., North Holland

Burleigh P, (2001), The Sunday Times, 30th September

Burnham P, (2001), Marx, 'International Political Economy and Globalisation', *Capital and Class*, Special Issue, Vol. 75, Autumn

Byrne D, (2001), 'Class, tax and spending: problems for the Left in post-industrial and post-democractic politics or why aren't we taxing the fat cats till the pips squeak?', *Capital & Class*, special issue, 75, Autumn

Cabinet Office, (1999), 'Modernising Government', CM4310, Stationery Office, London

Callaghan J, (2000), *The Retreat of Social Democracy*, Manchester University Press, Manchester

Cammack P, (2002), 'Attacking the Poor', *New Left Review* 13, Jan/Feb

Campen C E, (1999),'Change within the Conservative and Labour Parties', Interstate Online http:www.a er.ac.uk/ scty34/49/bpol.htm

Cooper and Jackson S, (eds.), *Creating Tomorrow's Organizations: A Handbook for Future Research in Organizational Behavior*, 207-230. New York: John Wiley

Casey C, (1998), *Work, Self and Society After Industrialism*, Routledge, London

Castells M, (1996), *The Rise of the Networked Society*, Oxford

Castells M, (1997), *The Power of Identity*, Oxford

Chamberlayne P, Cooper A, Freeman R, and Rustin M, (eds) (1999), *Welfare and Culture in Europe: Towards a New Paradigm in Social Policy*, Jessica Kingsley, London

Chan S, (1996*)*, *Romancing the Peace Dividend*, BICC Conversion Survey, Bonn

Child J, (1969), *British Management Thought*, Allen and Unwin, London

Chomsky N, (1998), 'Power in the Global Arena', *New Left Review*, 230, pp.3-27

CIA (2000), *World Factbook, Germany*

Clarke J, and Newman J, (1997), *The Managerial State*, Sage, London

Clark J B, (1914), *Social Justice without Socialism*, Riverside Press Boston, MA: Houghton Mifflin, cited in McHugh, Francis P., (1988, *Business Ethics*, Mansell Publishing Limited, London

Coase R, (1937), 'The Nature of the Firm', *Economica,* 4; November, pp. 386-405

Coates D, (2000), 'The Character of New Labour' in Coates D, and Lawler P, (eds), *New Labour in Power,* Manchester University Press, Manchester

Coddington A, (1983*)*, *Keynesian Economics: The Search for First Principles*, George Allen and Unwin, London

Commission on Global Governance, (1995), Report

Commission on Public Policy and British Business, (1997), *Promoting Prosperity: A Business Agenda for Britain*, Vintage, London

Compston H, (1998), 'The End of National Policy Concertation: Western Europe since the Single European Act', *Journal of European Public Policy*, vol. 5, n.3, pp. 507-526

Corfe R, (2000), *Reinventing Democratic Socialism for People Prosperity*, Arena Books, Bury St. Edmunds

Cox R, (1997), 'Economic globalization and the limits to liberal democracy', in McGrew A, *The Transformation of Democracy?* Polity Press, Cambridge

Dahrendorf R et al., (1995), *Report on Wealth Creation and Social Cohesion in a Free Society,* London: The Commission on Wealth Creation and Social Cohesion

Davey K, (1996), The Impermanence of New Labour, in Perryman, M, (ed) *The Blair Agenda*, Lawrence & Wishart Limited, London

Denny C, and Brittain V, *The Guardian*, 12th July, 1999

Dowding, K, (1996), *Power*, Open University Press, Buckingham

Draper D, (1997), *Blair's Hundred Days,* Faber and Faber, London

Durkheim E, (1933), *The Division of Labour in Society*, Collier-Macmillan, London

Eisenhower Dwight D, Speech on the Military Industrial Complex – for an interesting discussion of this see Black GS, and Black, BD, (1994), *The Politics of American Discontent,* pp. 69-70, John Wiley and Sons Inc., New York

Eldman P, (1999), Welfare and the "Third Way", *Dissent,* Winter 1999, pp. 14-16 Ivan R Dee, Chicago

Elliot L, and Atkinson D, (1998), *The Age of Insecurity*, Verso, London

Equal Opportunities Commission, Report, 2000

Esping-Andersen G, (1990), *The Three Worlds of Welfare Capitalism*, Polity Press, Cambridge

Etzioni A, (1997), *The New Golden Rule: Community and Morality in a Democratic Society*, Profile Books Ltd, London

European Commission, Report, 1997

Ewing D, China Needs Labour Flexibility, *Far Eastern Economic Review*, March 14th 2002

Faux J, (1999), 'Lost on the Third Way', *Dissent,* Spring

Felice W E, (1998), Militarism and Human Rights, *International Affairs*, 74, 1, pp. 25-40

Field F, (1995), *Making Welfare Work: Reconstructing Welfare for the Millennium*, Institute of Community Studies 1995, p. 20, London

Finance and Development, 1998

Fletcher, M and Webster P, (2000), *The Times*, 15th December

Flynn N, (2000), Managerialism and Public Services: Some International Trends, in Clarke J, Gewirtz S, McLaughlin E, (2000), *New Managerialism, New Welfare?* Sage, London

Forsberg R, (1992), Defense Cuts and Co-operative Security in the post-Cold War World, *Boston Review* 17, pp. 3-4, May-July

Friedland J, *The Guardian*, 8th November, 1999

FT World Desk Reference, 2002 Dorling Kindersley Limited, London

Fukuyama F, (1995), *Trust: The Social Virtues and the Creation of Prosperity*, Hamish Hamilton, London

Fukuyama F, (1992), *The End of History and the Last Man*, Free Press, New York

Gamble A, and Kelly G, (1997), Stakeholder Capitalism: Limits and Opportunities, http://www.netnexus.org/library/papers/gamkel.htm

Gamble A, (2001), Neo-Liberalism, *Capital and Class*, Special Issue, vol 75, Autumn, pp.127-134

Gansler J, (1998), Military and Industrial Cooperation in a Transformed, NATO-Wide Competitive Market, XVth International NATO Workshop on Political-Military Decision Making, Vienna

Geddes M, (2001), What about the workers? Best Value, employment and work in local public services, *Policy and Politics*, Volume 29/4, October, pp. 497-508

Gewirtz S, and McLaughlin E, (eds), (2000), *New Managerialism, New Welfare?* Sage Publications, London

Giddens A, (1994), *Beyond Left and Right: The Future of Radical Politics*, Polity Press, Cambridge

Giddens A, (2000), *The Third Way and its Critics*, Polity Press, Cambridge

Giddens A, (1999), *Runaway World: How Globalisation is Reshaping Our Lives*, Polity Press, Cambridge

Giddens A, (1998), *The Third Way: The Renewal of Social Democracy*, Polity Press, Cambridge

Gill S and Law D, (1997), *The Global Political Economy, Perspectives, Problems and Policies*, Harvester Wheatsheaf, London

Goldblatt D, (1999), *Will Hutton: the Stakeholding Society*, Polity Press, Cambridge

Gray J, (1998), *False Dawn: The Delusions of Global Capitalism*, Granta Publications, London

Hall S, (1998), 'The Great Moving Nowhere Show', *Marxism Today*, November/December, pp. 9-14

Hall S, (1991), 'The Local and the Global', in King A.D (ed.) (1991), *Identity, Community, Culture, Difference*, Lawrence and Wishart Ltd., London

Harris P, (1999), 'Public Welfare and Liberal Governance', in Petersen, A., Barns, I., Dudley J., and Harris, P., *Postructuralism, Citizenship and Social Policy*, Routledge, London

Hartley K, Bhaduri A, Bougrov E, Deger S, Dessouki A, Fontanel J, de Haan H, Intriligator M, and Egea A, (1993), *Economic Aspects of Disarmament: Disarmament as an Investment Process*, United Nations Institute for Disarmament Research (UNIDIR), New York

Hayes R, and Watts R, (1986), *Corporate Revolution: New Strategies for Executive Leadership*, Heinemann: London

Held D, (ed), (2000), *A Globalizing World? Culture, Economics, Politics*, Routledge in association with the Open University, London

Held D, (1995), *Democracy and the Global Order: From the Modern State to Cosmopolitan Governance*, Polity, Cambridge

Hine S, (2000), 'Why don't we hit the rich tax avoiders?' *The Daily Express*, March 10th

Hirschman, A, (1997), 'Exit, Voice and Loyalty', cited by Barnett, (1997), op.cit., p.90

Hirst P, and Thompson G, (1996), *Globalization in Question*, Polity Press in association with Blackwell, Cambridge

Hirst P, (1999), 'Has Globalisation Killed Democracy?', in Gamble A., and Wright T., *The New Social Democracy*, Blackwell, Oxford

Hobsbawm E, (1998), 'The Death of Liberalism', *Marxism Today*, Nov/Dec, pp. 4-8

Hoogevelt A, (1997), *Globalisation and the Postcolonial World: the New Political Economy of Development*, MacMillan Press Ltd, London

Hughes G. and Lewis G, (eds), (1998), *Unsettling Welfare: the Reconstruction of Social Policy*, Routledge in association with the Open University, London

Hutton W, (1996), *The State We're In*, Vintage, London

Hutton W, and Giddens A, (eds), (2000), *On the Edge: Living with Global Capitalism*, Jonathon Cape, London

Iacobs M, (1991), *The Green Economy*, Pluto

James A, (1995), 'Peacekeeping in the post-Cold War Era', *International Journal*, 1, Spring

Jameson F, (1991), *Postmodernism or the Cultural Logic of Capitalism*, Verso, London

Jessop B, (1994), Post-Fordism and the State, in Amin A, (ed.), (1994), *Post-Fordism: A Reader*, Blackwell, Oxford

Jessop B, *Good Governance and the Urban Question: On Managing the Contradictions of Neo-Liberalism*, published by the Department of Sociology, Lancaster University at: http://www.comp.lancs.ac.uk/sociology/soc075rj.html see page 115

Kaufmann W, and Steinbruner J, (1991), *Decisions for Defence: Prospects for a New Order*, The Brookings Institution, Washington D.C., p. 70

Kay J, (1997), The Stakeholding Corporation, in Kelly, Kelly and Gamble, ibid

Keane J, (1988), *Democracy and Civil Society*, University of Westminster Press, London

Kelly D, (l997), An International Perspective, in Kelly G, Kelly D, and Gamble A, *Stakeholder Capitalism,* MacMillan Press Limited, London

Keynes J M, (1936), *The General Theory of Employment, Interest and Money*, MacMillan, London

Kleinman M, (2002), *A European Welfare State? European Union Social Policy in Context*, Palgrave, Hampshire

Knipe M, *The Times*, March 12th, 2002

Kondrake, M, (2001) How will Washington's new administration settle in ? The Economist, Special Issue, The World in 2001

Kuttner R, (1991), *The End of Laissez-Faire: National Purpose and the Global Economy after the Cold War*, University of Pennsylvania Press

Kuttner R, (l997), An American Perspective, in Kelly, Kelly and Gamble, ibid

Lachmann L M, (1986), *The Market as an Economic Process*, Basil Blackwell

Lasch C, (l996), *The Revolt of the Elites and The Betrayal of Democracy*, W.W. Norton and Company Inc., New York

Latham A, (1995), The Structural Transformation of the US Defence Firm: Changes in Manufacturing Technology, Production Process, and Principles of Corporate Organisation, in (eds.) Latham A, and Hooper N, *The Future of the Defence Firm: New Challenges, New Directions*, NATO ASI Series, Mower Academic Publishers

Leijonhufvud A, *Information and Co-ordination: Essays in Macroeconomic Theory*, Oxford.

Levitas R, (l996), The Concept of Social Exclusion and the New Durkheimian Hegemony', *Critical Social Policy*, 16, pp. 5-20

Lind M, (l995), *The Next American Nation*, New York, p. 216

Ling T, (2000), Unpacking Partnership: The Case of Health Care, in Gewirtz S, and McLaughlin E, ibid

Lister R, (1997), Social Inclusion and Exclusion, in Kelly, Kelly and Gamble op.cit. MacMillan Press, London

Loescher G, (ed.), (1992*), Refugees and the International Asylum Dilemma in the West*, Penn. State University Press: Pennsylvania

Lorenz, (l999), *Social Work and Cultural Politics: The Paradox of German Social Pedagogy*, in Chamberlayne P. et al, 1999, JKP, London

MacKintyre, A, (l990), *Three Versions of Moral Enquiry*, Duckworth, London

Maddox, *The Times*, 12th October, 2001

Maddox, *The Times*, 26th September, 2001

Maile S, and Hoggett P, (2001), Best Value and the Politics of Pragmatism, pp. 509-520, *Policy and Politics*, Volume 29, number 4, October

Maile S, (l995), A Gendered Managerial Discourse, *Journal of Gender, Work and Organization*, 22, 2, pp. 76-87 Sage, London

Mallaby S, (2001), A decidedly bad idea. Two million Americans behind bars, The Economist, Special Issue, The World in 2001

Mallaby S, (2002), The Reluctant Imperialist, *Foreign Affairs*, March/April, pp. 2-7

Maltby J, and Wilkinson R, (1998), Whither Stakeholding?, *New Economy*, 5 (2), pp. 114-118

Markusen A, (1997), Understanding American Defence Industry Mergers, *Rutgers* PRIE *Working Paper No. 247,* May

Marshall TH, (l981), The Right to Welfare and Other Essays, Heinemann, London

Marx K, (1844), On the Jewish Question

McGrew T, (ed.), (1997), *The Transformation of Democracy?* Polity Press, Cambridge

Micklethwaite and Wooldridge, (2000), 'Global warriors strike back', Economist Special Issue, November

Milward B, (1994), *The New Industrial Relations*, Policy Studies Institute, London

Minford P, (1998), *Markets not Stakes*, Orion Business Books, London

Mintzberg H, (1996), Harvard Business Review, May-June

Monbiot G, (2001), Introduction in Bircham E and Charlton J (eds), *Anti-capitalism: A Guide to the Movement*, Bookmarks Publications, London

Monbiot G, (2000), *Captive State: The Corporate Takeover of Britain*, MacMillan, London see also Monbiot G, (2002), 'Very British Corruption', *The Guardian*, January 22nd

Mulhall S, and Swift A, (1992), *Liberals and Communitarians*, Blackwell Publishers, Oxford

Newman J, (2000), Beyond the New Public Management? Modernising Public Services in Clarke J, op.cit.

Nichols T, (2001), The Condition of Labour-A Retrospect, *Capital and Class,* Special Issue, Vol. 75, pp. 185-198

Nick Gardner in the *Sunday Times,* May, 2000

Novak T, (2001), *Rich and Poor: The Growing Divide*, Garnet Publishing Ltd, Reading

Nuti D. Mario, (1999), Making Sense of the Third Way, *Business Strategy Review*, Volume 10 Issue 3 pp. 57-67

OECD Annual Economic Survey, 1995; Germany

OECD Report (1997) *The World in 2020: Towards a New Global Age*, OECD Publications, Paris

Ohmae K, (1990), *The Borderless World*, Collins, London

Open University Study Guide, p. 22

Ormerod P, (1994), *The Death of Economics*, Faber and Faber

Ormerod P, (2001) *Butterfly Economics*, Basic Books

Perkin H, (1997), The Third Revolution, in Kelly G, Kelly D, and Gamble A, *Stakeholder Capitalism*, Macmillan Press Limited, London

Perkin H, (1996), *The Third Revolution: Professional Elites in the Modern World since 1945*, Routledge, London

Peters T J, and Waterman R H, (1982), *In Search of Excellence*, Harper Row, New York

Pilger J, (1999), *Hidden Agendas*, Vintage, London

Piore M J, and Sabel C F, (1984), *The Second Industrial Divide: Possibilities for Prosperity*, Basic Books, New York

Plant R, (2001), 'Blair and Ideology', in Seldon, A (ed) *The Blair Effect*

Plant R, (1998), Citizenship, Rights, Welfare, in Franklin, J, *Social Policy and Social Justice*, Polity Press, Cambridge

Plender J, (1997), *A Stake in the Future: The Stakeholding Solution*, Nicholas Brealey Publishing, London

Polanyi K, (1944), *The Great Transformation: The political and economic origins of our time*, Beacon Press, Boston

Porte A, (1990), cited in Thompson and McHugh, 1995, ibid

Preston L, and Sapienza H, (1990), *Promoting Prosperity: A Business Agenda for Britain*, IPPR, 1/2

Radice H, (2001),Globalization, Labour and Socialist Renewal, *Capital and Class*, Special Issue, Vol 75, Autumn, pp. 113-126

Ralston-Saul J, (1997), *The Unconscious Civilization*, Penguin Books, London

Ramsay R, (1998), *Prawn Cocktail Party: The Hidden Power Behind New Labour*, Vision Paperbacks, London

Reich R, *The Observer*, 24th October, 1999

Reich, R, (1991), *The Work of Nations: Preparing Ourselves for 21st Century Capitalism*, Alfred, A

Renner M, (1996), *Cost of Disarmament: An Overview of the Economic Costs of the Dismantlement of Weapons and the Disposal of Military Surplus*, Brief 6, Bonn International Centre for Conversion, March

Rhodes M, (1996), Globalisation and the West European Welfare State: A Critical Review of Recent Debates. *Journal of European Social Policy* 4, pp. 305-327

Roddick A, (1996), 'Openness: the true meaning of business and stakeholding', *The Times* September 28$^{th.}$

Rose N, (1996), The death of the social, *Economy and Society*, vol.25, no.3, pp.327-56

Rustin M, (1997), Stakeholding and the Public Sector, in Kelly, Kelly and Gamble op. cit., MacMillan Press, London

Rustin M, (1991), Life Beyond Liberalism? Individuals, Citizens and Society, in Osborne P, (ed) *Socialism and the Limits of Liberalism*, Verso, London

Sandel M, (1982), *Liberalism and the Limits of Justice*, Cambridge University Press, Cambridge

Sennet R, (1998), *The Corrosion of Character: The Personal Consequences of Work in the New Capitalism*, W.W Norton and Company, London

Shackle G L S, (1972), *Marginalism: The Harvest*, History of Political Economy, Fall

Smith D, (2001), *The Sunday Times*, 21st January

Smith Ring P, and Van de Ven A H, (1994), Developmental Processes of Cooperative Interorganizational Relationships', *Academy of Management Review;* 19/1; pp. 90-118

Smith A S, (1995), *Nations and Nationalism in a Global Era*, Polity Press, Cambridge

Strange S, (1997), *Casino Capitalism*, Manchester University Press, Manchester

Taylor C, (1990), *Sources of the Self*, Cambridge University Press, Cambridge

Teague P, (1998), 'Monetary Union and Social Europe', *Journal of European Social Policy*, 8 (2): 117-38

Seldon A, (2001), *The Blair effect: The Blair Government, 1997-2001*, Little, Brown and Company, London

The Guardian, 20th March, 2002

The Times Power List, 1999

The Times, 15th December, 2000

The Times, 21st April, 1999

The Times, 4th March, 2000

Thompson P, and McHugh D, (1995), *Work Organisations: A Critical Introduction* (Second Edition) MacMillan, London

Thompson G F, (2001), Are There Any Limits to Globalisation? International Trade, Capital Flows and Borders, (mimeo), Open University

Thurow L, (1996), The Future of Capitalism: How Today's Economic Forces will Shape Tommorrow's World, Allen and Unwin, London

Toffler A, (1980), *The Third Wave*, Pan, London

Toynbee P, (1996), *The Independent*, 31st January

Travers T, (2001), Local Government, in Seldon A, (ed) *The Blair Effect: The Blair Government 1997-2001*, Little, Brown and Company, London

TUC Stakeholder Task Group, (1996), '*Your Stake at Work – TUC proposals for a Stakeholder Economy*'

UMIST/Institute of Management annual survey for 1999

Vallely P, (1997), How Blair can save billions on defence, *The Independent*, Monday 10th February

Vershbow A, (1999), from a speech by the US Permanent Representative on the North Atlantic

Webster P, (2000), *The Times*, May 24th

Weitzman M, (1984), *The Share Economy: Conquering Stagflation*, Harvard University Press, Cambridge

Wheeler D, and Sillanpaa M, (1997), *The Stakeholder Corporation: A Blueprint for Maximising Stakeholder Value*, Pitman Publishing, London

Wheeler W, (1996), Dangerous Business: Remembering Freud and a Poetics of Politics, in Perryman, M (ed.) op.cit.

Williamson O L, (1981), The Economics of Organisation: The Transaction Cost Approach, *American Journal of Sociology*, Vol. 87, No. 3., November

World Health Report, 2001

Wyatt S, Henwood F, Miller N, and Senker P, (2000), *Technology and Inequality: Questioning the Information Society*, Routledge, London and New York

Index

Afghanistan, 18, 108, 109, 113, 125
alienation, 7, 76, 93, 125, 131
Al-Qaida, 108, 114
Anglo-Saxon, 1, 2, 4, 52, 59, 64, 66, 67, 74, 136, 143, 146, 148
anomie, 13, 133
arms trade, 18

Best Value, 135, 144
Big Bang, 44
Bosnia, 104, 107, 110, 112
Bretton Woods Agreement, 28
business cycle, 35, 36

capitalism, 2, 4, 5, 9, 11, 17, 25, 31, 32, 41, 46, 52-54, 56, 58, 59, 63, 65, 69, 70, 71, 73, 75, 86, 92, 130, 134, 136, 137, 139
central planning, 32
China, 8, 19, 87, 118
Civil Society, 3
classical economics, 2, 39, 40
Cold War, 2, 4, 5, 92, 93, 94, 106, 107, 110, 112, 113, 115, 120, 121-123, 137, 141
collective bargaining, 1, 102, 140, 146
communitarian philosophy, 124, 142
communitarianism, 5, 124, 129
competitive edge, 56, 58, 73, 85
'concertation', 81
consumer segmentation, 90
consumption, 13-15, 36, 71, 90, 97
corporate restructuring, 43
cultural, 2, 3, 4, 5, 9, 13, 16, 17, 23, 24, 25, 26, 29, 53, 70, 76, 89, 90, 95, 98-100, 102, 104, 124, 126, 128, 130-132, 136-138, 140, 141, 147

democracy, 2, 3, 4, 8, 11, 15, 25, 27, 28, 41, 42, 53, 75, 77, 78, 102, 106, 112, 124, 130, 131, 136, 138, 141-144
de-regulation, 17, 20, 29, 50, 74, 75, 80, 87, 100

'economic citizenship', 73
economic cyberspace, 47
elites, 106
Enlightenment, 7, 127, 128, 130, 134
Enron, 98
ethics, 94, 126, 127, 130
European Monetary Union, 60-62, 74
euro-zone, 60, 61, 62

FDI. See Foreign Direct Investment
flexible employment, 12, 13, 26
flexible firm, 85, 87, 88, 90, 102
flexible manufacturing, 57, 85
Foreign Direct Investment, 20
free enterprise, 32, 42, 101
full spectrum dominance, 119

GDP, 20, 22, 43, 45, 61, 62, 63, 114
General Agreement on Tariffs, 38, 81
general hysteria, 14
global economy, 17, 19, 28, 29, 31, 37, 42-46, 49, 51, 53, 58, 63, 64, 68, 70, 73, 74, 78, 80, 81, 83, 84, 87, 90, 92, 96, 97, 99, 138, 142, 144, 147
global reach, 119
globalisation, 2, 3, 4, 5, 7, 8, 9, 10, 12, 17, 19, 20, 21, 23, 24, 25, 26, 27, 44, 48, 63, 64, 70, 76, 78, 84, 94, 97, 98, 104, 106, 128, 131, 137, 138, 139, 141

golden age, 38, 66
governance, 2, 5, 12, 14, 22, 28, 50,
    55, 70, 73, 95, 96-98, 101, 106,
    135, 138, 142, 148, 149
Great Depression, 28, 35
Gulf War, 18, 107-110, 113

incentive mechanisms, 40
income inequality, 23, 36
India, 17, 18, 22, 105, 113
individualisation, 12, 13, 70, 141
individualism, 1, 2, 12, 13, 55, 60, 66,
    94, 95, 141, 142
industrial restructuring, 64, 89, 115
inflation psychology, 39
information technology, 85, 106, 138
interdependence, 17, 23
International Monetary Fund, 27, 37,
    38, 74, 81
'invisible continent', 46
Iran, 113
Iraq, 8, 18, 23, 107, 109, 110, 113,
    136, 148
Israel, 108, 113, 114
Italy, 8, 62, 63, 65, 66, 82, 118, 119,
    132

Japan, 8, 20, 26, 28, 45, 54-56, 72, 83,
    118

Keynesianism, 1, 2, 5, 39, 81
knowledge economy, 139
Kosovo, 23, 107
Kuwait, 107, 114

laissez-faire, 11, 32, 81
liberalisation, 23, 39, 41, 44, 65, 74,
    81, 96, 120

Maastricht Agreement, 60
market economics, 5, 31, 33-37, 41,
    50, 59, 81, 145
market efficiency, 9
markets, 1, 2, 9, 10, 11, 13, 15, 17, 19,
    20, 21, 29-33, 35-37, 39-45, 47, 50,
    52, 53, 57-59, 63, 65, 66, 69, 70,

72, 74, 78, 86, 87, 92, 97, 99, 102,
    103, 117, 134, 135,   137-140
modernity, 141
monetary union, 62
multinational corporations, 11, 20, 89,
    133

NAFTA, 26
nation state, 2, 3, 27, 28, 98, 99, 125,
    126, 135
natural equilibrium, 32, 47
neo-liberalism, 1, 2, 5, 7, 28, 39, 42,
    50, 59, 60, 84, 92, 101, 129, 140,
    143
New Deals, 100
new industrial revolution, 115
New Labour, 70, 78, 100, 131
New World Order, 25, 107, 112, 113
non-governmental organisations, 3, 22

OPEC, 10, 28

Pakistan, 113
Palestinian issue, 113
Palestinians, 10, 25, 114, 125
partnership, 32, 35, 50, 57, 58, 59, 72,
    73, 78, 79, 83, 85, 95, 99, 116, 123,
    133
Partnership for Peace, 120
peace dividend, 2, 71, 120-123
peace-keeping, 106
pessimistic globalists, 26
Phillips Curve, 38
plantation production, 21
positive globalists, 26
post-Fordism, 41
poverty, 10, 16, 18, 19, 22-24, 27, 37,
    69, 71, 72, 76, 78, 92, 95, 96, 105,
    108, 121, 139, 145
pressure groups, 10, 27, 93, 101
privatisation, 17-19, 41, 65, 70, 105,
    134
public expenditure, 7, 44, 62, 63, 71,
    80, 105, 140
public-private partnerships, 144

rationalisation, 43, 115-117
reduced form model, 31
Regionalism, 106
Rhenish, 1, 31, 54, 55-59, 65, 71, 86, 92
risk society, 12
'runaway capital', 87
Russia, 8, 18, 111-113, 118, 120

Saudi Arabia, 10, 113, 114, 118
Say's Law, 33
Scandinavian economies, 1
self-empowerment, 3, 13
September 11, 8, 113
shareholder, 39, 51, 55, 58, 70, 101, 143, 144
short-termism, 72, 101
social capital, 2, 78, 79, 94
social exclusion, 96
social inclusion, 73, 142
social policy, 77, 94, 95, 101, 124, 128, 129, 130-132, 144
social responsibility, 39, 94, 130, 142
Soviet Union, 49, 93, 105, 107, 120, 123
stakeholding, 1, 2, 4, 5, 9, 14, 16, 21, 29, 31, 39, 53, 56, 58-60, 68, 70, 72-74, 78, 79, 80, 83, 86, 92, 94, 99, 101-103, 105, 109, 124, 127, 136, 145, 148
sub-contractors, 53
supply chain, 53, 85
supply-side school, 40

Taliban, 18, 108

terrorism, 7, 8, 19, 108, 109, 111, 114, 135
Thatcherism, 2, 67, 78
the axis of evil, 18
The New Economy, 49
Third Way, 2, 3, 5, 9, 18, 73, 102, 124, 132, 133, 134, 136-138, 140-143, 145, 146, 148
trade unions, 1
transaction costs, 34
transformationalists, 26
Trans-national corporations, 20

unemployment, 17, 22, 32, 36, 37, 38, 40, 59, 63-66, 68, 72, 83, 95, 96, 141, 144, 145
United Nations, 22, 24, 25, 106, 109, 110, 111
United States, 8, 21, 39, 71, 74, 81, 94, 102, 107, 108, 116, 118

Walrasian general equilibrium, 33
welfare, 1, 3, 4, 5, 12, 18, 28, 41, 44, 52, 54, 59, 60, 62, 63-71, 73-78, 80, 81, 84, 86, 87, 96, 97, 100, 101, 121, 122, 124, 125, 129, 130, 133, 135, 136, 140, 141, 142, 144
welfare state, 1, 5, 12, 18, 41, 52, 64, 69, 71, 86, 96, 130, 133, 135
'welfare to work', 74
workfare, 100, 135, 137
World Bank, 18, 26, 27, 38, 50, 70, 74, 81, 92, 100, 104, 135
World Trade Organisation, 8, 19, 22, 48, 74, 114